The Westreich Family Tree

Putting the Puzzle Pieces Together Using Traditional and
Genetic Genealogy

Editor: Allan H. Westreich, Ph.D.

JewishGen
מרכז עולמי לגנאלוגיה יהודית
The Global Home for Jewish Genealogy

A Publication of JewishGen, Inc.
Edmond J. Safra Plaza, 36 Battery Place, New York, NY 10280
646.494.5972 | info@JewishGen.org | www.jewishgen.org

An affiliate of New York's Museum of Jewish Heritage – A Living Memorial to the Holocaust

MUSEUM OF
JEWISH HERITAGE
A LIVING MEMORIAL
TO THE HOLOCAUST

The Westreich Family Tree
Putting the Puzzle Pieces Together Using Traditional and Genetic Genealogy

Editor: Allan H. Westreich, Ph.D.

Cover Design: Irv Osterer

Library of Congress Control Number (LCCN): 2023946209

ISBN: 978-1-954176-87-4 (hard cover: 232 pages, alk. paper)

About JewishGen.org

JewishGen, an affiliate of the Museum of Jewish Heritage - A Living Memorial to the Holocaust, serves as the global home for Jewish genealogy.

Featuring unparalleled access to 30+ million records, it offers unique search tools, along with opportunities for researchers to connect with others who share similar interests. Award winning resources such as the Family Finder, Discussion Groups, and ViewMate, are relied upon by thousands each day.

In addition, JewishGen's extensive informational, educational and historical offerings, such as the Jewish Communities Database, Yizkor Book translations, InfoFiles, Family Tree of the Jewish People, and KehilaLinks, provide critical insights, first-hand accounts, and context about Jewish communal and familial life throughout the world.

Offered as a free resource, JewishGen.org has facilitated thousands of family connections and success stories, and is currently engaged in an intensive expansion effort that will bring many more records, tools, and resources to its collections.

Please visit https://www.jewishgen.org/ to learn more.

Executive Director: Avraham Groll

About JewishGen Press

JewishGen Press (formerly the Yizkor Books-in-Print Project) is the publishing division of JewishGen.org, and provides a venue for the publication of non-fiction books pertaining to Jewish genealogy, history, culture, and heritage.

In addition to the Yizkor Book category, publications in the Other Non-Fiction category include Shoah memoirs and research, genealogical research, collections of genealogical and historical materials, biographies, diaries and letters, studies of Jewish experience and cultural life in the past, academic theses, and other books of interest to the Jewish community.

Please visit https://www.jewishgen.org/Yizkor/ybip.html to learn more.

Director of JewishGen Press: Joel Alpert
Managing Editor - Jessica Feinstein
Publications Manager - Susan Rosin

The Westreich Family Tree

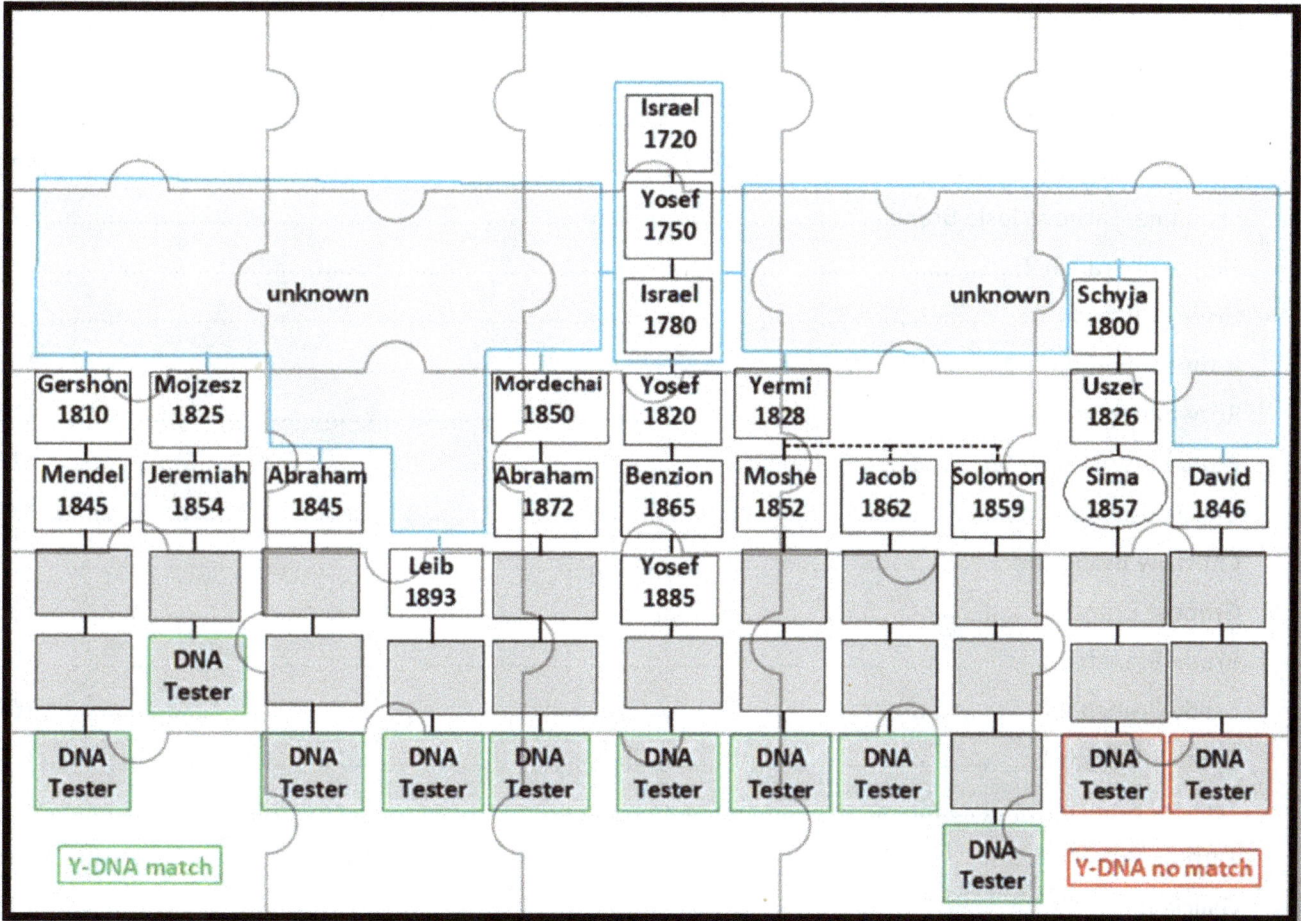

Israel 1720

Yosef 1750

Israel 1780

unknown

unknown | Schyja 1800

Gershon 1810 | Mojzesz 1825 | Mordechai 1850 | Yosef 1820 | Yermi 1828 | Uszer 1826

Mendel 1845 | Jeremiah 1854 | Abraham 1845 | Abraham 1872 | Benzion 1865 | Moshe 1852 | Jacob 1862 | Solomon 1859 | Sima 1857 | David 1846

Leib 1893

Yosef 1885

DNA Tester

DNA Tester | DNA Tester | DNA Tester | DNA Tester | DNA Tester | DNA Tester | DNA Tester | DNA Tester | DNA Tester

DNA Tester

Y-DNA match

Y-DNA no match

Putting the Puzzle Pieces Together
Using Traditional and Genetic Genealogy

Edited by Allan H. Westreich, Ph.D.

Table of Contents

The Westreich Family Tree
Introduction

by Allan Westreich

I was merrily going along, hunting down the genealogy (family history) of the Westreich side of my family. With the help of the Internet, I was even getting records from the "old country." But eventually I got stuck. I couldn't find out anything earlier than my great-great grandfather Gershon Westreich, born approximately 1810 in the town of Brzesko in Galicia, Austria (currently in modern-day Poland). I learned that getting stuck around this time frame is typical for many Jewish genealogists, as Jewish records typically did not exist before the 1800's and most Jews did not even have surnames earlier than that.

Then I became aware of a 7-generation Westreich line of Galician rabbis that was documented back to the early/mid-1700's. This is also typical of Jewish genealogy -- if you want to go back before 1800, it's often easiest to connect to a line of rabbis, the Jewish royalty whose lives and family trees were relatively well-documented. And then I learned that this line of rabbis lived in my ancestral town of Brzesko at some point, and that there were some shared first names between my line and the rabbinical line which could indicate being named after common deceased ancestors, a very frequently-used Jewish naming tradition. It was looking more and more like there was a family connection between my ancestors and the rabbis.

The next step was to identify and contact a living descendant of the rabbinical line. However, after sharing our separate family trees, we were not able to connect our trees together. And so the only way I could figure out to try to determine if we were related or not was to use DNA. If two males compare their male Y-DNA, they can tell if it is likely that they have a common ancestor. This only works if all the ancestors from each living person to the common ancestor are also male, i.e., a true patrilineal line; but that is usually the case if they have the same surname (except in Galicia where Jewish children were, at times, given their mother's maiden name as their surname because the parents were married in a religious ceremony but possibly not in a civil ceremony).

So the idea was born to create a Westreich surname study and use Y-DNA to help determine if my branch, the rabbinical branch, and other separate Westreich branches might be related to each other (see Appendix A for more details). More than 15 separate Westreich families were identified. They all reportedly descended from Jewish ancestors in relatively nearby towns in modern-day Poland and Ukraine, formerly known as Galicia, Austria (1772-1918). The question is: do all of these people descend from a single family? Or from multiple non-related families that happened to adopt the same surname of Westreich? (Jews in Galicia were mandated to adopt surnames in the late 1700's / early 1800's, and German surnames, e.g., Westreich [riches/empire in the west], were preferred by the then-Austrian government.)

The results of the Y-DNA testing indicate that 9 of 11 seemingly-separate Westreich family branches are very likely related, including my branch and the rabbinical branch. And it seems quite possible that the other two Westreich branches are also related but this was not revealed by the male Y-DNA test because these two branches may have had a female Westreich (whose maiden name was used by her children) in the line of ancestors back to the common ancestor. In addition, the Y-DNA of two families not named Westreich matched the Westreich group, indicating that these are likely related to the Westreich family but the connection is before the adoption of Jewish surnames around 1800.

And so it is looking more and more like the Westreich name may belong to a single family tree with separate branches that have been unaware of their long-lost connections to each other (see figure below -- "Using DNA to Reconnect the Westreich Family Tree"). The earliest known patriarch at the top of this tree would be Rabbi Israel Hillel Westreich, born circa 1720, who served as the rabbi of Sedziszow Malopolski (aka Shendishov in Yiddish). He would be the most recent common ancestor of all of the Westreich branches.

The purpose of this document is to record the connections between the seemingly separate branches of the Westreich family tree and to record the details of each of the branches in order to bring them to life -- with both "the facts" (e.g., names, dates of birth/marriage/death, locations, ...) and, as much as possible, "the feel, " which is conveyed through things like photographs, family stories, personal insights, ... Each chapter focuses on a particular branch of the tree, and, in most cases, significant input has been provided by living members of that branch. Whether or not the Y-DNA of each branch is a match with the vast majority of the other Westreich branches is indicated. The rabbinical branch is presented first since it has the earliest/deepest known roots, followed by the branches in the order they were "discovered" by the editor (with the exception of branches from the same ancestral town being grouped together).

What I've learned from working on this document is that despite the horrific effects of the Holocaust on the world and specifically on the Westreich family (the extent of which was previously unknown to me), there are many, many living Westreich descendants who are thriving throughout the world today -- primarily in North America, western Europe, and Israel. And, of lesser significance, I've also learned that technology has made the world a much smaller place and enables things like worldwide genealogy projects to happen.

I would like to thank the members of the Westreich community who have joined in this genealogical journey for their curiosity and collaboration. In addition, I'd like to acknowledge: Jewish Records Indexing – Poland for their invaluable resources for identifying lost ancestors; Anna Brzyska for being my "go to person" for all things related to Brzesko; and all those who granted me permission to include their work in this publication. And last, but not least, I'd like to thank my immediate family for putting up with my all-too-frequent "genealogizing." Genealogy is truly a team sport.

Future teamwork is also encouraged. Please feel free to email any comments, additions, corrections, etc. to: allanwestreichphd@gmail.com.

Goal: Fill in the Family Tree Using Traditional and Genetic Genealogy[1]

Using DNA to Reconnect the Westreich Family Tree

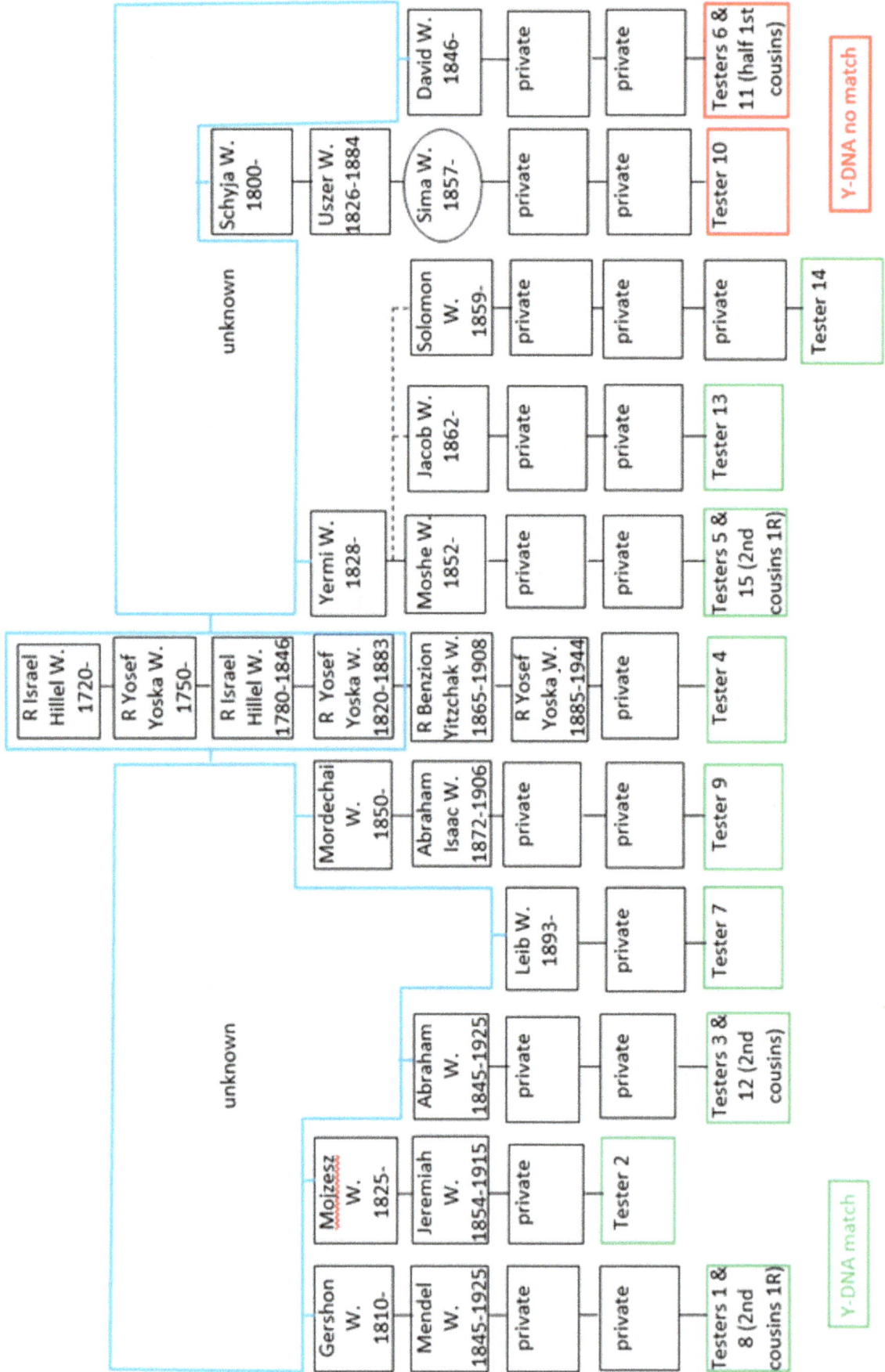

R Israel Hillel W. 1720-
R Yosef Yoska W. 1750-
R Israel Hillel W. 1780-1846

Upper branch (unknown):
Schyja W. 1800-
Uszer W. 1826-1884
Sima W. 1857-
David W. 1846-
private — private — Testers 6 & 11 (half 1st cousins)
private — private — Tester 10

Yermi W. 1828-
Solomon W. 1859-
Jacob W. 1862-
Moshe W. 1852-
private — private — private — Tester 14
private — private — Tester 13
private — private — Testers 5 & 15 (2nd cousins 1R)

R Yosef Yoska W. 1820-1883
R Benzion Yitzchak W. 1865-1908
R Yosef Yoska W. 1885-1944
private — Tester 4

Mordechai W. 1850-
Abraham Isaac W. 1872-1906
private — private — Tester 9

Lower branch (unknown):
Leib W. 1893-
private — Tester 7

Abraham W. 1845-1925
private — private — Testers 3 & 12 (2nd cousins)

Moizesz W. 1825-
Jeremiah W. 1854-1915
private — Tester 2

Gershon W. 1810-
Mendel W. 1845-1925
private — private — Testers 1 & 8 (2nd cousins 1R)

Y-DNA no match
Y-DNA match

4

Rabbinical Branch
of the Westreich Family Tree

Y-DNA match

Rabbi Israel Hillel of Sedziszow Malopolski/Shendishov

(c. 1720 - ?)

|

Rabbi Yosef Yoske of Brzesko/Brigel

(c. 1750 - ?)

|

Rabbi Israel Hillel of Brzesko/Brigel and Grybow

(1780 - 1846)

m. Fradel

|

Rabbi Yosef Yoske of Grybow and Kanczuga

(c. 1820 - 1883)

m. Beile Landau

|

Rabbi Benzion Yitzchak of Kanczuga

(1865 - 1908)

m. Genendel Zwanziger

|

Rabbi Yosef Yoske of Kanczuga

(1885 - 1944)

m. Serka Rokeach

|

Rabbi Benzion Yitzchak of Bilkamin

(1910 - 1941)

m. Sprinca Sapir/Horowitz

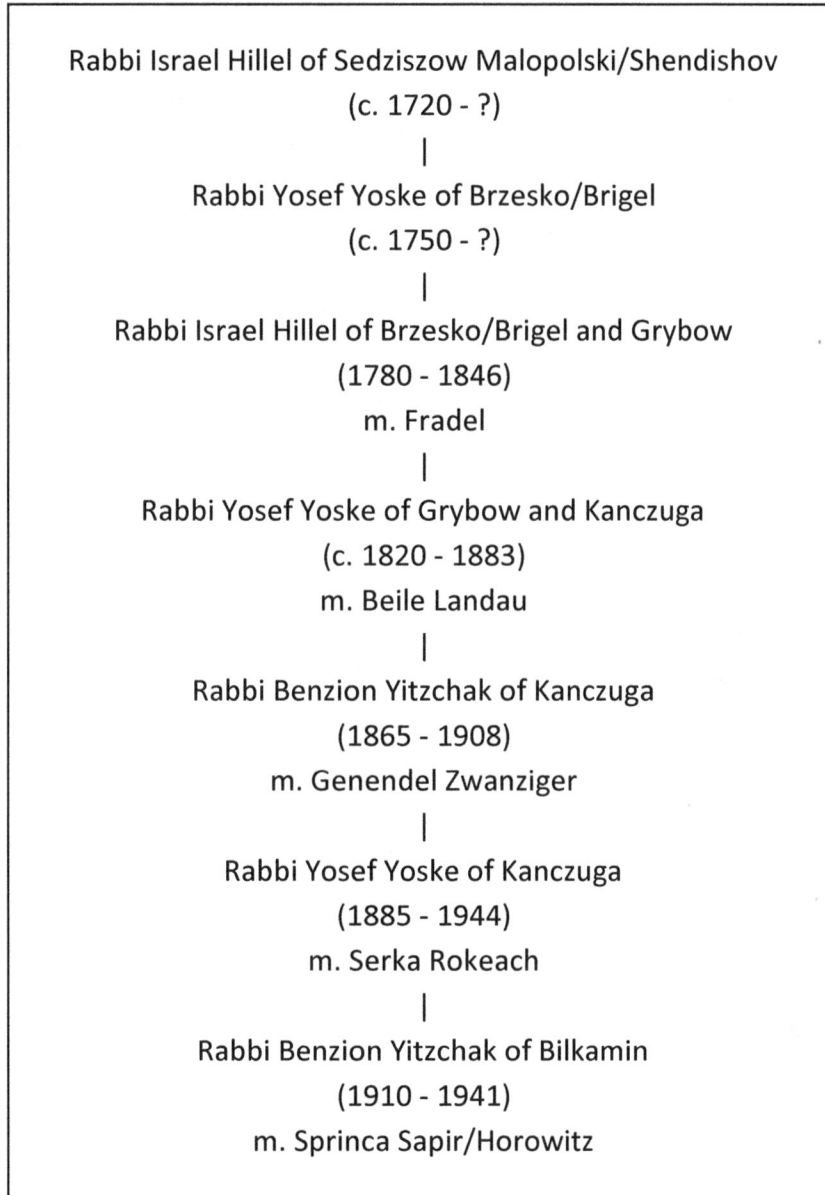

Primary sources include:
Meorei Galicia: Encyclopedia of Galician Sages (Wunder, 1978-1997)[2]

Edited by Allan Westreich

Introduction

The Westreich rabbis were a 7-generation father-to-son line of rabbis from the mid-1700's - mid-1900's. They lived in modern-day Poland, known as Galicia, Austria in 1772-1918. Galicia was the birthplace of Chassidic Judaism in the late 1700's. As living conditions for Jews worsened there, some family members left and immigrated to places such as North America (United States, Canada), western Europe (England, France, Belgium, the Netherlands), and Palestine/Israel. Unfortunately, many remained in Poland and were killed in the Holocaust, including the last two Westreich rabbis. The following biographical information focuses on the religious and family history of each of the rabbis.

Rabbi Israel Hillel Westreich of Sedziszow Malopolski/Shendishov (circa 1720 - ?)

Rabbi Israel Hillel is the earliest known of the Westreich branch of rabbis. He was the Chief Rabbi (Av Beit Din) of Sedziszow Malopolski (aka Shendishov in Yiddish). He was visited by Rabbi Naftali Tzvi Horowitz, leader of the Ropshitz Chassidic dynasty.

Israel Hillel may not have used the surname Westreich since most Jews in that part of Poland/Galicia did not adopt surnames until the late 1700's - early 1800's.

Rabbi Yosef Yoske Westreich of Brzesko/Brigel (circa 1750 - ?)

Rabbi Yosef Yoske was the son of Rabbi Israel Hillel of Sedziszow Malopolski/Shendishov. He was the Rabbi of Brzesko (aka Brigel in Yiddish).

Rabbi Israel Hillel Westreich of Brzesko/Brigel and Grybow (1780 - 1846)

Rabbi Israel Hillel was the son of Rabbi Yosef Yoske of Brzesko/Brigel. He was the Chief Rabbi (Av Beit Din) of Brzesko/Brigel and Grybow. He was the brother-in-law of Rabbi Yosef Charif Lichtag of Zborow (though unknown how).

He was openly the student of Rabbi Tzvi Hirsch Charif Heller and Rabbi Aryeh Leib Lipschutz (aka Hiddushei Aryeh-de-Vei-Ilai) of Brzesko/Brigel. In secret, he was the student of Rabbi Kalonymus Kalman Halevi Epstein of Krakow and was responsible for the original publishing of Rabbi Halevi's highly-esteemed book, *Maor Vashemesh*. He travelled with Rabbi Chaim

Halberstam (aka the Divrei Chaim), founder of the Sanz Chassidic dynasty, to visit Rabbi Naftali Tzvi Horowitz of Ropshitz.

Israel Hillel married Fradel. His known children were Rabbi Yosef Yoske (c. 1820 - 1883, see below) and Sara Lieba (1821 - 1881). Sara Lieba married Rabbi David Klagsbrun of Nowy Wishnitz (1819 - 1879), aka Rabbi David Klagsbrun-Graf because of his wealth. However, their possessions were destroyed by a fire and they went to Jerusalem. They had 4 known children -- Abraham Abisz (1846 - 1919, see photograph below), Isaac Meir (1854 - 1937), Fraidl, and Mindl -- from which long lines of rabbis descended.

Abraham Abisz Klagsbrun (c. 1916), son of Rabbi David Klagsbrun and
Sara Lieba Klagsbrun, daughter of Rabbi Israel HIllel Westreich[3]

Israel Hillel died in Rymanow on May 27, 1846 (2 Sivan on the Hebrew calendar) and was buried next to the tent (ohel) of Rabbi Menachem Mendel of Rymanow.

Rabbi Yosef Yoske Westreich of Grybow and Kanczuga (circa 1820 - 1883)

Rabbi Yosef Yoske was the son of Rabbi Israel Hillel of Brzesko/Brigel and Grybow. He was the Chief Rabbi (Av Beit Din) of Grybow (where he succeeded his father) and Kanczuga (where he succeeded his father-in-law Rabbi Yehoshua Landau in 1849).

He married Beile Landau. They had 6 known children -- Feiga Reisel, Frymeta Scheindla (1837 - 1905), Israel Hillel (c. 1849 - 1853), Schyja (1854 - 1855), Rabbi Uscher Alter Yeshayahu (1858 - 1917), and Rabbi Benzion Yitzchak (1865 - 1908, see below). Feiga Reisel married Melech Kauf and had 9 known children. Frymeta Scheindla married Rabbi Yaakov Yitzchak Horowitz of Radomysl/Radomishla and had 8 known children. Rabbi Uscher Alter married Sarah Weinberger in 1906 in Kanczuga and had 11 known children, all born in the town of Pruchnik. Uscher Alter and Sarah's daughter Frimet (1879 – 1967) married Dov Berisch Endzweig, and immigrated to Buenos Aires, Argentina along with her sons Josef (1906 – 1976), Yehoshua/Osias (1909 – 1990), Israel Hillel (1916 – 2004), and Alter Aszer (1919 – 2011), resulting in a growing South American family branch.

Rabbi Yosef Yoske died on June 25, 1883 (20 Sivan) and was succeeded by his son Rabbi Benzion Yitzchak in Kanczuga.

Rabbi Benzion Yitzhak Westreich of Kanczuga (1865 - 1908)

Rabbi Benzion Yitzchak was the son of Rabbi Yosef Yoske of Grybow and Kanczuga.   He succeeded his father as the Rabbi of Kanczuga in 1883.

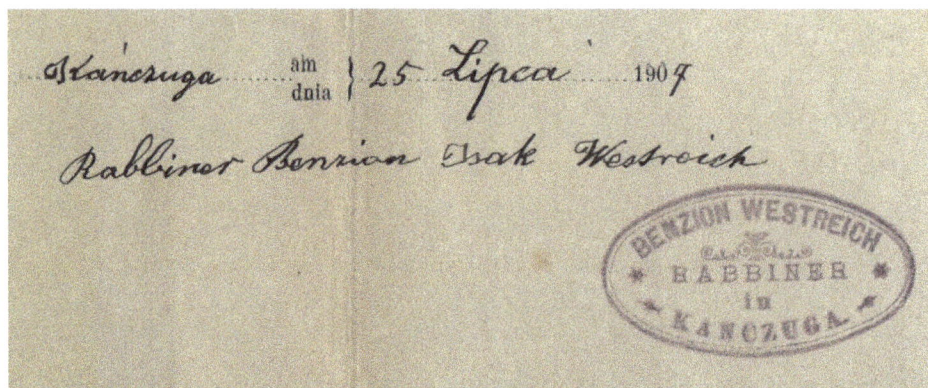

Signature and stamp of Rabbi Benzion Yitzchak Westreich, July 25, 1907[4]

He married Genendel Zwanziger. They had 6 known children -- Rabbi Meir Mechunah (1878 - ?), Sarah Fradel (1880 - ?), Sima (1882 - 1882), Israel Hillel (1883 - 1928), Rabbi Yosef Yoske (1885 - 1944, see below), and Gittel (1890 - ?). Rabbi Meir Mechunah (see photograph below) married Memel Sprung and had 9 known children. Rabbi Meir compiled a genealogy (yicchus) that traced his family (not through the Westreich side) back to King David and then further back to Jacob, son of Abraham. Sarah Fradel married Rabbi Moshe Aharon Horowitz, and, after being widowed, married Rabbi Israel Berger of Bucharest. Rabbi Berger, in 1910, supplied many details of the genealogy of the Westreich rabbis. Israel HIllel (see photograph below) married

Sarah and had 3 children, including Oscar Westreich, who changed his name to Yehoshua Bar-Hillel (see photograph below), went to Palestine/Israel, and became a world-renowned linguist, philosopher, and mathematician. Gittel married Rabbi Yosef Moshe Fuhrer of Rymanow and had 3 known children.

Rabbi Meir Westreich (son of Rabbi Benzion Yitzchak Westreich) and wife Memel Westreich from their Palestine Naturalization Application, 1941[5]

Israel Hillel Westreich, son of Rabbi Benzion Yitzchak Westreich[6]

Yehoshua Bar-Hillel, grandson of Rabbi Benzion Yitzchak Westreich[7]

Rabbi Benzion Yitzchak died at the young age of 43 on October 29, 1908 (4 Chesvan) and was succeeded by his son Rabbi Yosef Yoske in Kanczuga.

Rabbi Yosef Yoske Westreich of Kanczuga (1885 - 1944)

Rabbi Yosef Yoske (see photograph below) was the son of Rabbi Benzion Yitzchak of Kanczuga. He was the Chief Rabbi (Av Beit Din) of Kanczuga, where he succeeded his father.

Rabbi Yosef Yoska Westreich[8]

He studied under his father's tutelage as well as autodidactically. He traveled to study with Rabbi Tzvi Elimelech Shapira of Blozhov (author of "Tzvi LaTzadik" and grandson of the author of "Bnei Yissaschar"). He received his rabbinical ordination from Rabbi Shalom Mordechai Schwadron (aka the Maharsham) and Rabbi Yehoshua Horowitz of Dzikov. He was in frequent communication with, and noted in the writings of, Rabbi Dov Berish Weidenfeld, the Chief Rabbi of Tshebin (author of "Dovev Meisharim" on Jewish law). He succeeded his father as Chief Rabbi (Av Beit Din) of Kanczuga in 1909.

He married Serka Rokeach, the daughter of Chief Rabbi Elazar Rokeach of Uhnow (aka Hivniv in Yiddish), a descendant of Chief Rabbi Elazar Rokeach of Amsterdam (author of "Maaseh Rokeach"). They had 9 known children -- Shmuel Shmelka (1908), Rabbi Benzion Yitzchak (1910, see below), Moshe (1912), Frimeta Scheindla (1913 - 1913), Yehoshua/Osias (1918), Genendel (1919), Rifka Chava (1921), Meshulam Simche (1921), and Eliyahu/Eliasz (1922).

During World War I, he fled with his family to Hungary. He lived in Debrecen and worked as a rabbi in a neighboring town. At the end of WWI, he returned to his home town of Kanczuga and dedicated himself to the needs of the community. By order of his relative Chief Rabbi Yissachar Dov Rokeach, leader of the Belz Chassidic dynasty, he established a Yeshiva for students and dedicated himself to their education and other needs. He rose early every morning to learn Torah and continued his studies until past midnight. He busied himself in matters of charity and donated to the needy from his meager salary as well as convincing others to help.

He was of easy temperament and received all people softly and with affection. His learning ability came to the fore in the many religious disputes regarding the laws of Torah brought before him. His learning was marked with both reason and feeling. He was a talented prayer leader, sermonizer, and excellent scribe. He had a broad perspective and was well versed in worldly matters. He was active in the Agudat Yisrael political organization and served as their delegate to their national conferences and to their three major gatherings. He was a personal friend of Rabbi Aryeh Levin and Rabbi Meir Shapiro (aka the "Lubliner Rav" and institutor of the "daf yomi" initiative of Talmud study). He was active in promoting the Chachmei Lublin Yeshiva as well as being politically active in the elections for Polish parliament.

He left the country on 3 occasions: (1) In 1923, he sailed to the United States to raise money for a building for his yeshiva in Kanczuga. He remained in the US for half a year and turned down the repeated requests by his community there to stay in the US and be their rabbi. (2) He made a successful trip to Rome to meet with the Pope and convince him to issue orders to Galician Catholics not to oppose the erection of a fence/string (eruv) around Kanczuga for Jewish religious purposes. (3) He visited Amsterdam in order to visit libraries ("Etz Chaim" and "Rosenthaliana") to study old manuscripts of the books "Kanfei Yona" and "Maaseh Rokeach" which he was interested in publishing new editions of.

At the outbreak of the World War II, he fled to Lvov in Ukraine and continued his Torah studies while under Soviet occupation. He later moved to Zbarazh -- another Ukranian city -- with his wife and 2 of his sons. Students began flocking to him.

When the Nazis invaded on June 23, 1941, they suffered great trials and tribulations together with the rest of their Jewish brethren. In exchange for a watch and gold chain, they were able to afford to build themselves a bunker in which they hid for a long time. Alas, several days before the liberation, the Nazis discovered their hiding place by accident and all the Jews hiding there were murdered, including Rabbi Yosef Yoska.

His whole life was dedicated to the education of his children. His son Rabbi Benzion Yitchak (see below) was the Chief Rabbi of Bilkamin. Of all of his children, only his son Yehoshua survived the Holocaust. Yehoshua was a student of the Yeshivas of Stanislav ("Ohr Torah") and Tarnow, where he received his rabbinical ordination. He practiced as a rabbi for two years in post-war Europe and then moved to America, but did not practice there.

Rabbi Benzion Yitzchak Westreich of Bilkamin (1910 - 1941)

Rabbi Benzion Yitzchak (see photograph below) was the talented son of Rabbi Yosef Yoske of Kanczuga. He was the Chief Rabbi (Av Beit Din) of Bilkamin (today known as Belyy Kamen, Ukraine).

Rabbi Benzion Yitzchak Westreich, c. 1937[9]

He studied in Tarnopol under the tutelage of Rabbi David Menachem Mensch, author of "Chavatzelet HaSharon." He received rabbinical ordination from Rabbi Mensch, Rabbi David Horowitz of Stanislav, Rabbi Schmuel Firer of Krosno, and others. He also studied in Tshebin under Chief Rabbi Dov Berish Weidenfeld. He married the daughter of Rabbi Mordechai Yosef Sapir, Chief Rabbi (Av Beit Din) of Sanz, and served by his side as a court judge (dayan) and teacher of righteousness. He was later appointed as the Chief Rabbi (Av Beit Din) of Bilkamin.

Rabbi Benzion Yitzchak married Sprinca Sapir/Horowitz (see photograph of wedding invitation below). They had two known children -- Tzipora and Liba.

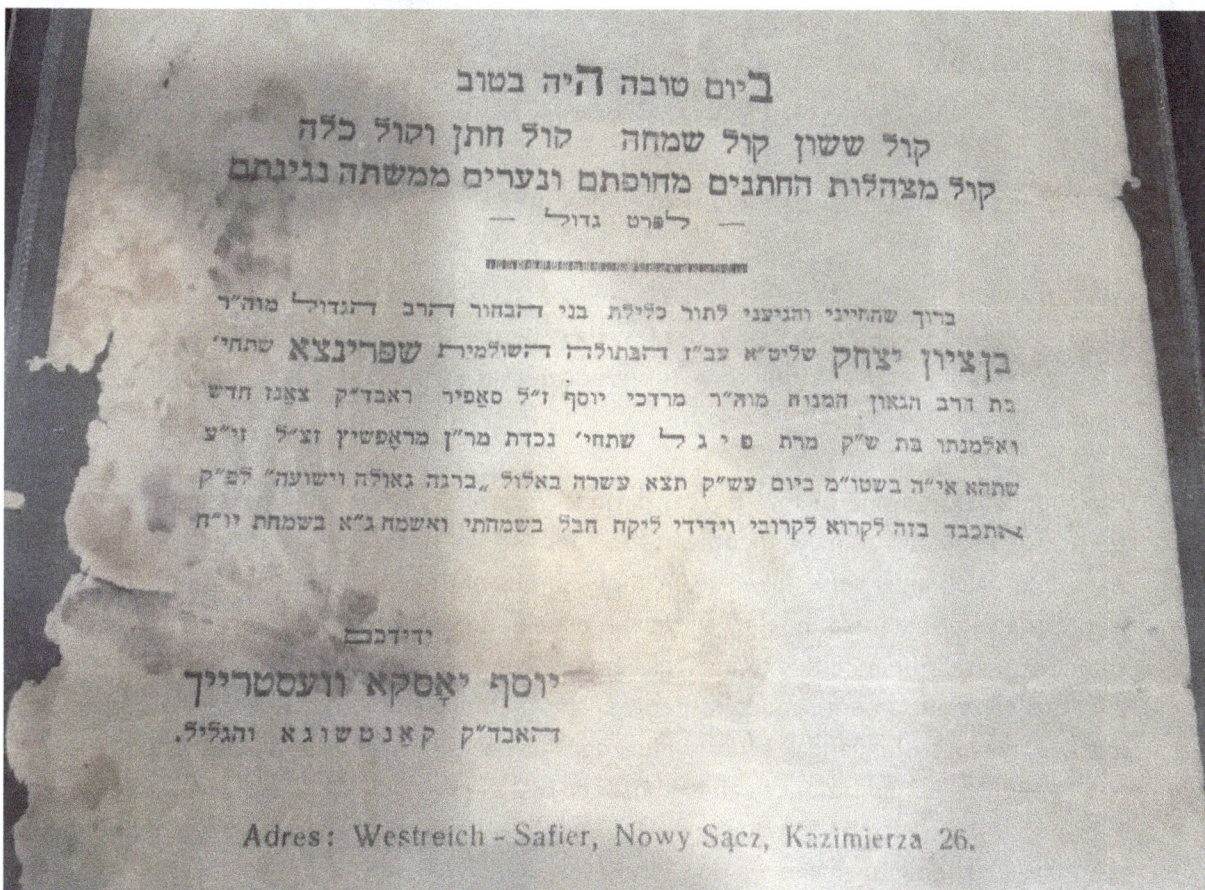

Wedding invitation of Rabbi Benzion Yitzchak Westreich and Sprinca Sapir, 1931[10]

He was "arrested" and imprisoned in Auschwitz for 2-3 days (see "mug shot" below), before being killed there (not in the gas chamber) on December 20, 1941 (30 Kislev).

Auschwitz "mug shot" of Benzion Yitzchak Westreich, 1941[11]

In 2023, below is the articulate response[12] of Benzion Yitzchak's great nephew Elie Westreich to seeing the mug shot:

> This is my great uncle's mugshot just a few days before he was brutally killed. His story is an inspiration for me to improve the world just a little bit each day by spreading kindness and love.
>
> The Holocaust was one of the darkest periods in human history, marked by the mass genocide of millions of Jewish people at the hands of the Nazi regime during World War II. People of all ages were taken from their homes and sent to concentration camps where they were starved, beaten, and even executed. Surviving the Holocaust became an act of extraordinary courage and resilience, with countless families destroyed in an effort to wipe out an entire race of people. The memory and lessons of the Holocaust must not be forgotten, and the world must continue to strive towards an understanding of how hatred and indifference can lead to such horrific atrocities.
>
> What are you doing to ensure we don't forget?
> How are you changing the world?

Concluding Thoughts

The Westreich multi-generation rabbinical family lived a fulfilling life dedicated to family and religion for 200 years in Poland/Galicia from the mid-1700's - mid-1900's. Sadly, that era came to an end with the Holocaust. Fortunately, enough Westreich family members left eastern

Europe and survived, resulting in a significant number of living descendants today spread throughout the world.

Rabbinical Sub-Branch 1:
Yehoshua Bar-Hillel

Y-DNA match
(based on match with the Rabbinical Branch)

by Mira Bar-Hillel

Rabbi Israel Hillel of Sedziszow Malopolski/Shendishov
(c. 1720 - ?)
|
Rabbi Yosef Yoske of Brzesko/Brigel
(c. 1750 - ?)
|
Rabbi Israel Hillel of Brzesko/Brigel and Grybow
(1780 - 1846)
m. Fradel
|
Rabbi Yosef Yoske of Grybow and Kanczuga
(c. 1810 - 1883)
m. Beile Landau
|
Rabbi Benzion Yitzchak of Kanczuga
(1865 - 1908)
m. Genendel Zwanziger
|
Israel Hillel Westreich
(1883 - 1928)
m. Sarah Dominitz
|
Oscar Westreich / Yehoshua Bar-Hillel
(1915 - 1975)
m. Frederika Shulamit Aschkenazy
|
Mira Bar-Hillel

Yehoshua Bar-Hillel, born Oscar Westreich,
was a world-renowned philosopher, linguist, and mathematician.

My father would have been 100 years old today.

Here's to the memory of a Very Great Man.

Blog post on September 7, 2015 by <u>mirabarhillel</u>[13]

An old Jewish joke tells of an old Jewish man saying: "If I'd known I was going to live this long, I would have taken better care of myself."

Had he lived longer, my father would be 100 years old today, and still not taking any care of himself.

Born on 8th September 1915 in Vienna, he lived through the worst of times – two World Wars – but also through the best of times, for him, as philosophy and technology were converging to enable his breakthroughs to impact on all our lives. I believe that his work in Linguistics was instrumental in allowing to talk to computers in *our* languages – not theirs.

Born to a well-to-do family on the move from Poland to Germany, Oscar Westreich was able to sing soprano in the Vienna Opera Choir. It gave him a fondness for the songs of Schubert and as his voice turned to a mellow baritone, he would entertain us by singing Roslein von der Heiden alongside the traditional Friday night Jewish chants he was to learn later.

Growing up in Berlin in the 20s as the baby of a family whose wealth was in property, Oscar's sister Berta was 10 years his senior and his brother Shmuel older still. But before he was 12 his father died on the operating table of peritonitis (burst appendix), not uncommon in pre-antibiotics times. His mother died not long after, at least partly of a broken heart. They were both only in their 40s.

Young Oscar attended both the Berlin Gymnasia (top high school) and Yeshiva (Jewish seminary) and graduated from both in 1933 with the highest grades ever achieved. But as he was celebrating, he saw the Reichstag go up in flames (a Nazi provocation falsely blamed on "Jews and Bolsheviks") and realised the writing was on the wall. With literally nothing but the shirt on his back he left his comfortable middle-class home and family and went to Palestine.

Although his aim was to pursue his studies, being penniless meant that for the first few years he had to work on the land on a kibbutz. Life was nothing like the fun holidays people go on nowadays: the work was backbreaking and spades were bloody shovels. He acquired a nice tan in time for the arrival, in 1936, of his saviour in the shape of my mother.

They had become engaged as 18-year-olds as Berta [Oscar's older sister] had married my mother's cousin and the youngsters met on family holiday in the Polish resort of Zhakopane. My mother, too, was the baby of her family with far older brothers and a sister with families of their own. But having my father waiting for her in Palestine enabled her to leave a loving family and go to join him, which literally saved her life.

As soon as she got a job as a school teacher in Jerusalem my father was able to resume his studies. But in January 1943, when news of the fate of the Jews of Europe was reaching Palestine, my father could not hide behind his books. He joined the British Army and spent the next three years training and rising to the rank of sergeant in the Jewish Brigade. I have written about this fascinating part of his life and the brigade separately and will be happy to send a copy to anyone who may be interested.

Demobbed in early 1946, it was back to the books for a while. But then the Israeli/Arab war broke out and Oscar was in uniform again, now as a lieutenant in the Israel Defence Force, and now known as Lt Yehoshua (his Hebrew name from birth) Bar-Hillel (after his late father Hillel).

With that war over, Yehoshua Bar-Hillel completed his PhD and took his young family (I was four, my sister Maya seven) to MIT in Cambridge, across the ocean, for his post-grad. We were supposed to stay for a year but ended up staying for three.

My memories are patchy (Chicken Pox ruining my debut as a ballet dancer (!), whooping cough, climbing street lamps like a monkey and watching the neighbours' 3" television while they yelled at each other in the kitchen). But I do remember walks along the Charles River and my father making up stories for us about the adventures of two naughty squirrels, Anushka and Bulbula. After a while I acquired so much faith in his story-telling abilities that for a long time I believe he had actually written The Jungle Book. Even now whenever I hear the name Riki-Tikki-Tavi I think not only of the intrepid cobra-slaying mongoose but of my intrepid father as well.

During those three years I became bilingual in English and Yehoshua met Noam Chomsky and began a lifelong relationship and working partnership. Much as I would like to, I cannot tell you what it is that they did – although history can. I shunned the academic world in favour of the realities of news and became a reporter which I still am.

The best compliment ever came one day when, after hearing one of my reports on the evening news, he turned to my mother and said: "She doesn't talk rubbish".

Having lost around five years of his career to the wars, Yehoshua finally caught up and got the rewards due to him before – and remarkably even more so after – his tragically early death just after his 60th birthday. I was already living in London then and was amazed, reading his incredible obituaries, to find how many people knew of him and his work and how highly they all thought of him. I should not have been.

Forty years on I still have a life-size photo of him above my computer and I often look to him for advice and guidance. It never fails.

I am totally his daughter in many ways, but not this: my father had no malice in him. His total inability to suffer fools (it's not easy being a genius) and his utter lack of tact could have been confused for malice, but I knew – and know – better. His wit could be cutting, even wounding, but never with malicious intent.

I try to be more like him, and fail, and try again. I will keep trying.

Thank you, Yehoshua, for all you've been and done for me. I love you and always will.

Mira

Photos[14]

(L-R) Oscar Westreich with mother, brother-in-law Natan, and sister Berta in 1920's Berlin

Yehoshua Bar-Hillel (bottom left) with the Jewish Brigade of the British Army, circa 1944 in North Africa

Yehoshua Bar-Hillel with 3-year-old daughter Mira

Yehoshua Bar-Hillel, world-renowned scholar

Rabbinical Sub-Branch 2:
Klagsbrunn Family

Y-DNA match
(based on Rabbinical Branch)

by Michael Naor

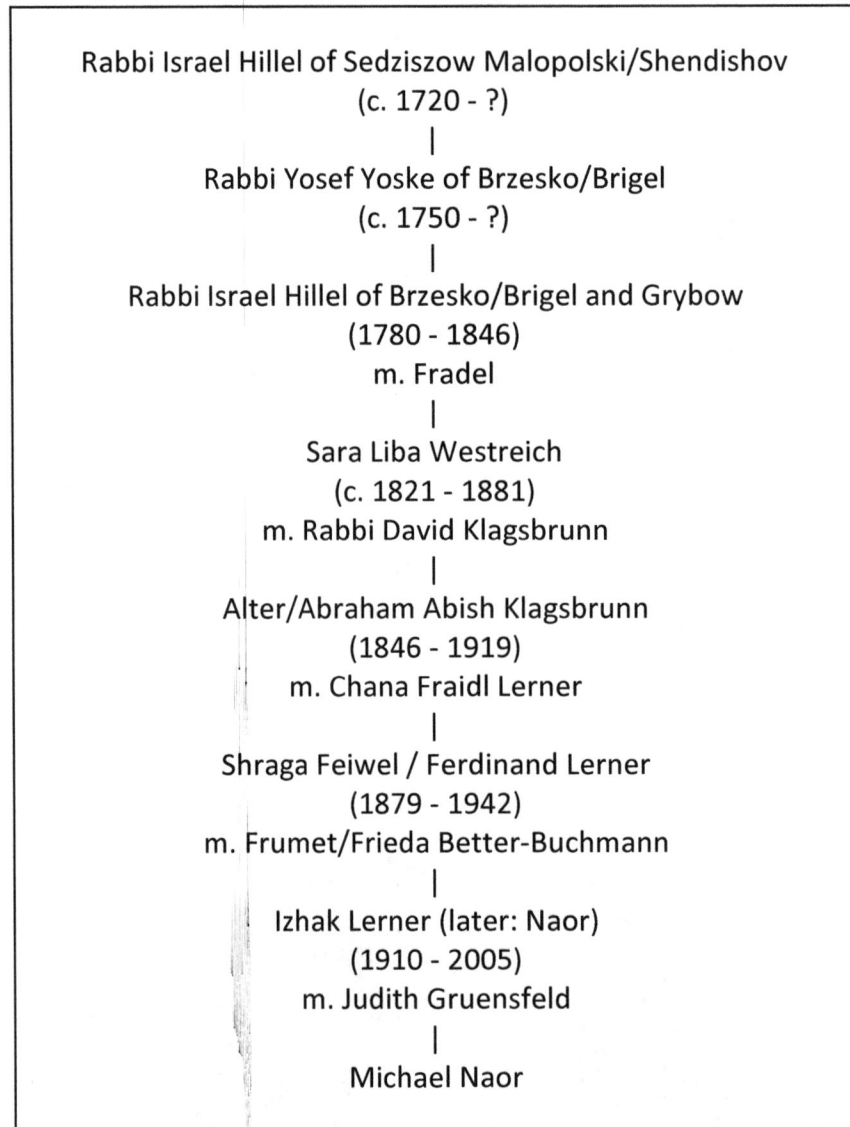

Rabbi Israel Hillel of Sedziszow Malopolski/Shendishov
(c. 1720 - ?)
|
Rabbi Yosef Yoske of Brzesko/Brigel
(c. 1750 - ?)
|
Rabbi Israel Hillel of Brzesko/Brigel and Grybow
(1780 - 1846)
m. Fradel
|
Sara Liba Westreich
(c. 1821 - 1881)
m. Rabbi David Klagsbrunn
|
Alter/Abraham Abish Klagsbrunn
(1846 - 1919)
m. Chana Fraidl Lerner
|
Shraga Feiwel / Ferdinand Lerner
(1879 - 1942)
m. Frumet/Frieda Better-Buchmann
|
Izhak Lerner (later: Naor)
(1910 - 2005)
m. Judith Gruensfeld
|
Michael Naor

Sara Liba Westreich, daughter of Rabbi Israel Hillel Westreich,
married into the Klagsbrunn family.

Preface

It was only after my father wrote his memoirs, which were published in 2003 under the title *Dem Leben Wiedergegeben – Ein Neuer Tag Beginnt* (*Back to life – a new day begins*), that I started to get interested in family history. My father died in 2005 and I was left with more questions than answers. So I started to work and research in libraries, on the internet and even visited the archives in Bochnia, Poland.

I was born in 1951 in Tel Aviv and have been working for many years as a Psychologist and Psychotherapist. Since the end of 1987, I live with my family in Duesseldorf, Germany. I am married to a physician and an expert on Diabetes. My wife's family came from the Bukowina, which today is a part of Ukraine. We have two sons -- one is a lawyer, the other an investment manager.

The name

My paternal family's name was KLAGSBRUNN from Galicia, more specifically from Nowy Wisnicz. The name Klagsbrunn does not seem to correspond with the regular criteria applied by the Austrian officials when they were giving Jews their surnames around 1800. It is neither the name of a place nor an occupation. Even Alexander Beider calls it "artificial". According to his *Dictionary of Jewish Surnames from Galicia* the name can be found in a number of Galician towns like Biala, Wielizka, Chrzanow, Krakow, Dabrowa, Rapczyce, Mielec.

The name Klagsbrunn consists of 2 German words: Klag/s which means a complaint or complaining and Brunn(en) - a fountain or a well. So it could perhaps be a personal characteristic of someone who complained a lot at the time the name was given. My own guess is that it might be derived from "a litigated well", Klags-Brunn. It is possible that the family lived near a well or was involved in a litigation/complaint concerning a well. Years ago I have discussed this interpretation with Prof. Aaron Demsky from the Bar Ilan University in Israel, who found it plausible.

The town

Nowy Wisnicz (*Yiddisch: Vishnitza*) is a small town in the Krakow region. After the Jews were expelled from Bochnia in 1606 for allegedly having desecrated the host, the local Lord Lubomirski invited them to settle in Wisnicz. In the middle of the 18th century, the community included several towns such as Brzesko, Czchów, Niepołomice and Limanowa as well as numerous villages and had 2380 members. It became one of the largest and most significant Jewish communities in the region of Małopolska, with as many as 150 villages from the area belonging to it.

The Klagsbrunns in the 19th century

In the State Archives in Bochnia, a district town 40 km east of Krakow, I found very little about the Klagsbrunn family of Nowy Wisnicz. The first mention is of Isac (Yitzchak) Klagsbrunn - my great great great grandfather, whose birth I estimate at around 1794. His wife's name was Chaje, and she died in 1879. There is no further information in the archives.

Isac's son, my great great grandfather, was Rabbi David Klagsbrunn, born in Nowy Wisnicz in 1819. He married Sara Liba (or Lieba) Westreich (1821-1881), the daughter of Rabbi Israel Hillel Westreich (1780-1846), Chief Rabbi (Av Beit Din) of Brzesko and Grybow. Oral tradition describes David Klagsbrunn as being very wealthy, so that people used to call him "Graf" -- German for Count or Earl. He was also very generous and spent regularly for Tzedaka (charity). There would be 30 poor persons dining at his table daily, so it is told. A booklet written by the Brim branch of David Klagsbrunn's descendants and published within a private circle under the name *Shnot Chayim* (*Life Years*) reports that he eventually lost all his wealth. Only an expensive goblet remained in his possession. It was a gift from one of the noblemen he was dealing with. This goblet still exists and is being kept by the Brim family in Israel.

David Klagsbrunn's goblet (courtesy of the Brim family)[15]

The above booklet goes on to tell that following his financial disaster, David Klagsbrunn went in 1867 together with his youngest child (or possibly nephew) Izchak Meir to Eretz Hakodesch, then Palestine, and lived in Jerusalem. Sara Liba and the other children very likely joined him in Jerusalem. His gravestone at the cemetery on the Mount of Olives in Jerusalem indicates that he died on 5. May 1879. Sara Liba died in 1881.

Gravestone of Rabbi David ben Rabbi Izhak Klagsbrunn, Mount of Olives, Jerusalem[16]

Oral traditions in the family tell that the descendants of David Klagsbrunn additionally received the unofficial surname BARDAK – acronym of Ben Rabbi David Klagsbrunn, which shows a high respect towards the person David Klagsbrunn.

Rabbi Izchak Meir Klagsbrunn (1854–1937), son (or possibly nephew) of David Klagsbrunn but not my direct ancestor, lived all his life in poverty in Jerusalem. His sharp mind and comprehensive knowledge of the Thora were renowned and so was his strict observance of the Halacha (*Jewish law*). According to Sefer Me'orot Galizia (*Book of the Lights of Galicia*) he became the principal of the Galicia Yeshiva (*Koylel Galizia*) and contributed a lot to that institution, which was mostly dependent on donations from the Diaspora.

Rabbi Izchak Meir Klagsbrunn[17]

Gravestone of Rabbi Izhak Meir Klagsbrunn,
Mount of Olives, Jerusalem[18]

My direct family

Back to my branch: My great grandfather Alter/Abraham Abish Klagsbrunn, the son of Rabbi
David Klagsbrunn, was born in Nowy Wisnicz in 1846. He married Chana Fraidl Lerner, also born
in 1846. The 1880 Census of the Jews in Nowy Wisnicz shows that both the Lerner and
Klagsbrunn families lived in house Nr. 32.V. The only thing I know about him is from my father's
childhood memories that whenever he came for a visit, as for Pessach, he used to spend many
hours in his room reading and studying the Thora. He died in 1919. I can only suppose that he is
buried in Nowy Wisnicz.

Abraham Klagsbrunn, circa 1916[19]

Abraham and Chana Fraidl Klagsbrunn had 3 children, all of them born in Nowy Wisnicz:

Mordechai Chaim (Markus), b. 1874. He lived in Krakow, where he owned a shop for leather goods. He and his wife Estera had about 8 children.

Zipora Feigil, b. 1876, married Mordechai Pacanowski from Radomsko, where he had a shop for leather goods. They had 2 girls.

Shraga Feiwel (Ferdinand) - my grandfather - b. 1879, married Frieda Better-Buchmann from Oswienczim. Since he had to wait a very long time to receive an official marriage certificate, he adopted his mother's surname Lerner. They had 3 sons: Leo (Arje Lejb) b. 1906, Isac (Izhak - my father) b. 1910, and Jakob b. 1916.

Shraga Feiwel Lerner started already at the age of 18 his own business manufacturing paper and carton goods. At first, his workshop was located in Bielsko-Biala. During WWI, he moved with his family to the Czech town of Moravska Ostrava (*German: Maehrisch-Ostrau*), where he eventually built a factory that supplied clients from in and out of the country. In 1938 the Czech authorities expelled all persons with Polish citizenship back to Poland. My grandparents went to Krakow, where after the German occupation they were put into the Ghetto. I could only find out that they were transported to Bochnia in 1942, where their tracks disappear.

The Lerner family in Ostrava around 1923 (my father standing in the middle)[20]

Shraga Feiwel's son Leo, along with Leo's wife and son (later they had another son), went to Palestine in 1938 in the hope to build a new start there for the family, that was supposed to follow. My father Isac and his younger brother Jakob were arrested in Prague, where they were waiting for the certificate to leave for Palestine. They were arrested on the second day of Rosh Hashana as they came out of the Altneu Shul and put first in prison and later transported to an improvised concentration camp in the east of Poland. After several months of imprisonment, they were set free due to the intervention and bargaining of the Jewish leadership of Slovakia. They went to Bratislava, the Capital of Slovakia. There my father met and married Judith Gruensfeld. In the summer of 1942, Judith's parents were arrested and transported to an unknown destiny.

The Shoa

Both my paternal grandparents -- Shraga Feiwel and Frieda Lerner -- and my maternal grandparents -- Michael Zwi (Hermann) and Elizabeth Gruensfeld -- were murdered in 1942. Mordechai (Shraga Feiwel's brother) and Estera Klagsbrunn along with most of their children, as well as Zipora (Shraga Feiwel's sister) and Mordechai Pacanowski along with one of their 2 daughters, were also murdered (the other daughter left earlier to Palestine to work as a pioneer). My own parents spent around 2 years in a forced labor camp in Slovakia and afterwards several months of hiding in the mountains and forests until the end of the war. They joined a group of young people organized by the Haganah heading to Palestine on one of the illegal routes. Already in the port of La Spezia in Italy, where they were supposed to board the Haganah ships Dov Hoz and Eliyahu Golomb, they were arrested by British soldiers. After having conducted a hunger strike of 72 hours, the international public opinion pressed the British government to allow them to leave. On the 18th of May 1946, they arrived in Haifa.

During the hunger strike in La Spezia (my father in the front with eyeglasses)[21]

Brzesko Branch 1
of the Westreich Family Tree

Y-DNA match

by Allan Westreich

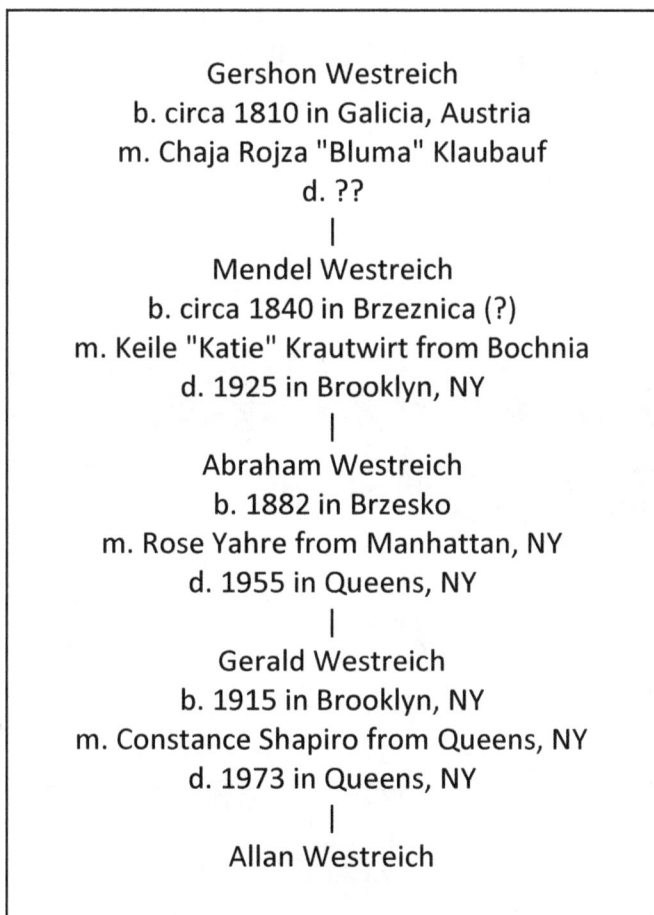

Gershon Westreich
b. circa 1810 in Galicia, Austria
m. Chaja Rojza "Bluma" Klaubauf
d. ??
|
Mendel Westreich
b. circa 1840 in Brzeznica (?)
m. Keile "Katie" Krautwirt from Bochnia
d. 1925 in Brooklyn, NY
|
Abraham Westreich
b. 1882 in Brzesko
m. Rose Yahre from Manhattan, NY
d. 1955 in Queens, NY
|
Gerald Westreich
b. 1915 in Brooklyn, NY
m. Constance Shapiro from Queens, NY
d. 1973 in Queens, NY
|
Allan Westreich

Brzesko is a small town in modern-day Poland,
formerly part of Galicia, Austria (1772 - 1918),
located 31 miles east of Krakow.

I've been interested in my family history for a long time. My first active questioning about it was back in high school when my three living grandparents were over for dinner. My one deceased grandparent was my paternal grandfather, Abraham "Abe" Westreich, who died before I was born and I was subsequently named after. I was told that night by my grandmother that the name of Abe's father (my great-grandfather) was Mendel and that he was from Austria. And that Mendel had a sibling named Angel who had emigrated to England and that is where his descendants live. This was the first I had heard of relatives living in a different country. And I remember getting confused about the name Angel, thinking this was a sister but really it was a brother (full name of Anschel). And this was also the first time I drew a family tree, eagerly trying to capture all this new and interesting information which started me on a lifelong (on-and-off) genealogical journey. If only I had asked more questions of my grandparents back then!

Gershon Westreich, born circa 1810, is the earliest-known patriarch of this branch. Gershon married Chaja Rojza "Bluma" Klaubauf (see picture below), daughter of Dawid and Rifka Klaubauf. Bluma was born circa 1812 and died in Brzesko in 1907 at age 95. She is buried in the New Jewish Cemetery in Brzesko -- see gravestone (restored in 2020) and translation below.

Chaja Rojza "Bluma" Westreich, wife of Gershon[22]

אשהזקנה צנועהוישרה
יראתד'הי תמיד אוצרה
גמלהחסד בטוב לבה בימי
חיי'חסידהוזריזה היתהאל
מצותי מ'חי רוזא בהמנוה
מו'דוד זל'נפט ערב ה'
שבט ש'תרסז תנצ'צב'ה

Here lies
An elderly, modest, and honest woman
Always treasured and feared God
Compassionate and kind with a good heart
Was pious and quick to observe the
commandments
Mrs. Chaya Rojza daughter of our departed
teacher David of blessed memory
Passed away on the evening of ?? Shevat
5667 [Feb. 12, 1907]
May her soul be bound up in the bond of
eternal life

Gravestone of Chaja Rojza "Bluma" Westreich[23]   Translation

Gershon and Bluma had 4 known children, all sons -- **Joseph**, **Mendel**, **Israel Hillel**, and **Anschel**.

I.   Little is known about **Joseph Westreich**, the oldest son of Gershon and Bluma. According to a family letter, he changed his surname to Koenigsberg to avoid getting drafted into the military and lived to 112. Since the Y-DNA of this Westreich line matches the Y-DNA of the rabbinical Westreich line, perhaps he was named after the rabbi Yosef Yoska Westreich.

II.   My great-grandfather **Mendel Westreich** (c. 1840 - 1925) was the next son of Gershon and Bluma. Reports of his livelihood in Poland include owning a "saloon," making cabinets, and owning a small farm. He married Keile "Katie" Krautwirt (from Bochnia) and they had 6 known children -- Gustav (c. 1868 - 1928), Rebecca "Beckie" (1876 - 1939), Chana/Anna "Annie" (1878 - 1968), Abraham "Abe" (1882 - 1955), Marjem (1888 - 1889), and Schewe (1888 - ?). The last 2 children probably died in childhood -- Marjem and Schewe. Below is a family picture of Mendel, Katie, Beckie, Annie, and Abe, most likely taken in Brzesko circa 1890.

(L-R) Katie, Mendel, Abe, Beckie and Annie Westreich in Brzesko, circa 1890[24]

Based on the birth and death records of Mendel and Katie's children, it appears that the family moved often, which apparently was common for families of modest means, primarily in the towns of Brzesko and nearby Nowy Wisnicz and Brzeznica. Abe was born in Brzesko in House #313 in 1882, likely the family residence at the time. See the photograph below for this location in current day, although it is likely that the original (wooden?) house was burned down in the major fire in 1904 in Brzesko and rebuilt as shown.

Location of residence of Mendel and Katie's family
(corner of Okocimska Street and Rzeznicza Street)
where their son Abe was born in 1882 in Brzesko, in 2022[25]

Based on the birth and death records of their children, Mendel and Katie were never married in an Austrian civil ceremony, although no doubt they had a Jewish/religious wedding ceremony. This was quite common among Galician Jews who, by and large, were not eager to assimilate into the Austrian/Polish culture.

Mendel's oldest son, Gustav (c. 1868 - 1928, see picture below), appears to be the pioneer of the family. As a child, Gustav attended public school for 3 years and also went to a cheder, an elementary Jewish school where he was taught the basics of Judaism and the Hebrew language. He also learned to read, write, and speak German, Polish, and Yiddish. As an adult, the story goes, he was a faithful reader of German, Jewish, and English newspapers. Family lore also reports that one of his public school teachers offered to instruct the children to play the violin if they brought a violin to school. Gustav related this to his father Mendel who made him a violin. So he had musical instruction at a fairly young age.

Gustav Westreich, son of Mendel[26]

Family lore also says that Gustav went AWOL from the Austrian army, buried his uniform, and left Austria in 1887 to live in England with Mendel's brother Anschel and his family. (Although the less glamorous version of this story is that he simply left Austria for England when he received an order to join the Austrian army.) After a year in England, living in his uncle's home, which was not an affluent one, and finding himself unable to earn a living in the glass and window business, Gustav decided to go to the US in 1888, first settling into the lower east side of Manhattan. He began working as a house painter, and then in 1895 decided to go into business with a friend (Isidor Greschler), who each invested their life savings of $300 into a paint store at 1674 Broadway in Brooklyn. As the business prospered, Gustav added hardware. (In fact, many Westreich's from this branch went into the hardware business.) Gustav later built 2 buildings nearby, at 1664 Broadway in Brooklyn, each 4 stories high with a store, a loft, and a 7-room apartment. He moved his business and his family residence into one of these buildings.

Gustav married Augusta "Gussie" Spinard in 1889 in Manhattan (see picture below). They had 6 children -- Bertha (1890 - 1985), Ann (1892 - c. 1989), Pearl (c. 1894 – 1920, died in the flu pandemic), Miriam (1896 - 1981), Jonas (1898 - 1974), and Abe/Albert/Al (1901 - 1982).

Wedding of Gustav Westreich and Gussie Spinard, 1889[27]

Bertha, the eldest, was the source for much of the family history of Gustav. In describing the household where she grew up, Bertha told of a father who was very successful in business and a mother who, without help from relatives or servants, successfully ran a home and raised 6 children. Her parents lived very carefully and would be described as middle class. Religion was not an important factor in family life. Although Gustav, and presumably Gussie, had a Jewish upbringing, their children did not. Gustav was a free thinker and a socialist. Religious education was not made available to the children and neither of their sons had a Bar Mitzvah, which was very unusual at the time. Both sons followed in their father's footsteps and opened their own retail business – Jonas, a clothing store in Keyport, NJ and Al, a paint/hardware store in Brooklyn, NY (see newspaper clippings below).

1903 Westreich & Greschler[28]

1929 Westreich & Greschler ad[29]

1923 Opening of Jonas Westreich's clothing store[30]   1929 Opening of Al Westreich's hardware store[31]

Gustav's move to the US (1888) was followed by his sister Beckie (1890) and then his sister Annie (1895). Mendel, Katie, and their youngest son Abe followed (1896) when Abe was approaching draft age. According to a fanciful family story, they snuck over the Austrian border in the middle of the night to board a boat to Ellis Island, NY. Immigration records indicate that they departed from Hamburg, Germany, approximately 600 miles from Brzesko, in steerage class on a ship named *Persia*, arriving at Ellis Island on May 29, 1896.

Beckie married Zelig/Sigmund Plapinger and they had 3 children -- Mathilda "Tillie" (1898 - 2000), Anna (1899 - 1976), and John "Edward" (1907 - 1978). Tillie, who lived to the ripe old age of 102, supplied several of the above family stories. Edward owned a hardware store.

Annie married Henry Halbkram and had 2 children -- Flora (1907 - 1990) and Abraham "Albert/Al" (1908 - 1981). Flora supplied the above early pictures of Bluma and of Mendel's family. Al owned a hardware store on 42nd Street, Manhattan.

Mendel, Katie, and Abe initially settled in the lower east side of Manhattan in a small 2- or 3-room apartment at 107 Pitt Street and later moved to 2998 Fulton Street in Brooklyn. Mendel reportedly did not work once coming to the US, financially supported by his sons Gustav and Abe. Mendel has been described as "smart" and "shrewd." He often smoked a pipe.

Abe (see picture below), my grandfather, initially went into business with a partner, Mr. Moscowitz, who he later bought out. Abe then had his own hardware business, A. Westreich Co., in 1906 at 3134 Fulton Street in Brooklyn (see picture below), which was apparently very successful as it expanded to 3 store fronts. Abe has been described as "ambitious."

Abe Westreich, son of Mendel, circa 1950[32]

A. Westreich Co., Inc. at 3130 - 3134 Fulton Street
in 3 adjacent buildings in Brooklyn, 1940[33]

Abe married Rose Yahre in 1914 (see picture below) and had two sons -- Gerald and Harold. The family moved to 208 Norwood Avenue, around the corner from the store. When the sons were old enough, the entire family of four worked in the hardware store ... a true "family business." The family and the business all relocated to Jamaica, Queens, NY in the 1950's, all living and working within blocks of each other yet again. The store existed into the 1970's.

1914 Wedding of Abe Westreich and Rose Yahre[34]

III.   The next son of Gershon and Bluma was **Israel Hillel Westreich** (1850 -). He was born in 1850 in Brzeznica, a small village near Brzesko. He operated a seltzer factory and was a wine dealer. He died relatively young, in his early 50's (?), leaving his wife Ruchel to care for their 9 living children, all (but the first) born in Brzesko -- Gershon (1877 -), Chaim/Henry (1879 - 1980), Leib/Leo (1881 - 1966), Mendel (1883 -), Natan (1886 – 1886), Rifka/Regina (1887 - 1942), Josef Salamon (1889 - 1939), Isaak/Izzie (18792 -), Laje Freide (1893 -), and Dawid/David (1898 -).

Similar to his brother Mendel's family, Israel Hillel's children's birth records indicate several different residences. Therefore, Israel Hillel's family moved relatively often, which again was common for families of modest means. Another similarity with his brother Mendel, Israel Hillel did not have a civil marriage ceremony before having children, although no doubt had a Jewish/religious wedding ceremony then. However, Israel Hillel and Ruchel did eventually have an Austrian civil marriage in 1900 in the nearby town of Klasno. Perhaps this was done because

Israel Hillel was in failing health and he wanted to legitimize his children in the eyes of the Austrian government before he passed on.

Since the Y-DNA of this Westreich line matches the Y-DNA of the rabbinical Westreich line, it seems very likely that Israel Hillel was named after the rabbi Israel Hillel Westreich who died 4 years before he was born.

Israel Hillel's wife Ruchel (nee Jakob, see picture below) lived to over 100 years old, when she was taken from her daughter Regina's house in Jaworzno by the Nazis. Regina's daughter Natalie recalled her grandmother Ruchel as always dressed in black and never wearing glasses, yet being able to sew on black material at a ripe old age. She was religious and every Friday night would cook food, deliver it to the poor, and spend a little time with them.

Ruchel Westreich, wife of Israel Hillel[35]

Israel Hillel and Ruchel's family suffered the most at the hands of the Holocaust because they had not left Austria/Poland. Although Israel Hillel had already passed, Ruchel and 6 of their 9 children were killed in the Holocaust along with their families.

The surviving children were Henry, Leo, and Izzie. Henry (see picture below) married Dora Gawrilowicz in 1905 in Tarnow and moved to Frankfurt, Germany in 1908 where he opened a bicycle business. They had 3 children -- Joseph, Rosalie (see picture below), and Regina. Henry and Dora moved to London, England with the help of Angel's family in 1939, and then to the US in 1943. Henry lived to the ripe old age of 101. Their son Joseph worked for Warner Brothers in Paris, France and was able to relocate to California. Their daughter Regina barely managed to escape from Germany in 1939 to Manhattan with the aid of Jack Warner, her brother Joseph's employer.

(R-L) Henry Westreich (son of Israel Hillel) and daughter Rosalie in NY[36]

Henry and Dora's daughter Rosalie emigrated to Paris in 1937, where she lived with her brother Joseph and his wife and worked as a nanny. A few months later, she accepted a job as a secretary and translator with the Joint Distribution Committee (JDC) and worked for them until the German invasion. She escaped to Bordeaux, France and made her way to England. In 1939, she emigrated to the US and continued working for the JDC, whose primary function was to help Jews emigrate to safe places. After the war, she was sent back to Europe in 1945, where she worked at the head JDC office in Munich, Germany helping displaced persons until 1949. In 1954, she was sent to Tehran, Iran by the JDC to observe and help the progress of Jewish communities in Iran. She later moved back to Manhattan.

Leo came to the US in 1914. He worked in the hardware business in the Bronx. He married Rifka/Ruth Gutfreund from Brzesko and they had 2 children -- Ira and Sylvia. Ira and his wife Elaine were the first Westreich genealogists, spending much time and effort in this endeavor and generously sharing their information (see picture below). Their quest was spurred on by a letter in 1975 from Ira's uncle Henry (above) who laid out the foundation of this branch.

(L-R) Allan Westreich (great grandson of Mendel) meets with Elaine and Ira Westreich (grandson of Israel Hillel) for a "genealogy brunch" (1991)[37]

Izzie came to the US in 1914. He was a businessman and a "go getter," initially owning an Italian-American grocery and later a hardware store. He married Esther Nussbaum and had 1 daughter, Selma.

IV.   The last son of Gershon and Bluma was **Anschel "Angel" Westreich** (c. 1857 - 1936, see picture below). He was the first Westreich of this entire branch to leave Austria when he emigrated to London, England, appearing in the 1881 England Census as a "lodger." He anglicized his surname to "Westrich," reportedly to not appear of German origin. He worked as a "master tailor." He married Betsy Perrich at the Princes Street Synagogue in London in 1882, living in the impoverished and overcrowded (with immigrants) neighborhoods of Whitechapel and Stepney Green in the East End of London. (In fact, they lived there during the time of the infamous serial killer Jack the Ripper.)

Anschel "Angel" Westreich/Westrich[38]

Angel and Betsy had 9 known children -- George (1883 - 1965), Joseph (1885 - 1958), Kate (1887 - 1960), Davis "David" (1889 - 1921), Paulina (1892 - 1892), Annie (1893 -), Fanny "Faye" (1895 - 1984), Solomon (1897 - 1901), and Leah "Lily" (1902 - 1933).

Son George married Charlotte "Lottie" Ostrowiecki/Hyman (see picture below) and had 1 daughter, Evelyn "Betty." He owned a cinema (movie theater). He reached out to save his first cousin Henry Westreich and wife Dora (above) by helping them emigrate from Germany to London in 1939.

George Westrich (son of Angel) and wife Lottie[39]

Son Joseph married Kate "Kitty" Lefcovitch and had 4 children -- Cyril, Lillian "Lilykins" (see wedding picture below), Rosalind, and Doreen. Kitty, Lillian, and Rosalind immigrated to Canada and then to the US (California) in the 1950's.

Wedding of Lillian Westrich (daughter of Joseph) and Jack Linder, 1942[40]

Joseph died in 1958 seemingly a very poor man, as evidenced by his extremely meager gravestone (see picture below).

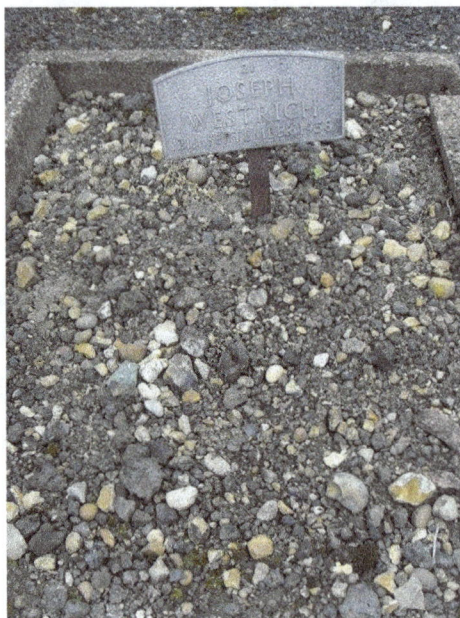

1958 gravestone of Joseph Westrich at East Ham Jewish Cemetery in London, 2013[41]

Daughter Kate married Sid Solomon/Somerston and had one son, Eric.

Son David (see picture below) emigrated to Manhattan, married Deborah "Dolly" Epstein, and had one daughter, Leona. He died at the young age of 31 of cancer. His daughter was just 3-1/2 years old.

Passport pictures of David and Dolly Westreich, 1919[42]

Daughter Annie married Sidney Myers and had 3 sons -- David (political cartoonist), Geoffrey, and Michael.

Daughter Faye (see picture below) married Charles "Chas" Barnett and had 1 daughter, Gilda (1930 – 2019, see picture below).

Faye Barnett nee Westrich, daughter of Angel[43]   Gilda Bogod nee Barnett, daughter of Faye, 2013[44]

Daughter Lily married David Davis and had 1 daughter, Patricia "Pat." Lily passed away at the young age of 31, resulting in her sister Faye helping to raise Pat.

And that's what is known today about this branch of the Westreich family tree ... but who knows what new discoveries will surface in the future :-)

Brzesko Branch 2
of the Westreich Family Tree

Y-DNA untested

by Eveline Witjas

Mordechai/Markus Westreich
b. circa 1789
m. Malke
d. ??
|
Issachar Ber/Berl Westreich
b. circa 1819
m. Sarah Rifka Weisbart
d. 1879 in Brzesko
|
Szyja Westreich
b. 1851 in Brzesko
m. Rachel Blaugrund from Brzesko
d. ??
|
Berl Westreich
b. 1881 in Brzesko
m. Chawa Ruchel Klipper from Krakow
d. 1958 in Antwerp, Belgium
|
Erna Westreich
b. 1916 in Metz, France
m. Joseph Witjas from Amsterdam
d. 1997
|
Eveline Witjas

Brzesko is a small town in modern-day Poland,
formerly part of Galicia, Austria (1772 - 1918),
located 31 miles east of Krakow.

My and my sister's story of being hidden children during World War II

I, Eveline Witjas, was born on April 22, 1939 in Liege, Belgium.
My sister Edith Witjas was born on August 3, 1940 in Arras, France.

My parents:
My mother Erna Westreich-Witjas was born in Metz, France on August 8, 1916.
My father Joseph Witjas was born in Amsterdam, The Netherlands on January 21, 1904. My father's ancestors go all the way back to 1604, all Dutch Jews!

In 1940, my parents and my father's parents fled Belgium to France. My mother was 8 months pregnant, and I was 1 year old. They later came back the same year to Brussels, because the Germans also invaded France.

Until the end of 1943, we were all together. My parents obtained a false identity and were named "Pascal". My parents felt it was more and more unsafe, and they decided to look for a place for us. They had Christian friends and they found a convent first in the North of France.

At that time, I was 5 years old and Edith was 4. My mother always told me how difficult it was for her to give us away to a place she did not know. We stayed approximately 6 months in that convent. The nuns were not nice to us and we were very unhappy there.

My mother, who was a very courageous young women of 27 years old, came during 1944 to visit us. I have no idea how she managed this. We did not recognize her because she had blond hair which made her look not that Jewish. Originally, she had black hair. You can imagine how she felt that her own children did not recognize her. We told her that we were not happy there. How she did it I don't know, but we went in 1944 to a small Belgian village called Londerzeel, and there again in a convent.

My mother also told us that we will never see our father again. She said he was gone. We did not really understand what that meant.

My mother, as I said, was very brave. When my father was taken by the Gestapo, she had no money whatsoever. She had the courage to sell butter from the black market to the German soldiers. She spoke German and was very good looking!

In the convent in Londerzeel we were quite happy. The nuns loved us, specially Edith who was the youngest of all the girls who lived there. Of course, we did not know we were Jewish. There were another 5 Jewish girls there, but we only knew that after the war. When there were school holidays, we were the only ones who could not go to their parents. We felt odd but took it for granted. We went to mass, and I even went to confess. I had nothing to say to the priest, so I lied sometimes and said I was not nice to the nuns. With a few *Ave Maria*'s and *Our Father*'s, my sins were gone!!!

After the war, my mother left us there until 1947. She could not financially take us home. I was for some years angry at her, but later I understood why she did it. She knew we were ok there.

At the end of 1947, she decided to move us to a Jewish home in Antwerp. We even went to a Jewish school. But in 1949 the whole home went to Israel.

At that point, my mother finally took us home. I was 10 years old and Edith was 9. It was difficult for my mother and us to have a warm relationship. She did everything she could, but it was always in a materialistic way. I missed a warm nest.

I will always respect her courage to raise us without a father. She passed away in 1997, and I still miss her. She was not an easy person but had a strong personality. She lost 2 brothers during the war.

And my paternal Dutch grandparents lost 2 children -- my father and his brother Jacob. My grandmother never recovered from that loss.

In the 1960's, Edith and I went back many times to Londerzeel. The nuns who were still alive remembered us very well, and we were so grateful to them. They saved our lives. Of course we named them at Yad Vashem. One of the nuns, sister Jeanne, passed away 2 years ago. Each Christmas we talked, and she said to me that we were like her own children.

That, in a nutshell, is my story.

Joseph and Erna Witjas, Eveline's parents[45]

Eveline Witjas visiting the grave of her great-great grandfather Issachar Berl Westreich
in the New Jewish Cemetery in Brzesko, 2022[46]

Brzesko Branch 2a
of the Westreich Family Tree

Y-DNA untested

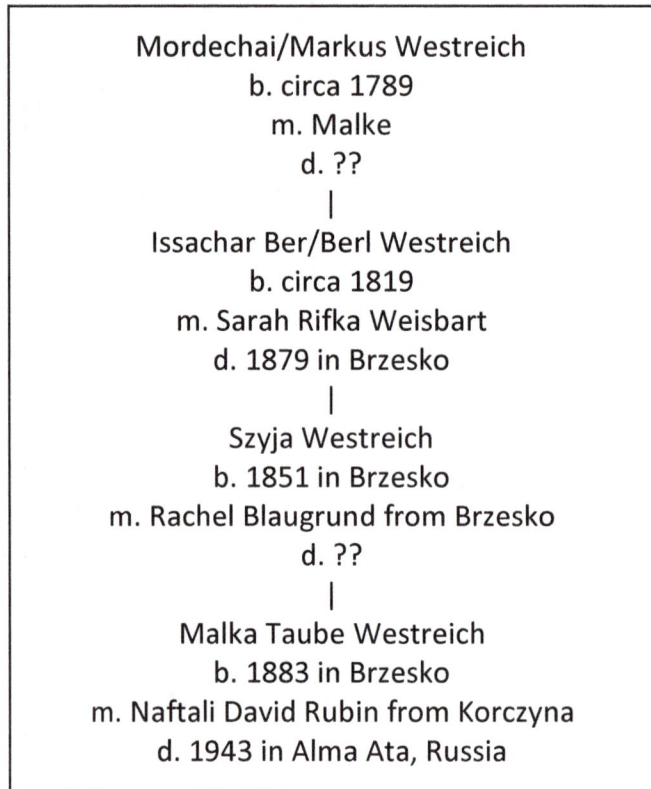

Mordechai/Markus Westreich
b. circa 1789
m. Malke
d. ??
|
Issachar Ber/Berl Westreich
b. circa 1819
m. Sarah Rifka Weisbart
d. 1879 in Brzesko
|
Szyja Westreich
b. 1851 in Brzesko
m. Rachel Blaugrund from Brzesko
d. ??
|
Malka Taube Westreich
b. 1883 in Brzesko
m. Naftali David Rubin from Korczyna
d. 1943 in Alma Ata, Russia

Brzesko is a small town in modern-day Poland,
formerly part of Galicia, Austria (1772 - 1918),
located 31 miles east of Krakow.

Primary source:
Memory of the Rubin Family
by Jan Haag, grade 12 student of the Lessing-Gymnasium,
from the website
Gendenkbuch für die Karlsruher Juden (*Memorial Book for the Karlsruhe Jews*),
July 2004[47]

Edited by Allan Westreich

Memory of the Rubin Family

Personal Data

Taube Malka Rubin

Surname:	Rubin
Born:	Westreich
First name:	Taube Malka
Date of birth:	December 1, 1883
Place of birth:	Brzesko / Galicia (Austria-Hungary, now Poland)
Marital status:	married
Parents:	Schya and Rachel, née Blaugrund, Westreich
Relationship:	Wife of Naftali Rubin
Mother of:	Joshua, Esther, Helene (1908-1908), Recha and Sara Regina
Address:	1907-1909: Kronenstr. 56
	1910: Kaiserstr. 65
	1911: Kronenstr. 8
	1912-1920: Schützenstr. 89
	1920-1938: Winterstrasse. 50
	1938: Herrenstr. 22
Job:	Housewife
	Commercial traveler (in husband's shop)
Deportation:	October 28, 1938 deported to Poland (Poland)
Date of death:	1943
Place of death:	Alma Ata (formerly Soviet Union, now Kazakhstan)

Biography

Naftali and Taube Rubin

Today the history of National Socialism is dealt with in detail. Such destruction of human existence and dignity must never happen again. Victims were all those who did not meet the "Aryan" ideal of a person, especially so-called "Gypsies" and above all Jews. They were all defenseless against the arbitrariness and terror of National Socialism.

One of these families was the Jewish Rubin family. It consisted of the members Naftali David Rubin, the father, the mother Taube Malka Rubin, née Westreich, and their five children Esther, Helene, Recha, Joshua and Sara Regina.

Naftali David Rubin was born on March 15, 1883 in the Austrian-Hungarian city of Korczyna as one of six children of Benjamin Rubin, a merchant, and his wife Maria, née Schipper. In the same year, on December 1, 1883, his future wife Taube Malka Westreich, daughter of Schya and Rachel, née Blaugrund, Westreich was born in Brzesko. Both small towns are located in Galicia, where the proportion of the Jewish population was very high due to the medieval migration movement. The former Polish territory was first divided between Russia, Prussia and Austria in 1772; this brought the inhabitants of this part of Galicia under Austrian control. As a result of the Treaty of Versailles after the First World War, it came back to Poland, which had been rebuilt.

Nothing is known about the meeting of the Rubin couple, but it can be assumed that they got to know each other before their decision to emigrate to Germany, since in 1901 they both had the goal of Strasbourg, which at the time was still part of the German Empire. Naftali Rubin decided at the age of 18 to leave his parents' home and wanted to start his own life far away in the west. The exact reasons remain hidden, perhaps there were closer or more distant relatives on whom his decision was based; it can be assumed that he had a portion of courage and determination. Naftali struggled as a traveling salesman. In Strasbourg, Naftali and Taube decided to marry, but only in the synagogue according to the Jewish rite, not at a civil registry office.

In 1907 the couple moved to Karlsruhe together and initially lived at Kronenstrasse 56. Shortly thereafter, on February 17, 1908, the twin sisters Esther and Helene were born. Unfortunately, Helene passed away the following month, March 23. The death register does not specify the exact circumstances of the death, perhaps a sudden child death can be assumed. On May 27, 1909, Recha saw the light of day, followed by Joshua, the only son, on May 1, 1911 and finally Sara Regina Rubin, on June 6, 1912. After the children were born, the family moved to Südstadt, in the first floor of Winterstrasse 50, where they stayed for the next twenty years.

While Naftali Rubin initially earned enough money to survive as a traveling salesman, he now attempted his own business by dealing with enlarging photographs. Since 1926, he became the owner of a relatively large laundry mail order business, which also seemed to have gone well until the boycott during the Nazi era. After all, he could temporarily employ eight travelers. Taube Rubin was initially a housewife. After opening the mail order business, she was not "just helping family members", but as a commercial traveler made a significant contribution to its sales. At that time, the Rubins also had a maid, not only a sign of professional effort, but also of striving for the bourgeois lifestyle of the time.

Several career changes for Naftali and frequent moves within Karlsruhe in the first few years are striking; it is therefore reasonable to assume that the parents fought very hard for the existence of their family by trying to adapt to the given circumstances. The residential areas were not in an exceptional location, neither particularly wealthy, nor were they characterized by poverty. The fact that Naftali was involved in the Orthodox Chewra Kadisha brotherhood, which provided the strictly religious Jewish funeral ritual, suggests a religious Orthodox lifestyle.

On January 26, 1915, the Rubins who had previously only been married in the synagogue decided to now also say yes in the civil registry office. The reasons for this can only be speculated: either they wanted to create the conditions for naturalization later - they were still Austro-Hungarian citizens - at an early stage, or the legal wedding should be carried out quickly before the expected military conscription of Naftali. The witnesses are an indication of the second. In the marriage register, the caretaker of the town hall and an office worker are indicated, which speaks to the hurry. On the other hand, a lack of acquaintances could also be the reason for this; it is also unknown whether family members lived in Karlsruhe or the surrounding area.

When Italy declared war on Austria-Hungary on May 23, 1915, Naftali was obliged to serve on August 16 due to his nationality, and continued to do so in Rifle Battalion No. 18 until the end of the war; he survived the war and was finally released on December 5, 1918.

Since their Galician place of origin was incorporated into the Polish state after the First World War, the Rubin family applied for German citizenship in mid-April in 1920. Naftali Rubin based his decision on the fact that "under no circumstances would he want to become a Polish citizen". The application was processed by the Karlsruhe Police Headquarters by researching any anomalies, clarifying financial circumstances and checking the persons concerned for possible bankruptcy, criminal proceedings and welfare relationships.

The officials came across the only entry in the criminal record of Naftali Rubin, which says that in 1911 he was fined 50 marks, or a five-day prison term, for fraud. According to the job description of this report, he had also been a bag dealer at the time, but this name can only be found in this register. The fraud was decisive for the following decision: "Even though this punishment is relatively small, it has to be based on the assumption that the lifestyle is no longer undamaged, because after the Rubin judgment the photographer tried to bring inferior photographic enlargement with all sorts of inaccurate offers thereby harming a number of people, thus putting the audience at risk.

Naftali, not discouraged, made another application on March 22, 1929, to obtain German citizenship for himself and his family on March 22, 1929; daughter Esther, who was now an adult, submitted a separate application at the same time. Although from the police point of view there were no objections, his livelihood was secured, no state support payments were received, the trivial penalty mentioned had long since been deleted from the criminal record, the request was rejected with the objection of the Karlsruhe City Council that Naftali Rubin would not properly fulfill his duties as a taxpayer. At the same time, the application of his daughter Esther was processed, the city council raised no concerns about her naturalization. However, the police headquarters informed her three days later in writing without further explanation, that it did not meet the requirements of section 8 of the Reich and Citizenship Act of 1913 and therefore the application for naturalization could not be met. This law stipulates that foreigners who have settled in Germany must be able to do business without restriction according to the laws of their old homeland, as well as those of Germany, that they have not borne any guilt in previous life and also that they have their own accommodation at the place of establishment to own and be able to feed any relatives. Since Esther Rubin had not yet learned a profession and lived with her parents, there can be talk of a subsequent decision that results from the parents' application rejection. Shortly thereafter, on May 27, 1930, Esther married Salomon Bergmann, born May 1908 in Brzesko near Poznan. Their son Max was born in Karlsruhe, on March 22, 1931. In the same year, the young couple moved to Ludwigshafen, where the second son Oskar was born on November 20, 1934. Salomon Bergmann ran a bag shop.

With Hitler's seizure of power in 1933, the Rubins mail order business gradually went downhill. The business suffered from the boycott and the busy travelers could no longer work. As Jews, their travel permits were withdrawn in 1934. In 1938, Naftali Rubin tried to resist the inclusion of his business by the National Socialist Ordinance in the list of Jewish businesses. Hopeless. In this matter, the only thing left for the chief of police to say was that Taube Rubin dissolved the business after her husband's deportation in December 1938.

On October 28, 1938, Naftali Rubin was deported by rail from the Karlsruhe loading station via Mannheim to Zbaszyn, a Polish city on the border with Germany. The number of Jewish inmates rose from 52 to around 6,100 after the time of deportation to Poland on 28/29. October. The reason was that on this date the Nazi regime intended to deport all male Jews in Germany, whom it described as "Polish citizens", to Poland.

Naftali's wife also had to leave the Reich, but she was given a deadline of July 31, 1939. When she actually left Karlsruhe in order to forcibly follow her husband to Poland remains unknown. Every trace of her is lost. Alone, as the year and place of death for Taube Malka is Alma Ata in Kazakhstan, 1943. But if there is no paper proof for this, it remains completely in the dark where this information comes from. It is also not understandable how and why she should have gone there, and under what circumstances she died. At the beginning of the German attack on Poland in September 1939, did she flee to eastern Poland, which was occupied by the Soviets in accordance with the so-called Hitler-Stalin Pact? If so, she was certainly not persecuted as a Jew in the Soviet sphere of control, however, for reasons of strategy, the Soviet regime carried out various population deportations during the war, which resulted in unspeakable suffering for the victims and also resulted in deaths. One can only say with certainty that her death would not have happened without the brutal persecution of the Nazi regime.

Naftali's place and date of death are unknown; he is considered a missing victim of the Nazi regime.

From the "reparation files," you can roughly understand what happened to the children. In 1932, daughter Recha had married Salomon Mohl, born in Lancut in 1903 and living in Düsseldorf since 1922, where the couple also lived. The marriage gave birth to a son, Oskar, who was born on June 14, 1935 in Düsseldorf. In May 1939, the family of three was forced to leave Düsseldorf and go to Poland. Recha died on January 12, 1947 in a DP (Displaced Person) camp, a shelter for many of the persecuted who survived the war, in Bad-Reichenhall. This suggests that she was also a victim of Nazi terror but survived the immediate end of the war. The DP camp intermediate station may be on the way to a hoped-for emigration. According to lawyer Cohn, her siblings Esther and Joshua did not return from the extermination camps to which they had been deported by the National Socialists. But how and when they had to go this way remains in the dark. Esther probably followed her husband Salomon Bergmann, who was probably also deported to Poland from Ludwigshafen in October 1938. On September 3, 1936, in Karlsruhe, Joshua had married Rosa Bergmann, two years his junior from Ludwigshafen, from the same family to whom Esther had married. Then he must have left Karlsruhe.

Only the youngest daughter Sara Regina had survived the cruel years of the dictatorship. She later lived in Brooklyn / New York, USA, was married and had a child.

On February 5, 1959, an application for compensation for deprivation of liberty due to the deportation to Poland was rejected because, according to the officials of the "reparation authority", it could not be proven that Naftali Rubin could be affected by Nazi measures after "leaving the territory of the Reich."

A compensation sum was later only granted for the loss of the furniture left behind, but only after an objection to the first rejection decision. The occupational restriction was subsequently recognized by the Nazi measures and "balanced" with a sum of money.

During the official research in connection with the "reparation procedure" it was found that in 1938 none of the children in Karlsruhe had lived with their parents. A couple living at the last address still remembered that the Rubins housing stock, such as furniture, had been auctioned publicly by the Nazi authorities.

Probably only the grandchildren of Naftali and Taube Malka Rubin are still alive today, who are certain to have missed their grandparents and who, like us, cannot imagine how people could cause such brutal, terrible discrimination and enormous psychological and physical damage to other people.

Malka Taube Rubin, nee Westreich[48]

Brzesko Branch 2b
of the Westreich Family Tree

Y-DNA untested

Mordechai/Markus Westreich
b. circa 1789
m. Malke
d. ??
|
Issachar Ber/Berl Westreich
b. circa 1819
m. Sarah Rifka Weisbart
d. 1879 in Brzesko
|
Aron Joseph Westreich
b. 1848 in Brzesko
m. Alte Brucha Fischgrund
d. 1919 in Brzesko
|
Rachel Westreich
b. 1872 in Brzesko
m. Aron Wagschal from Nowy Sacz
d. 1940 in Jerusalem, Israel
|
Israel Ze'ev Wilhelm Friedrich Wagschal
b. 1906 in Dieburg, Hessen, Germany
m. Kate Esther Biberfeld
d. 1980 in Jerusalem, Israel
|
Julius Yekutiel Yehuda Wagschal
b. in Breslau, Germany
m. Celia Sabbath Sklar
|
Avigail Israela Wagschal Mertens

Brzesko is a small town in modern-day Poland,
formerly part of Galicia, Austria (1772 - 1918),
located 31 miles east of Krakow.

by Allan Westreich

The Wagschal family descended from Brzesko Branch 2 of the Westreich family tree. The earliest known ancestral couple is Mordechai/Markus (born circa 1789) and Malke Westreich. They had a son Issachar Ber/Berl Westreich, born circa 1819. Berl married Sara Rifka Weisbart, born circa 1825. Berl died in 1879 and is buried in the New Jewish Cemetery in Brzesko (see photo of gravestone below).

Gravestone of Berl Westreich (d. 1879)[49]

Berl and Sara Rifka Westreich had five known children – Aron Joseph (b. 1848), Szyja (b. 1851), Mojzesz Wolf (b. 1866), Abraham David (b. 1868), and Chane Gitel. Descendants of Szyja are discussed in the previous chapters. This chapter will discuss Aron Joseph and his descendants.

Aron Joseph Westreich married Alte Brucha Fischgrund (b. 1850). They had 12 known children – Gerschon, Rachel, Szymon, Chaim, Scheine, Hersch, Berl, Taube Itty, Laje, and triplets Sara, Rifka, and ?. All of the children were born between 1869 and 1891 in Brzesko. Six of them died in childhood. Aron Joseph died on August 25, 1919 and Alte Brucha Fischgrund/Westreich died on August 4, 1930. Both are buried in the New Jewish Cemetery in Brzesko (see photos of gravestones below).

Gravestone of Aron Joseph Westreich (d. 1919)[50]

Gravestone of Alte Brucha Westreich (d. 1930)[51]

Aron Joseph and Alte Brucha's daughter Rachel (b. 1872 in Brzesko) married Aron Wagschal (b. 1868 in Nowy Sacz) in Brzesko in 1900. They also had 12 known children. Based on the details of the lives of their children, it appears they moved from Nowy Sacz to Brzesko to Dieberg, Hessen, Germany to Israel. Rachel (d. 1940) and Aron (d. 1953) are buried in Jerusalem.

And the generations continue on.

Brzesko Branch 3
of the Westreich Family Tree

Y-DNA no match

Szyja/Osias Westreich
b. circa 1800
m. Sima Selinger
d. ??
|
Uszer Westreich
b. 1826 in Klasno
m. Gittla Ryfka Apter
d. 1884 in Brzesko
|
Sima Westreich
b. 1857
m. Leser Pipersberg
d. ??
|
Asher Pipersberg/Westreich
b. 1886 in Brzesko
m. Bella Wetstein from Wieliczka
d. 1942

Chaim Yosef Westreich	Osias "Sam" Westreich
b. 1911 in Wieliczka	b. 1919 in Wieliczka
m. Beila Bluma Horowitz	m. Bella Siegfried
d. 1995 in Bat Yam, Israel	d. 1978 in US
|	|
Elimelech Westreich	Henry Westreich

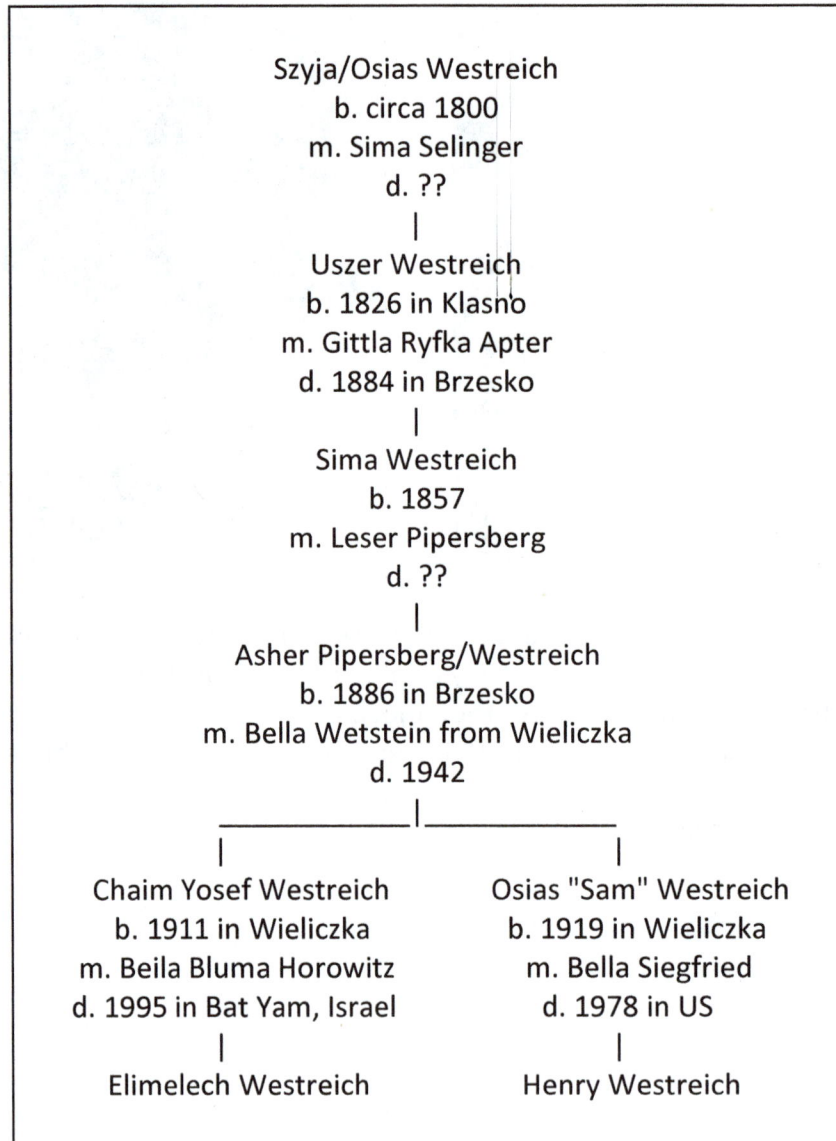

Brzesko is a small town in modern-day Poland,
formerly part of Galicia, Austria (1772 - 1918),
located 31 miles east of Krakow.

Sources include:
Email communications with Elimelech Westreich and Henry Westreich[52]

Edited by Allan Westreich

Although birth/marriage/death records have enabled this branch to be traced back to Szyja Westreich, born circa 1800, family stories are only known beginning with Asher Pipersberg/Westreich (1886-1942). He was one of eight known children born to Leser Pipersberg and Sima Westreich. Some of the children used the surname Pipersberg, and some used Westreich. The typical reason for this incongruity was many Galician Jews at that time only had a religious marriage ceremony and not a civil one; therefore, in the eyes of the Galician government, Leser Pipersberg was not recognized as the legitimate father. Hence, the mother's maiden name, Westreich, was used by some of their children. And hence, although the surname of Westreich was passed down to Ascher, the male Y-DNA does not match the other Westreich branches because this branch has the Pipersberg Y-DNA.

Asher was born in Brzesko. He married Bella Wetstein from Wieliczka, where they settled and had four known children -- Chaim Yosef, Markus Mordechai, Osias "Sam," and Gitle. Family lore has it that Asher was a war hero who fought in World War I and against the Russians through the 1920's. Asher, Bella, Markus, and Gitle perished in the Holocaust. Asher was beaten to death by a German soldier at the beginning of the war and was buried in the Jewish cemetery in Wieliczka.

Brothers Chaim and Osias survived the Holocaust, but endured the torturous route of multiple concentration camps. They managed to stay together. In August 1942, the Wieliczka ghetto was liquidated, with the bulk of Jews being placed on trains to the Belzec extermination camp. A small group, which included Chaim and Osias, was sent to work in the Plaszow labor and concentration camp. Chaim was a trained plumber and his services were in demand. Osias met his future wife, Bella Siegfried, in the Plaszow camp. Chaim's wife, Beila Horowitz, was also in the Plaszow camp. She survived the Holocaust by being placed on Schindler's List.

Chaim and Osias were later shipped to Mauthausen and its sub-camps, Melk and Ebensee. Mauthausen was one of the most notorious slave labor camps. It was known for its "Stairs of Death" where inmates carried blocks of granite up 186 steps to the top of the quarry.

After the liberation, Chaim and Osias went back to Poland to locate survivors, managing to locate their future wives. They next moved to displaced persons (DP) camps in the American zone of Austria, where they began their families. Osias was the Jewish Deputy Police Chief in the DP camp *Star of David* in Ebelsberg (near Linz, Austria). From the DP camps, Chaim immigrated to Israel in 1948, while Osias went to the US in 1949. And, as a result, future Westreich generations have prospered across the globe.

Family Photos/Documents

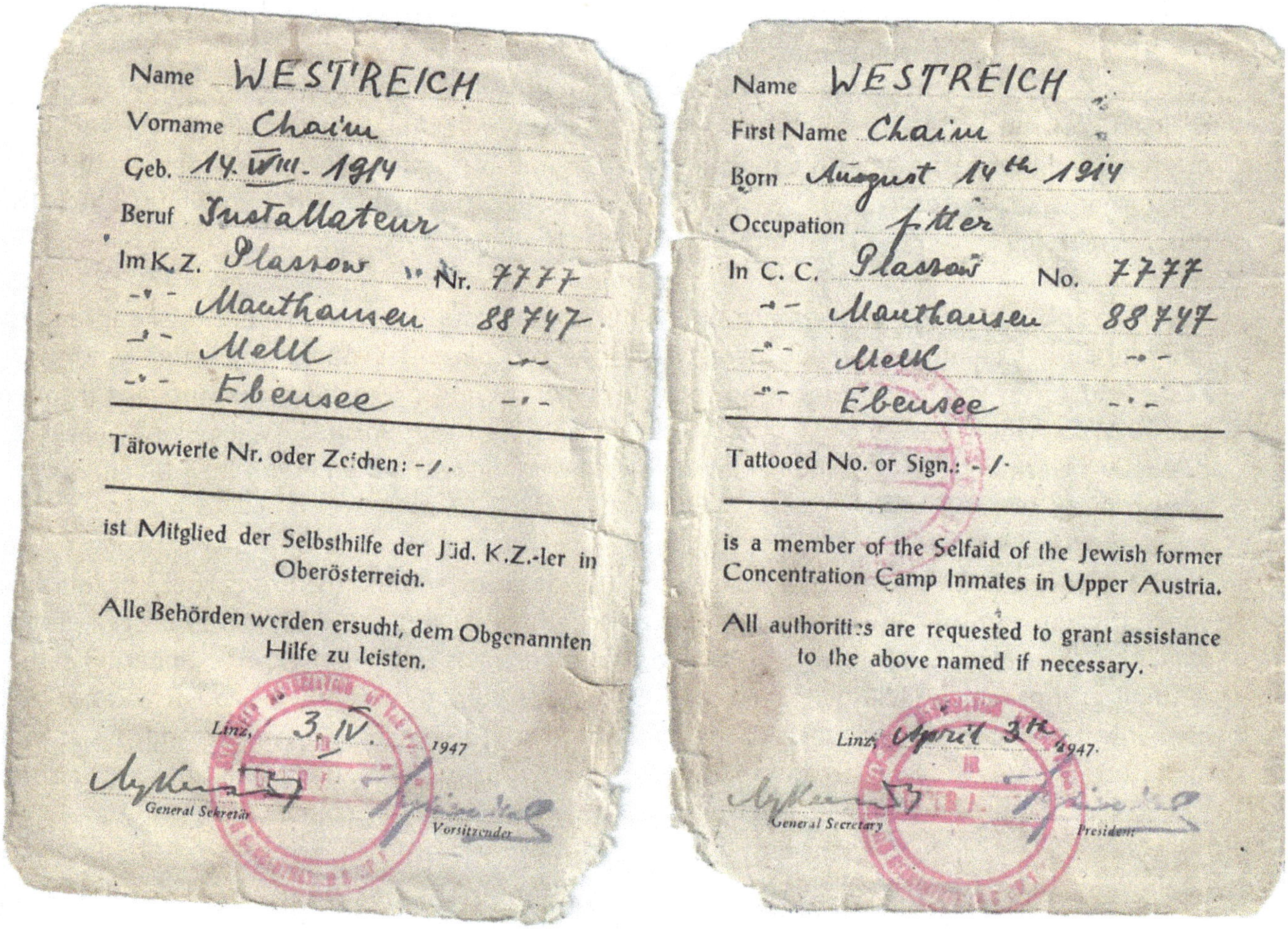

Name **WESTREICH**
Vorname *Chaim*
Geb. *14. VIII. 1914*
Beruf *Installateur*
Im K.Z. *Plassow* Nr. *7777*
-"- *Mauthausen* *88747*
-"- *Melk* -"-
-"- *Ebensee* -"-

Tätowierte Nr. oder Zeichen: -/-

ist Mitglied der Selbsthilfe der Jüd. K.Z.-ler in Oberösterreich.

Alle Behörden werden ersucht, dem Obgenannten Hilfe zu leisten.

Linz, *3. IV.* 1947

General Sekretär *Vorsitzender*

Name **WESTREICH**
First Name *Chaim*
Born *August 14th 1914*
Occupation *fitter*
In C.C. *Plassow* No. *7777*
-"- *Mauthausen* *88747*
-"- *Melk* -"-
-"- *Ebensee* -"-

Tattooed No. or Sign.: -/-

is a member of the Selfaid of the Jewish former Concentration Camp Inmates in Upper Austria.

All authorities are requested to grant assistance to the above named if necessary.

Linz, *April 3th* 1947

General Secretary *President*

Post-war ID of Chaim Westreich,
listing the Concentration Camps where he was imprisoned[53]

Osias Westreich in the vicinity of *Star of David* DP camp
in Ebelsberg, Austria, with Austrian Alps in the background,
circa 1948[54]

Osias W.'s team pin from the
Hakoach Linz soccer club for
Jewish players from DP camps[55]

Henry Westreich in the vicinity of *Star of David* DP camp
In Ebelsberg, Austria, circa 1949[56]

Brzesko Branch 3a
of the Westreich Family Tree

Y-DNA untested

by Lea Markson, Martin Markson,
and Allan Westreich

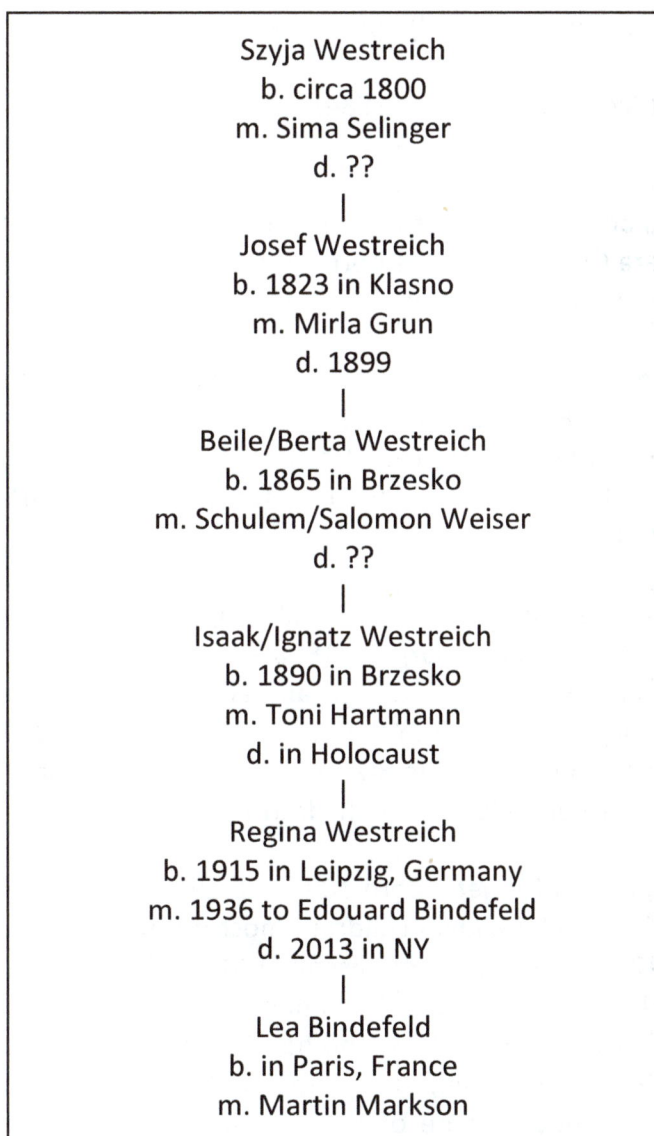

Szyja Westreich
b. circa 1800
m. Sima Selinger
d. ??
|
Josef Westreich
b. 1823 in Klasno
m. Mirla Grun
d. 1899
|
Beile/Berta Westreich
b. 1865 in Brzesko
m. Schulem/Salomon Weiser
d. ??
|
Isaak/Ignatz Westreich
b. 1890 in Brzesko
m. Toni Hartmann
d. in Holocaust
|
Regina Westreich
b. 1915 in Leipzig, Germany
m. 1936 to Edouard Bindefeld
d. 2013 in NY
|
Lea Bindefeld
b. in Paris, France
m. Martin Markson

Brzesko is a small town in modern-day Poland,
formerly part of Galicia, Austria (1772 - 1918),
located 31 miles east of Krakow.

The earliest known ancestral couple of this branch is **Szyja and Sima (nee Selinger) Westreich**, born circa 1800. They had 3 known children – Perl, Josef and Uszer Westreich, all born in Klasno, Poland. Klasno is a small village on the outskirts of the town of Wieliczka, about 10 miles southeast of Krakow.

Daughter **Perl Westreich** (1821 – 1881) was born in Klasno and died in Bochnia at age 60. She married David Flanzer and had 1 known child – Josef, born 1854 in Brzesko. Josef married Chaje Grobtuch (born 1851) and they had 5 known children, all born in Bochnia – Abraham Mojsesz (b. 1872), Schewa Ryfka (b. 1875), Perl (b. 1884, d. 1886), Freide Gittel (b. 1885), Feigel (b.1886, d. 1886), and Zina (b. 1891). Abraham Mojsesz had 2 known wives – Roza Plessner (married in 1899 in Krakow, later divorced) and Sara Feniger (married in 1902 in Bochnia).

For details on son **Uszer Westreich** (1826 – 1884) and his descendants, please see the previous chapter.

Son **Josef Westreich** was born 1823 in Klasno and died 1899 in Brzesko. He married Mirla Grun, daughter of Josef and Sara Grun. Mirla was born circa 1820 in Radomysl and died in Brzesko in 1900 at age 80. Josef and Mirla had 3 known children -- Israel Hillel, Beile, and Sara.

Their oldest known child was **Israel Hillel Westreich** (1850 - 1935). It seems very likely that Israel Hillel was named after Rabbi Israel Hillel Westreich of Brzesko (and later Grybow) who died 4 years before he was born. Therefore, it seems very likely that this branch is related to the rabbinical Westreich branch which descends from an even earlier Rabbi Israel Hillel Westreich, born circa 1720.

Israel Hillel married Chane Broder and had 10 children, all born in Brzesko -- Osias (1876 - 1877), Chaim Anschel (1878 - 1880), Marjem (1880 -), Mojzes (1883 - 1889), Reisel (1885 - 1909), Efroim (1887 - 1894), Gittel (1890 - 1891), Samuel Ber (1893 -), Chaje (1895 -), and Hene (1898 - 1997). The majority of the children did not live into adulthood. Israel Hillel and Chane were married in a civil ceremony in 1917 in Brzesko. It is very likely that they were married in a religious ceremony much earlier, before their children were born.

Israel Hill and Chane's daughter Marjem, born 1880 in Brzesko, married Yehuda/Juda Kapelner, born 1872 in Tarnow. They had 7 known children, most if not all born in Cologne, Germany – Sarah (1902 – about 1942/Auschwitz), Yosef/Joseph (1905 – 2002/Israel), Aaron/Arnold (1912 – 1996/Israel), Efraim (1914 – 2006), Helena, ? (died in Holocaust), and Max. Sarah, the oldest, married Wolf Israel Wajl/Weil (1901 – 1943) and had 2 sons – Julius (1925 – 2021) and Arnold (1929 – 1944), born in Germany. Sarah, Wolf, and Arnold (see photos below) perished in the Holocaust. Julius had the good fortune of escaping in 1939 on a Kindertransport with his classmates from Cologne to a hostel in London (see photo below). He died in Cardiff, Wales in 2021 at age 95.

Sarah and Wolf Weil (1924)[57]

Arnold and Sarah Weil (1939)[58]

Julius Weil (second from left) in front of hostel
at Minster Road 1, London (1939)[59]

Hene, the youngest child of Israel Hillel and Chane, immigrated to Argentina, married Abraham Isaac Neumann, and lived to the ripe old age of 99.

Israel Hillel died in 1935 in Brzesko at age 85. Below is a picture of his gravestone in the New Jewish Cemetery in Brzesko, followed by its translation (from Hebrew to English).

Gravestone of Israel Hillel Westreich (1850-1935)[60]

1. מ [=מורנו] ישר[אל] הילל   Our Teacher* Israel Hillel

2. וועסטרייך במ [=בן מורנו?]   Westreich BM (=the son of our Teacher)

3. יוסף עה [=עליו השלום]   Yosef, rest in Peace

אייר תרצה (1935 ;Iyar 5695=) Iyar TRZH

ל[ז] [=זכרונו לברכה]   of Blessed memory

4. איש זקן והלך במישרים   An old man and [=that] went in straight ways

5. תנצבה (=May his soul be bound up in the bond of eternal life) T.N.Z.B.H.

* Our teacher usually refers to rabbinic authority (rather than educational authority).

Translation of gravestone of Israel Hillel Westreich (1850-1935)

Josef and Mirla's daughter **Beile/Berta** was born 1865 in Brzesko. Berta married Schulem/Salomon Weiser (see photograph below), a traveling merchant/salesman born in Debica, Poland. Berta and Salomon were quite religious. They had 5 known children, all born in Brzesko – Pinkas (1887 - 1893), Isaak/Ignatz (1890 – Holocaust), Ascher (1893 - 1894), Sara/Sophie (1895 – 1988), and Mirla Feiga (1900 -). Many of their children used the surname Westreich which suggests that, similar to many Galician Jewish couples, Salomon and Berta had a Jewish marriage ceremony but not a civil one. Salomon died on a Nazi transport to Poland. Berta's fate is unknown.

Salomon Weiser in Germany, early 1930's[61]

Berta and Salomon's son Ignatz immigrated to Leipzig, Germany where he worked as a wine merchant and served in the German Army during World War I (see photograph below). Ignatz married Toni Hartmann (see photograph below) and had two daughters, Regina and Suzi. Sadly, Ignatz, Toni, and Suzi perished in the Holocaust. Regina married Edouard Bindefeld in Leipzig in 1936. They immigrated to Paris, France in 1938 following Kristallnacht and, along with their two daughters, immigrated to New York City in 1956.

Ignatz Westreich (1890 – Holocaust) in his WWI German Army uniform[62]

Ignatz and Toni Westreich on vacation in Czechoslovakia, early 1930's[63]

Berta's daughter Sara/Sophie also immigrated to Germany. She married Meier/Max Müntz and they lived in Gotha, Germany with their two sons, Joseph/Joe and Jacob/Jack[64]. The family left Germany to escape the Nazis, beginning a harrowing life during World War II of multiple moves/escapes. In 1939, Joe escaped to England via the Kindertransport. The rest of the family escaped to Belgium (Antwerp, 1939), followed by occupied France (Paris, 1942), then non-occupied France (Nice, 1942), then Switzerland (labor camps), and then a return to Belgium (Brussels, 1944). In 1948, they immigrated to the US (Manhattan). Max, Sophie, and Jack ended up in Long Island, NY and changed the family name to Minc to be "more American." Jack married a woman named Rose and had three children. They later divorced and Jack married again to Veronica "Ronnie." Jack's brother Joe joined the British Army and was hunting Nazis in Germany after the war. He eventually settled in London, where he changed his last name to Milton, married a woman named Vera, and had a son and a daughter.

Little is known about Josef and Mirla's daughter **Sara** who was born circa 1862 in Brzesko. She married Jakob Stechler in 1902 in Nowy Wicnicz.

Although the Holocaust surely took its toll on this Westreich branch, there are living descendants thriving across the world, specifically in the United States and England.

Brzesko Branch 4
of the Westreich Family Tree

Y-DNA untested

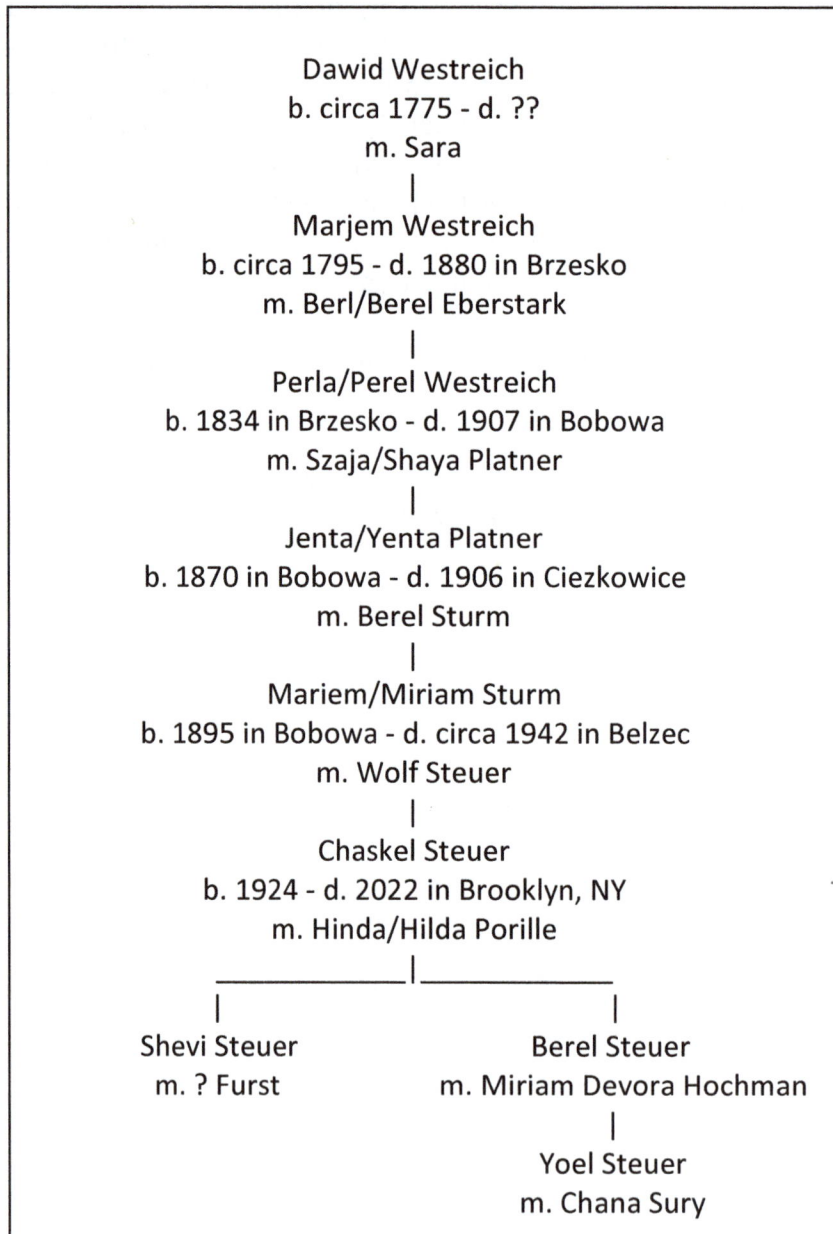

Dawid Westreich
b. circa 1775 - d. ??
m. Sara
|
Marjem Westreich
b. circa 1795 - d. 1880 in Brzesko
m. Berl/Berel Eberstark
|
Perla/Perel Westreich
b. 1834 in Brzesko - d. 1907 in Bobowa
m. Szaja/Shaya Platner
|
Jenta/Yenta Platner
b. 1870 in Bobowa - d. 1906 in Ciezkowice
m. Berel Sturm
|
Mariem/Miriam Sturm
b. 1895 in Bobowa - d. circa 1942 in Belzec
m. Wolf Steuer
|
Chaskel Steuer
b. 1924 - d. 2022 in Brooklyn, NY
m. Hinda/Hilda Porille

Shevi Steuer	Berel Steuer
m. ? Furst	m. Miriam Devora Hochman
	Yoel Steuer
	m. Chana Sury

Brzesko is a small town in modern-day Poland,
formerly part of Galicia, Austria (1772 - 1918),
located 31 miles east of Krakow.

Written by Yoel Steuer and Allan Westreich

74

This branch of the Westreich family tree can be traced relatively far back to the ancestral couple Dawid and Sara Westreich, born circa 1775. They had two known children – daughters Marjem and Rojsa.

Little is known about daughter **Rojsa.** She was born circa 1821 and died in 1906 in Brzesko. She married Isak Brandstatder.

More is known about daughter **Marjem** and her descendants. She was born circa 1795 and died in 1880 in Brzesko. She married Berl Eberstark[1] and had one known child – Perla/Perel Westreich. Perel was born in 1834 in Brzesko and married Szaja/Shaya Platner. Shaya Platner (1836 – 1913) was a landowner who was held in high esteem and, at times, called upon to apply his wisdom to mediate disputes. Perel and Shaya had 6 known children – Sura (b. 1859, m. Benjamin Hoenig), Berel (b. 1861, m. Chana Blumenkehl), Jossel (b. 1863), Chaim (b. 1865, m. Sara Gross), Pinkas (b. 1868 – d. 1910 in Tarnow), and Jenta/Yenta (b. 1870 – d. 1906 in Ciezkowice). All of these children were born in Bobowa.

Yenta Platner married Berel Sturm of Swieczany, and gave birth to her eldest, Mariem/Miriam, in 1895 in Brzana Dolna. Yenta died in 1906 in Ciezkowice[2] during the childbirth of twins. Miriam then assumed the role of surrogate mother to her siblings.[3]

Miriam married Wolf/Volf Steuer and gave birth to Yenta, Chaskel (see stories below), Shabsi, and Moshe Chaim in Ciezkowice. Miriam, Volf, and nearly all of their children perished in WWII. Chaskel Steuer survived and married Hilda/Hinda Porille. Together they had Miriam (Schachter), Shloma Volf, Sheva Rochel (Furst), and Berel. Berel married Miriam Devora Hochman and the family tree continued down to Yoel Steuer, accounting for 8 known generations from top to bottom.

---

[1] When I shared this tidbit with my grandfather Chaskel, he recalled he had learned of a Simcha Eberstark in Poland, and he had known they were distantly related, though he did not know how.

[2] It should be noted that the dead of Ciezkowice were buried in the cemetery of Bobowa.

[3] Her son Chaskel still remembers how his uncle Chuna would stop by nightly for tea with his mother, Chuna's older sister.

Tribute to Chaskel Steuer
by Shevi Furst[65]

Chaskel Steuer, born in 1924, grew up in the Galician town of Ciężkowice (in modern-day Poland), approximately 7 miles north of Bobowa/Bobov and 21 miles south of Tarnow, until his family moved to Cracow. He was sent at the age of 12 to learn in the Yeshiva in Sanz, in the shadow of the Kedushas Zion of Bobov (Rabbi Benzion Halberstam), zt'l Hy'd. When the war broke out, he was forced to return home. There he and his friends would still gather in secrecy to learn until they were resettled in a ghetto.

At that point Chaskel was forced into labor, where he helped build the Plaszow work camp, which he was later forced to dismantle. He miraculously survived -- physically and spiritually -- over 5 tortuous years during World War II -- in 6 different labor and death camps.

After spending some years with a cousin in Paris, he made his way to the house of his uncle, Avrohom Sturm, in New York. In 1951 he married Hinda Porille, the daughter of a prominent Rav of Rhode Island and later the East Side of New York. With Hashem's help, they raised a beautiful family, including many Bobover chassidim. They were fortunate to have great-great-grandchildren together, before Chaskel passed away in 2022 as he approached his 98th birthday.

Chaskel was a Baal Koreih (reader of Torah during synagogue services) for over 45 years, as well as the Chazzan (cantor) for Shacharis (morning prayer) on Yomim Noraim (High Holy Days). He was beloved by all for his warm, smiling and kind personality.

Staying Put for Shabbos

by Shevi Furst[66]

How beloved are Your dwelling places, God of Legions.
(Psalms 84:2)

My father, Chaskel Steuer, was just a teenager when World War II broke out and he *r"l* lost his entire family. He went through a few different concentration camps and was finally liberated from Bergen-Belsen at the end of the war. He didn't know of any surviving relatives.

One Shabbos, shortly after Pesach in 1945, my father was approached in the Bergen-Belsen DP camp by a French soldier who asked him to confirm his name, which he did. The soldier told him he was sent by my father's (not-*frum*) cousin to bring him to the cousin's house in Paris. The soldier had come by motorcycle and had brought along an extra soldier's uniform for my father to don so nobody would notice him and it wouldn't look strange having him ride the motorcycle with this soldier. My father told the soldier he couldn't leave till that night because it was Shabbos. The soldier said he didn't know what my father's talking about, all he knew was that this cousin had paid him a lot of money to leave his brigade and go pick up my father. My father again explained to him that it was his Shabbos and he couldn't leave until nightfall. The soldier said he couldn't wait until then because if they noticed him missing from his brigade he could get into big trouble. My father refused to leave and the soldier refused to wait.

At the end, the soldier left without my father! It took my father another six months until he was finally able to take a train to Belgium, from where he continued on to Paris to this cousin's house. When he arrived, he koshered the whole kitchen, bought two new sets of dishes, and ended up staying there four and a half years until he finally got a visa to come to America in 1950.

To me, the clincher is that when I heard the story (my father mentioned it once "in passing," telling how he ended up at this cousin, not thinking he did anything special), I asked my father how he had the ability, after everything he had been through, to stay so strong. He looked at me incredulously and said, "I don't understand your question! I was brought up in a *frum* house, it was Shabbos, the war was over — what's the question?"

May he and my mother live and merit to greet Mashiach with all Jews soon!

Skopanie/Tarnow/Jaslo Branch
of the Westreich Family Tree

Y-DNA match

by Rayna Gillman

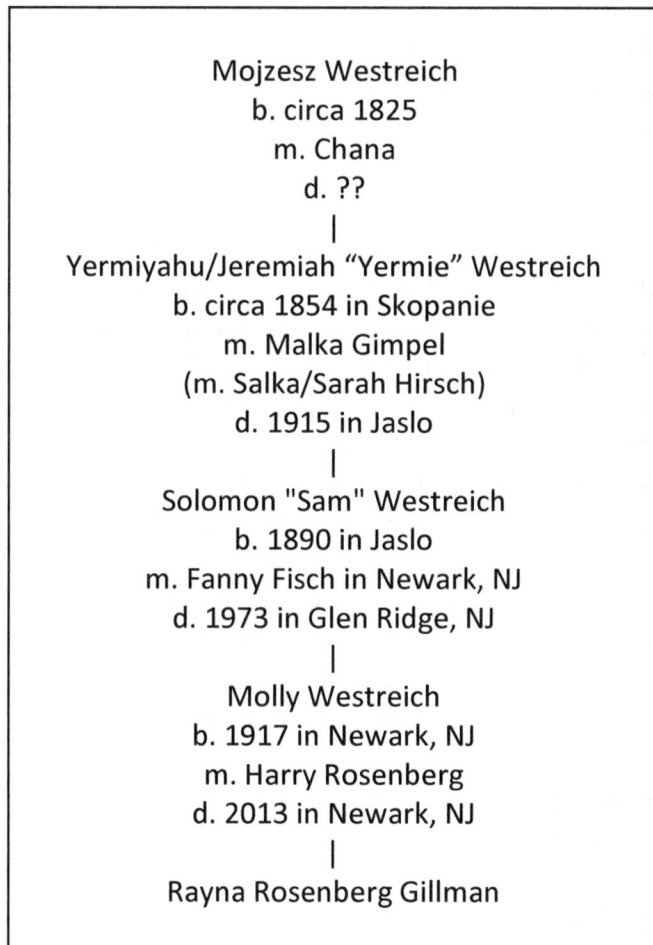

Mojzesz Westreich
b. circa 1825
m. Chana
d. ??
|
Yermiyahu/Jeremiah "Yermie" Westreich
b. circa 1854 in Skopanie
m. Malka Gimpel
(m. Salka/Sarah Hirsch)
d. 1915 in Jaslo
|
Solomon "Sam" Westreich
b. 1890 in Jaslo
m. Fanny Fisch in Newark, NJ
d. 1973 in Glen Ridge, NJ
|
Molly Westreich
b. 1917 in Newark, NJ
m. Harry Rosenberg
d. 2013 in Newark, NJ
|
Rayna Rosenberg Gillman

Skopanie, Tarnow, and Jaslo
are towns in modern-day Poland,
formerly part of Galicia, Austria (1772 - 1918).

My Westreich History (as I know it)

It seems that the Westreichs on my branch of the tree are the renegades! Totally secular, it seems impossible that we are descended from such an illustrious group of rabbis from centuries ago. Where we connect to the rest of you is a mystery that I hope will be solved some day. If all of us descended from Israel Hillel Westreich, there must be a connection somewhere. In the meantime, here's what I have...

My great-great grandfather Mojzesz Westreich, born circa 1825, is the earliest-known patriarch of this branch. Mojzesz married Chana, and their only known child was my great-grandfather Yermiyahu/Jeremiah "Yermie", who was born circa 1854 in Skopanie, Poland -- about 53 miles from Jaslo. *Since it is unlikely that Moshe was an only child and that his son Jeremiah was an only child, there must be other Westreich relatives descended from Mojzesz and Chana. Hello? Are you out there?*

> Breaking News: Jeremiah had a younger brother named Josef! Josef was born circa 1859 in Skopanie. He married Brandel Eilband/Alband (circa 1861 – 1933) and had 8 known children, most born in Tarnow – Leib Hersz (circa 1885), unnamed infant (1887 - 1887), Lezer (1892), Sarah (1894), Chana (1895), Aszer (1897), Mendel (1899 - 1900), and Abraham (1901). Most of the children were born in Tarnow and used the surname Eilband/Alband of their mother. While Josef and Brandel did not have a civil/Polish marriage until 1912 in Wojnicz, they undoubtedly had an earlier religious/Jewish marriage before their children were born (common among Galician Jews).

Jeremiah Westreich married Malka Gimpel, born circa 1853 in Tarnow, where they began raising their family. Their first 3 children -- Rifka (1880), Josef "Yussel" (1882), and Leib (1884) -- were born in Tarnow. Their next 5 children -- Chane (1886), Laje (1888), my grandfather Solomon "Sam" (1890), Gittel "Gittla" (1893), and Mojzesz (1896) -- were born in Jaslo.

According to family lore, <u>Gittel</u> ran away to Russia with an actor and died there. Rifka married an unknown "schlemiel" and moved to Tarnow. (*Children??*)

> Update: Rifka married Feiwel Orenstein in 1915 in Tarnow and had 4 known children, all born in Tarnow – Reizel (1901), Sarah (1903), Isak (1913), and Etel Gitel (1915). Rifka died in 1926 in Tarnow.

My grandfather Sam and his brother Josef were both artists. They painted a mural on the ceiling of the synagogue in Jaslo. Sam painted in oils, watercolors, and pastels. He made his living painting murals in the homes of wealthy people. Later, in the U.S., he made his living painting interiors and hanging wallpaper and continued to paint on canvas and paper. His paintings are on my family's walls.

Sam Westreich arrived in the US on December 15, 1912 at age 23 by himself with $27 in his pocket. He married Fanny Fisch (born in London, England) in 1913 in Newark, NJ. Their mothers (Malka and Leah Gimpel) were half-sisters, making my grandparents cousins with a common grandmother (technically, half first cousins). Grandpa called his mother-in-law Leah, "tante" (aunt).

After Malka died in 1905 at the relatively young age of 52, Jeremiah married Salka/Sarah Hirsch, from Tarnow and 31 years his junior. They had 5 children (born in Jaslo between 1906 - 1913):

- Baila (Bertha) -- Escaped to Argentina. Married Joseph Frey and had 3 children: a daughter Marinia who moved to Los Angeles, a son who died, and a daughter Aida. Have lost track of them.
- Shindel -- Lost track of her.
- Baruch -- Went to Israel. Married Lisa ? and had one known daughter.
- Benek -- Went to Israel. Was a baker. Had 2 children. Lived in Tel Aviv when my grandparents went to visit him in the 1960's.
- Monek -- Was shot by the Nazis and drowned in the Jaslo River.

Unfortunately, Jeremiah died at about age 60 in 1915, shortly after the last of his children was born in 1913.

As stated above, Baruch and Benek Westreich immigrated to Israel - and were apparently alive there in 1979. I know my grandparents went to Tel Aviv in the early 1960's to visit "grandpa's brother." Baruch and Benek Westreich both had children in Israel and their grandchildren would probably be there today. Benek was a baker and had two children (by 1979) and was most likely in Tel Aviv - that's all I know.

To make the family tree even more complicated, (Sam's brother) Josef Westreich married his stepmother Salka's sister, Adela Hirsch. They moved to Tarnow and had 4 daughters and 2 sons – Amalia "Mala" (1910), Lola (1912), Bracha (1915), Gisele (1920), Mattias, and Moses. Josef perished in the Holocaust along with 3 daughters, except for Mala. I don't know what happened to the sons.

Mala Westreich went to Paris to study, married Josef Helçman, and had a daughter, France. Mala's husband was deported and died in a camp. Mala and France were hidden, survived the war, and returned to Paris. Mala then married her husband's brother, who brought up France. Mala died in her 90's. France married, had 2 children, and still lives in Paris. I met Mala in 1963 in Paris and still have a strong relationship with her daughter and grandchildren.

Also, Abraham Westreich, born in Tarnow in May 1902, could well be related to me, since I had Westreich relatives in Tarnow.

Nanny's Gift of Memories: Rayna Gillman[67]

I'm **Rayna Gillman** and I print my own cloth. (Sounds like the beginning of a 12-step program introduction and I'm so addicted to doing this that maybe I should consider it). You may be familiar with my book, *Create Your Own Hand-Printed Cloth*, published by C&T.

I never considered myself an artist: my seventh grade art teacher told me on the first day of school that I couldn't draw, after he saw my rendering of a tree.

Because my grandfather was an artist who drew and painted, I equated making art with the ability to draw, so that was THAT. I began quilting because I could use color, texture, and design without drawing. **My grandmother [Fanny Fisch Westreich]** was really my prime influence in several ways. First, she had an instinctive, fearless sense of color. Second, she improvised. Third, she gave me a raft of memories and a love for the past.

She used leftover threads and yarns and scrap cloth for whatever her next project was, which meant she never planned ahead. If she had orange, green, red and purple remnants at hand, that's what she used together and they always looked wonderful!

"Darling," she said to me, "you can put any colors together as long as you use them more than once."

That advice and ability to improvise were among the best gifts I got from her! This early "art" quilt put that advice to the test. (*Celebration*, 1997, first photo below)

If you look at the purple and green hand-dyes in this piece, you'll see I tried to cover them up with other fabrics. But I soon discovered that printing on them worked better. (*Postcards 2*, 2003, 2nd photo)

In my piece, *Cacophony* (2003, photo 3), my original intent was to cover up the blotchy raucous yellow fabric I had dyed. Without planning ahead, I just kept adding layers till I had covered the fabric and suddenly it was a whole-cloth quilt that was juried into Art Quilts at the Sedgwick (now Elements).

Once I discovered I could improve almost anything by printing in layers, I was off and running. And it became clear that if I didn't like one layer I could add another and another. But I learned it was better to stop before the fabric became mud and that if you have to ask yourself whether it needs more, the answer is usually "no." Improvisation is great but a little drop of thought as you go along can make something better.

If you were to ask which printing process I like best, the answer would depend on which day it is. This week it's screen printing; next week it might be soy wax batik. Sometimes I love using paint, other times, thickened dyes. I love it all and I love teaching it all.

I improvise when I'm designing, too: a legacy from Nanny. Scraps and leftovers, randomly pieced, cut up and reassembled and moved around on the wall till they pleased me. I don't know any other way to work: if I were to plan ahead I would feel as though I had already made the piece and I would never actually make it. (*Usha's Quilt*, 2005, photo 4)

The third way my Nanny influences my work is in my return, time and again, to memory and a sense of the past. A poignant photo of unknown relatives she gave to me led me to collect and use old photographs of people in my work. Sometimes I use image transfer, sometimes a screen: I don't know who they were – but they are alive for me.(*Kaddish detail*, 2003, photo 5)

An antique collector, she taught me to look beyond the first layer to see what was behind it: old buildings, passports, newspaper clippings, a piece of china: everything has a story. If we don't know what it is, we can invent one. (*Time and Again*, 2005, photo 6)

Layers. Whether It's layers of cloth, layers of meaning, layers of the past, or layers of paint and dye, my work explores it all – improvisationally and without worrying about whether the colors coordinate. I didn't start out to write about my grandmother's influence but it is there, beneath the surface – and even on the surface.

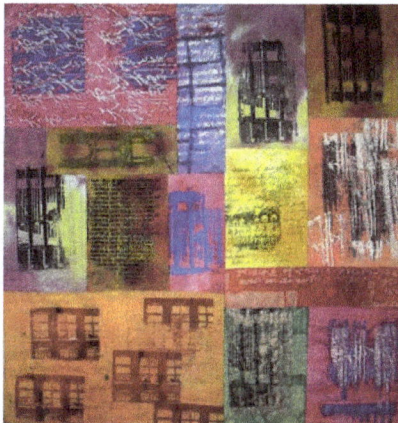

RAYNA GILLMAN

create your own
hand-printed cloth

STAMP, SCREEN & STENCIL WITH EVERYDAY OBJECTS

Baby Rayna's Family:
(Couples from L-R)
grandparents Sam and Fanny Westreich
parents Harry and Molly Rosenberg
great-grandparents Efroim and Leah Fisch

Fanny Fisch and husband Sam Westreich in Jaslo, 1909

(Sam's brother) Josef Westreich and wife Adela Hirsch in Tarnow

Josef, France, and Amalia Helcman (daughter of Sam's brother Josef Westreich), in Paris, France, 1941

Skopanie Branch 2
of the Westreich Family Tree

Y-DNA untested

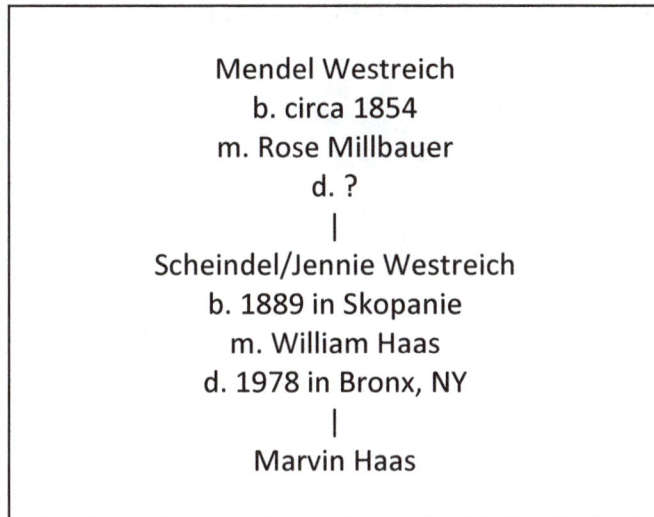

Mendel Westreich
b. circa 1854
m. Rose Millbauer
d. ?
|
Scheindel/Jennie Westreich
b. 1889 in Skopanie
m. William Haas
d. 1978 in Bronx, NY
|
Marvin Haas

Skopanie is a town in modern-day Poland,
formerly part of Galicia, Austria (1772 - 1918),
located 10 miles southwest of Tarnobrzeg.

Sources include:
email communications with Marvin Haas[69]

Edited by Allan Westreich

Mendel and Rose Westreich had 11 known children from 1874 through 1892: Morris, Lena, Bessie, David, Augusta/Gussie, Rachel, Anna, Jeremiah, Harry, Scheindel/Jennie, and Schije/Samuel. At least several of the children were born in the town of Skopanie. Many of the children immigrated to the United States and changed their surname to Westrich.

Harry started the long-time successful Westrich's Deli in Rockaway Park, Queens, NY. It was later taken over by Anna's son, Julius Gerstel, for several decades.

tongue in cheek (and foot in mouth)
I remember Mama, with love and regrets

BY MARVIN HAAS, *Sun Lakes Life*, May 5, 2016[70]

Each year, as Mother's Day approaches, my memories of her become stronger. One would think that memories fade with time but when it comes to Mother's Day the opposite is true. Previously forgotten incidents and events are remembered, stimulated by my aging nostalgia.

One overriding feeling this year is one of regret, regret that I never really sat down with her and asked her to tell me about her past, her childhood and adolescent years. The little I know is the result of brief conversations I had with her, and with my sisters who, typically, as in most families, were closer to her than I was.

My mother was born in Galicia, an oft contested Province in Eastern Europe alternately governed and controlled by Poland and the Austro-Hungarian Empire. One of my sisters did some research and discovered that in the Middle Ages Galicia was invaded by German tribes from the North. My mother's maiden name is Westreich, and my Dad's, and of course, my name attest to that historical fact.

I was born with blue eyes and stark blonde hair another verification of the German invasion and a genetic clue that sometime in the distant past a racial inter-marriage took place, or perhaps, judging by the violence of the Middle Ages, a sexual assault.

My mother had 12 siblings; 10 girls and two boys. She was born on a farm, and once proudly told me she had her own horse which she loved to ride. She came to America at about the age of 12, in the steerage of a ship called the Potsdam. I don't know much of the details of her early life in the U.S., except for the fact that she worked 12 hours a day sewing ladies' blouses in a sweat shop on the lower East Side. I would have liked to have known how she met my Dad, her courtship and wedding, etc.

And now, what I do know and recall...

On one rainy afternoon when I was about six years old, my Mom retrieved an old photo album hidden away in a closet and sat down next to me identifying the photos. When she came to a full page photo of a beautiful red-haired little girl she quickly turned the page. I asked who that was but she never answered.

Many years later one of my sisters went through the album with me, and she revealed the identity of the little girl. She was my sister, Frieda, who died at the age of eight from spinal meningitis. I then realized why my Mom, years before, had rapidly turned the page in the album. Frieda's death, I'm certain, was the understandable reason why my Mom was overly concerned with health and nutrition, and my welfare in general. I was never allowed to wear sneakers because she claimed they would hurt my feet. I played baseball wearing sandals and after a hit flopped around the bases embarrassed by the taunting of my friends. I was forbidden to eat hot dogs. When I came home from Ebbets Field after a ball game she would smell my breath. I consumed packages of SenSen to hide my smoky hot dog breath.

She wasn't a great cook, but her baking, though, was unsurpassed. She made the best strudel this side of Vienna. When she included her strudel in the packages she sent me when I was in the service, I shared them with my buddies, most of whom were from the South. They had never heard of strudel, and often asked me, "When is yo' momma gonna send some more of them cookies?"

My mom spoke perfect English without even the trace of an accent. She spoke Yiddish, Polish, and some German. The worst memories I have of my Mom are the times she suffered from migraine headaches so severe she screamed in pain. Her doctor tried everything except pain killers, and to this day, when I think about it, I wonder why he didn't. Once he recommended Karo Syrup. Another time he prescribed some "fizzy" stuff which my sister filled at the corner drug store. I can still see her running back to our apartment to administer the liquid before the "fizz" went away.

My mother was an avid reader of the daily papers, the Yiddish and English ones. She read some books when she managed the time between her household chores. Her favorite was "The Grapes of Wrath."

At the beginning of this column I expressed my regret for not learning more about her life, especially about her early years growing up in a "shtetl" (a small Jewish enclave or town) and suffering the effects of the anti-Semitism, violent at times, which was so widespread in Europe at the time. Another and more painful regret is that I never said "I love you" to her. I can't explain that neglect as I certainly did love her. She suffered from cancer twice and during my hospital visits I held her hand, and with my eyes tearing up I managed to say, "Don't worry, you're going to get better" which she did. Those visits would have been the appropriate time to add "I love you." Perhaps I felt that squeezing her hand and my optimistic words conveyed to her the compassion and love I felt without verbally expressing it. I hope so.

Another incident, or series of incidents I regret occurred during the times parents were invited to visit classes in the elementary schools during Open School Week. I was born late in my mother's life and she was always the oldest parent in the room, surrounded by youthful looking moms. I was embarrassed by her aging presence, and shied a bit away from her, an unthinking snub from an immature child. My only consolation is that I don't think she was fully aware of my embarrassment, probably attributing my cool reception to my general shyness when among people. My fond memories of my mom surpass my regrets, and that's a good thing.

Marvin Haas[71]

Scheindel/Jennie Westreich Haas, 1941[72]

OBITUARY
Marvin Haas
JULY 7, 1925 – FEBRUARY 6, 2021[73]

Marvin Haas passed away peacefully at home on February 6, 2021 at the age of 95. He was born to Jennie and William Haas on July 7, 1925 in New York City. Following high school, at 18 years old, Marvin joined the Army and proudly served our country as a sergeant fighting in Italy during WWII. He received many commendations for his service including the Bronze Star. Upon returning from the war, Marvin attended Long Island University on the GI Bill, earning a degree in English. He used his education in a long, successful career in advertising in Manhattan. Marvin married Betty Rae Reinhart on January 9, 1949. After raising their sons in Plainview, New York they headed west to the Sun Lakes Community in 1988. Marvin would become an active member of the Lifestyle Committee, and the Tennis, Yiddish Culture, and Dinner Dance Clubs. He also served on the advisory board for San Gorgiono Hospital. Marvin enjoyed using his love for the written word, writing witty articles about his experiences in life for the Sun Lakes Lifestyles section of the Record Gazette for many years. Marvin was predeceased by his wife Betty and sisters Esther Davidson and Rose Dinin. He is survived by his sons Richard and Jon, daughter-in-law Mona; three grandchildren Kaitlyn (Michael), Alexandra (Justin), and Jameson; and two great grandchildren Evelyn and Calvin. He is also survived by his three nephews, Robin and Stephen Davidson and Ken Dinin. All of these he loved and touched deeply. The family would like to thank Dorothy Taub and her family for their friendship and Paula Henson and her staff for their companionship and compassionate care. A private service will be held graveside at the Riverside National Cemetery, where he will be buried alongside his wife Betty. In lieu of flowers donations may be made in Marvin's memory to The American Diabetes Association, PO Box 7023, Merrifield, VA 22116-7023. Or on the web at Diabetes.org.

Westrich's Deli

By *Master Chef* on January 29th, 2018[74]

The No. 16 Sandwich is a classic invention of Westrich's Deli in Rockaway Park, New York (a part of Queens borough). The Gerstel family ran this 1930s-style establishment well into the 1980s. It is where our Publisher gained his love of great deli food, experimenting with a variety of classic recipes. The No. 16 Sandwich, one of many superb sandwich combinations, was his favorite.

This is not for the faint of heart, nor those who prefer to eat light. It's a mile-high pile of heavy-duty calories, rich in cholesterol. But, oh my, how good this is! You can see from the photo, it stands about 6 inches tall, weighing in at around two pounds, each. It is, most assuredly, big enough to share among two or three others.

Grybow Branch
of the Westreich Family Tree

Y-DNA match

by Robert Westreich

Abraham Westreich
b. 1845 in Grybow
m. Hinda Handwerker
d. 1925 in Gorlice
|
Szyja Westreich
b. 1892 in Grybow
m. Rifkah Handwerker from Gorlice
d. 1967 in Brooklyn, NY
|
Jitzhak (Izak/Jimmy) Westreich
b. 1923 in Gorlice
m. Sophie from Montreal, Canada
d. 2015 in Metuchen, NJ
|
Robert Westreich

Grybow is a small town in modern-day Poland, formerly part of Galicia, Austria (1772 - 1918), located 11 miles east of Nowy Sacz.

My family tree was traced back to the mid 1800's with my great grandfather, Abraham Westreich (born 1845 in Grybow, Malopolskie, Poland and died in 1925 in Gorlice, Malopolskie, Poland). He was married to Hinda Handwerker whose father was Wolf Handwerker. Wolf and his wife had 2 children that I am aware of: Hinda Handwerker (spouse of Abraham Westreich) and Eliyahu Handwerker (born 1865 in Gorlice, Malopolskie, Poland and died in 1942 in the Belzec concentration camp) who was married to Sarah Grun (born 1870 and died 1935 in Gorlice, Malopolskie, Poland). The Handwerkers were in the business of making stove pipes.

Abraham and Hinda had eight children:

(1) David Westreich (born 1874 in Grybow, Malopolskie, Poland and died in 1960 in Newark, New Jersey);

(2) Moses Westreich (born 1878 in Grybow, Malopolskie, Poland);

(3) Eliyahu Westreich (born 1880 in Grybow, Malopolskie, Poland and died in 1942 in the Belzec concentration camp) and had five children: Idys (Edith), Joseph, Sigmund, Solomon, and Ruchla;

(4) Mariem Laje "Marmalaya" Westreich (born 1885 in Grybow, Malopolskie, Poland and died in 1942 in the Belzec concentration camp) and was married to Jakob Ohrenstein;

(5) Berthold Leib Westreich (born 1887 in Grybow, Malopolskie, Poland and died in 1952 in Montreal, Canada), who was first married to a woman who perished in the Holocaust and later married Zyta (?) (born 1904 in Poland and died 1993 in Queens, New York);

(6) my grandfather Szyja Westreich (born 1892 in Grybow, Malopolskie, Poland and died in 1967 in Brooklyn, New York), who was first married to Rifkah Handwerker (born 1891 in Gorlice, Malopolskie, Poland and died in 1942 in the Belzec concentration camp). Rifkah was the daughter of Eliyahu Handwerker and Sarah Grun above, so they were cousins.

(7) Rifkah Westreich (died in 1942 in the Belzec concentration camp) and was married to Jakob Neugreshel; and

(8) Wolf Westreich (born 1900 in Grybow, Malopolskie, Poland and died in 1942 in the Belzec concentration camp).

My father, Jitzhak (Izak/Jimmy) Westreich (born in 1923 in Gorlice, Malopolskie, Poland and died in 2015 in Metuchen, New Jersey) was married to Sophie Westreich (born in 1935 in Montreal, Canada and died in 2002 in Brooklyn, New York).

In September 1939, my father was about to leave for school in Krakow, Poland when the Germans and Russians invaded Poland starting Word War II. In summary, he and his father ran away to avoid potential conscription and were captured by the German and Russian military, respectively. My grandmother, Rifkah, and uncle, Abraham, were sent to the death camps. My father ended up in multiple German concentration camps in Poland and my grandfather was sent to the gulags in Siberia. After the war, my father migrated to Israel where he fought in the Independence War of 1948 and later found out his father was alive and living in Montreal, Canada with his brother Berthold and his wife, Zyta where my father ultimately emigrated to.

In Montreal, my grandfather's brother, Berthold, passed away and my grandfather married his wife, Zyta. In the late 1950's, my father met my mother in Montreal and were married in 1960. After I was born, we emigrated to Brooklyn, New York.

I have included below more specifics about my father's experiences during and after the war from certain chapter summaries from the book I wrote and published, *I'm Still Alive*.

Book Excerpts from *I'm Still Alive* by Robert Westreich[75]

Chapter 3. Jimmy's Early Childhood

We journey back to Jitzhak Westreich's early life and his earliest memories in and around the town of Gorlice in southern Poland where he was born in 1923. The chapter includes in its entirety the only remembrances that Jimmy ever sat down and committed to written form – a little more than 2500 words. Perhaps the most poignant aspect of this brief narrative is the youthful Jimmy's vivid memories of his early schools, teachers, and classmates, and his yearning for the normal routine of school evidenced by the eagerness with which he seems to greet the start of each new term, against a troubling and increasingly fearful backdrop of the political turmoil leading up to the invasion by Nazi Germany in September of 1939. We learn about Jimmy's father, a hardworking man and good family provider who nonetheless was obliged to find work in distant villages and towns, and consequently, sadly, is rarely at home such that Jimmy barely knows him. And we learn of Jimmy's mother, a stalwart, confident and educated businesswoman and shopkeeper ahead of her time who was equally determined that her sons receive a superior education that included an appreciation for culture, music, and the arts, and that they become career professionals so that they do not have to labor in mills and factories and fields like their father's generation.

Chapter 3 concludes with dramatic and solemn counterpoint: a picturesque mind's-eye image of what was undoubtedly the very last wholly innocent and carefree days and weeks of Jimmy Westreich's young life, at age 16 basking and playing and chasing girls in an idyllic beach resort town on the Baltic Sea, over the midsummer days before war was to break out across all of Europe and ultimately all around the world, and the largest mass murder in human history was tragically just about to begin. As the calendar turns to September that summer, Jimmy is summoned home to Gorlice by his mother, ostensibly to get ready to go back to school, but as we will shortly learn, that is not what happens.

Chapter 7. The Camps

We trace Jimmy's odyssey through seven Ghettos and concentration camps, beginning with forced labor at a sawmill just outside his home town, but with particular focus on a lesser known camp called Pustków in Southern Poland, where he spent most of his time during his captivity. Pustków stands in somewhat atypical contrast to the usual public perception of these horrific places, having been originally converted from a munitions factory built by the Polish government to a massive training camp for SS troops, and later to a technical/industrial facility which manufactured parts for the V-1 and V-2 rockets and other new and sophisticated weaponry for the German war machine. Remarkably, even as a teenager Jimmy managed to convince the SS commanders that he had technical skills and knowhow that were needed in the manufacturing processes being designed and developed there, and even among the Jews, technicians were better fed and provided for, if only marginally.

Nevertheless, the forced labor at Pustków begins with clearing the forests—felling huge trees and digging out stumps to create drill fields and shooting ranges—all with hand tools like saws, axes and picks, some being forced to dig by hand when there weren't enough tools to go around. Many of the men, who are unskilled in this dangerous work, are routinely killed every day in accidents. Later Jimmy works as a carpenter building barracks for the 15,000 prisoners who would be interned in Pustków, virtually all of whom would die there. It is here that Jimmy has a dream in which he sees a vision of his mother, who tells him that he is not a carpenter, but rather he is a mechanic. The next day, when the SS muster the prisoners into the usual two lines of carpenters and mechanics, Jimmy queues into the mechanics line, and on that day, all the carpenters are taken into the forest and executed because the prisoner barracks are complete, and the carpenters aren't needed anymore!

While at Pustków, Jimmy stumbles upon a large box containing dozens of precision machine tools, which he manages to hide and then, one by one, trades each of the tools for food and other items with a SS guard. The guard was apparently fascinated with the tools, and never asked where Jimmy was getting them, and the additional food Jimmy received in trade helped him to keep his strength up, and survive.

However, in the wake of the promulgation of the "final solution to the Jewish question" embodied in the Wannsee Protocol adopted by the Nazi commanders, and with the military training base largely completed, most of the remaining Jewish workers in the camp were sent to their deaths in the newly created Belzec extermination camp, Yet Jimmy was among some 215 Jewish technicians who were kept alive to work in the armaments factory, until they too were shipped to Auschwitz. There yet another remarkable thing happened, when the former Commandant of the now evacuated Pustków camp interceded with Dr. Joseph Mengele himself, telling him that these inmates were technicians that could still serve Germany, and instead of the ovens of Birkenau, Jimmy was sent to the Auschwitz factory sub-camp of Blechhammer. It was from here that he was finally liberated by the Russian Army on January 27, 1945.

Chapter 11. The Long Walk to Nowhere

Liberated from Blechhammer in January of 1945 with the war in its final stages, Jimmy decides to do the only thing that seems to make sense; he proceeds to walk the nearly 400 miles back to his hometown of Gorlice. He travels through hostile territory, where marauding underground militias, of Polish nationals, organized Jewish refugees, and others continue to clash with pockets of remaining German troops, and to some extent, with each other, thus requiring Jimmy and his refugee compatriots to arm themselves with weapons in anticipation of potential trouble from just about any people they encounter on their long trek home.

When Jimmy finally makes it home to Gorlice, he finds his house destroyed, his family gone, and he encounters pervasive hatred from the people who still live there. Simply put, they don't want him there. The chapter ends with the heartbreaking story of the Polish woman who, upon seeing Jimmy standing in the snow looking at his burned-out home, gives him a small batch of family photographs, which his mother had entrusted to the woman for safekeeping before she was evacuated and sent to her death in the camps, asking her to give them to her son and husband when they returned home. Now, there being nothing left for him in Poland, Jimmy decides to go to Palestine to join the fight for an internationally recognized Jewish state.

Chapter 14. To Palestine via Italy

After leaving Gorlice, Poland forever, Jimmy journeys south in very zig-zag fashion across several countries toward the Mediterranean with the intention of crossing the sea to Palestine, where there is growing hope—and impetus—for establishing a Jewish Homeland. He eventually does so aboard a former US Coast Guard cutter that had been gutted and refitted to accommodate as many passengers as possible. The ship, renamed the Tradewinds (and later renamed Hatikvah —"the hope" in Hebrew – while at sea), was one of hundreds of vessels used by the Aliyah Bet arm of the Jewish resistance force known as the Haganah to attempt to run the British blockade and bring hundreds, even thousands, of Jewish settlers to Palestine in defiance of highly restrictive immigration quotas imposed by Great Britain under the Mandate for Palestine.

The chapter describes in detail the history leading up the British blockade, from the Balfour Declaration (and subsequent British reneging of that crucial document) to the establishment of the Mandate for Palestine, and to the infamous Chamberlain White Paper of 1939, as well as the early Zionist efforts of leaders like Ze'ev Jabotinsky. It goes on to describe increasing restrictions on Jewish immigration to Palestine and other countries—including the United States—even in the face of escalating persecution and extermination of the Jews at the Nazis over the war years from 1939 to 1945. It also describes Jimmy's harrowing 11-day Mediterranean journey on the passenger-overloaded Hatikvah, his subsequent capture by the British along with the other passengers, and his three-month internment in a "displaced persons" camp on Cyprus. Finally, the chapter describes the story of the Exodus, perhaps the most famous ship in the Aliyah Bet fleet. Turned back to port by the British Navy, it's Jewish passengers—after refusing to disembark in the French city of Port de Bouc—were eventually forced to disembark in Hamburg, Germany, a spectacle that so enraged the rest of the world that the British blockade of Jews attempting to immigrate to Palestine disintegrated virtually overnight. Jimmy made it to the port of Haifa in August of 1947, just in time to become a soldier in Israel's 1948 War of Independence.

Chapter 15. War and Peace

This chapter describes in detail the events at the UN and elsewhere around the world leading up to the dissolution of the British Mandate for Palestine and the establishment on May 14, 1948 of the State of Israel with David Ben-Gurion as the sovereign country's first Prime Minister—and consequently of course, precipitating the Arab-Israeli War of 1948-49. It describes the Arab terror campaign that followed the UN partition plan issued in November of 1947, as well as Jimmy's involvement in the Battle of Haifa, which represented a major Jewish victory months before the war itself actually commenced.

Having laid this groundwork, the chapter goes on to explore Jimmy's attitude toward the war and its meaning, and reveals what may by all accounts be his most startling philosophical statement. When his son Robert, still a young teenager at the time, learns that his Dad fought in the War of Independence, he remarks excitedly and proudly, "So you were a Freedom Fighter!" But Jimmy replies bluntly, "No, I was a terrorist." The discussion turns to an examination of Jimmy's ruthlessly pragmatic philosophy about war and human conflict. We learn that he is by no means beguiled by any manner of romantic notions about the "glory" of war even in the cause of Zionism and despite his dedication to that noble cause. He never sought any sort of recognition or congratulation, official or otherwise, for the part he played in the fiery cauldron of war from which the state of Israel was forged, and when it was over, he simply went on to the next thing; he went back to trying to live a good, productive life. His intention, we may conclude, was to become a working member of one kibbutz or another and to get on with his life as a regular citizen in his new country.

Chapter 16. Back from the Dead

However, in 1952, Jimmy learns that his father is still alive and living in Montreal, having somehow survived as many as six or more years in a Russian gulag somewhere in Siberia. His response is immediate, unquestionable, and irrevocable: He goes to Canada to rejoin his father, who now goes by the westernized name of Sam. In his heart Jimmy hopes to put himself under the care of Sam, to become a son again and for Sam to become the father again, making the kinds of decisions that parents are supposed to make, but which calamitous circumstances have forced Jimmy, who is now 29 years old, to make for himself for 13 onerous and burdensome years. Unfortunately, when he arrives in Montreal he discovers to his dismay that his father is a broken man from his years of brutal captivity, and it turns out that the son must take care of the father. In any case, we learn a bit about Sam's ordeal during the war, and about how, in the old tradition of yibbum (or levirate marriage), he has subsequently married his brother Berthold's wife Zyta, after Berthold died suddenly. Most importantly we are introduced to the woman that Jimmy ultimately marries—the author's mother.

Her name is Sophie and she comes from a very poor family in which she was the last of eight children. We may surmise that Jimmy always felt he "rescued" Sophie from her difficult family circumstances, but the truth is that her demure and acquiescent personality, as well as her ultimate devotion to her children after they were married were a fitting complement to his brash and domineering style, which in reality was really more a measure of his drive and determination to provide for the family, more than a desire to be some sort of dictatorial overlord of the house, though there was a little of that as well. The chapter paints a vibrant portrait of Sophie, the compassionate, loving, and gentle way she had about her in all of her concerns, and especially her dedication to her children. In sum, Sophie was a touchy-feely mother who passionately loved her children. And while the two of them began to enjoy an increasingly good life in Montreal, partying with new friends and reveling in some small measure of post-war victory euphoria, however measured, when Sam and Zyta moved to New

York City, Jimmy would obligingly follow in short order, which occurred in 1966 when the author of this book excerpt was three years old.

Family Photos[76]

Abraham Westreich (1845 - 1925), Robert's great grandfather

Szyja Westreich (1892 - 1967) in 1918, Robert's grandfather

Jimmy Westreich (1923 - 2015) circa 1955, Robert's father

Rozwadow Branch 1
of the Westreich Family Tree

Y-DNA match

Yermiyahu Westreich
b. circa 1828
m. Necha from Wielowies
d. ??
|
Moshe Westreich
b. circa 1852 in Rozwadow (?)
m. Esther Silber
d. ??
|
Leja/Leah Westreich
b. 1874 in Chwalowice
m. Mendel Perlman
d. 1960 in US
|
Necha/Naomi Perlman
b. 1910 in Chwalowice
m. Charles Kassenoff
d. 1991 in US
|
Melvyn Kassenoff

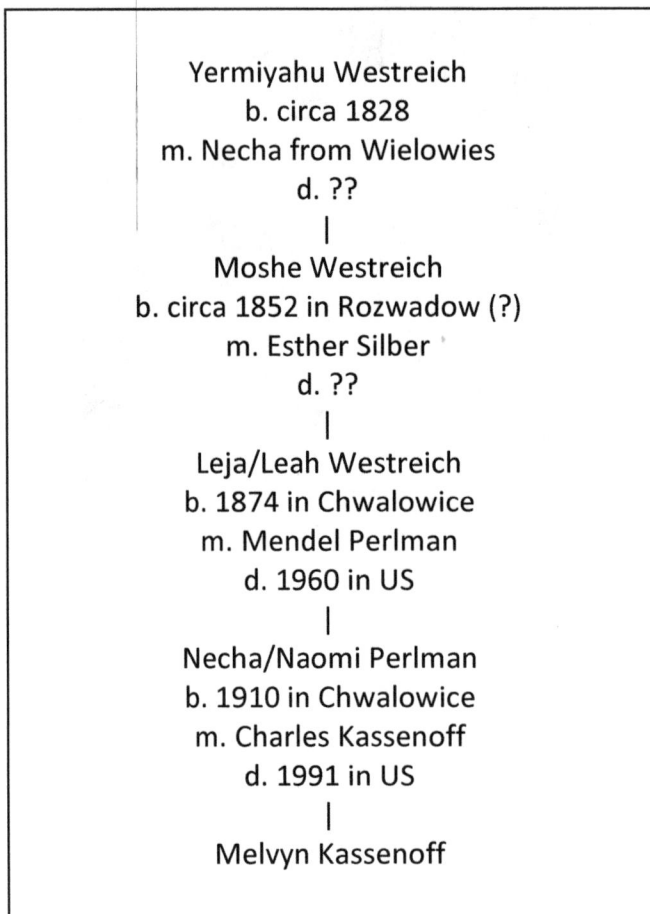

Rozwadow, previously a town of its own,
is now part of the town of Stalowa Wola in modern-day Poland,
formerly part of Galicia, Austria (1772 - 1918),
located 16 miles east of Tarnobrzeg.

Sources include:
email communications with Melvyn Kassenoff[77]

Edited by Allan Westreich

Yermiyahu Westreich, born circa 1828, is the earliest-known patriarch of this branch. Yermiyahu married Necha who was born circa 1828 in Wielowies and died in Dzikow on May 24, 1908 at age 80. They had 4 known children -- Moshe (born circa 1852), Chana, Itta, and Esther -- and 2 likely additional children -- Solomon (born circa 1859) and Jacob (born circa 1862).

Moshe Westreich, son of Yermiyahu, reportedly was born in Rozwadow. Moshe married Esther Silber (see photo below) and they lived in the village of Chwalowice, about 15 miles northwest of Rozwadow. They reportedly owned a tavern in Chwalowice and their customers included (were mainly?) residents of the Russian sector of Poland who would come to the Austro-Hungarian sector to buy liquor to smuggle into the Russian sector. Alcohol taxes were much higher in the Russian sector than the Austro-Hungarian sector, and Chwalowice was a border village just inside the Austro-Hungarian Empire.

Esther Silber Westreich, wife of Moshe, 1930's, in Chwalowice (?)[78]

Moshe and Esther had 7 known children -- Leja/Leah, Abraham, Chaim/Hyman, Ovadia, Leibesh/Leo, Yakov, and Beila/Berta Chaya. Leah (1920) and Hyman (pre-1910) immigrated to the US before World War II. In 1939, several of the siblings (Leibesh, Yakov, and Beila ?) along with their families fled east from Rozwadow to the Soviet Union (western Siberia) and survived the war. Unfortunately, their mother Esther was too frail to go with them and perished in the Holocaust. Ovadia also did not survive the Holocaust. It is unknown when Moshe died, but seemingly sometime between World War I and World War II.

Daughter **Leah** (1874 - 1960, see photo below), born in Chwalowice, was the eldest child of Moshe Westreich and Esther Silber Westreich. Leah married ? Konigsberg(?) and they had one child, Abraham (1896 - Holocaust/1942?). Subsequent to her husband's death, Leah married

Menachem Mendel Perlman, a widower with grown children. (There may have been another marriage that ended in divorce after less than a year between the death of her first husband and her marriage to Menachem Mendel Perlman.) Menachem Mendel managed a farm on which Austrian Lipizzaner show horses were raised.

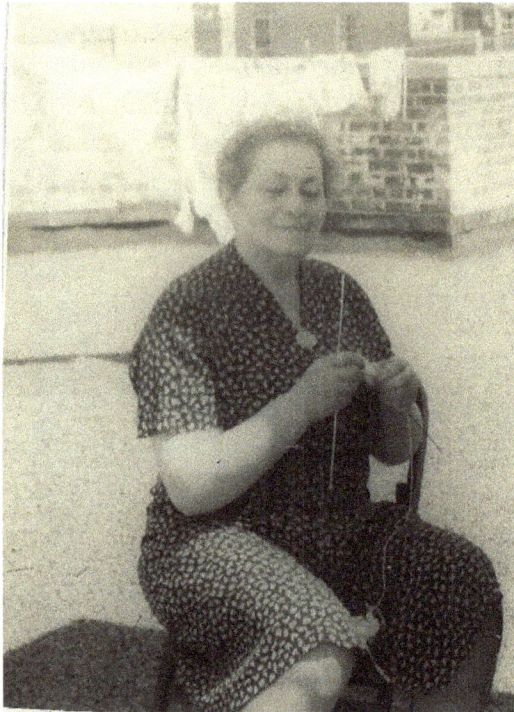

Laje/Leah Westreich Perlman, 1940's[79]

After Leah's marriage to Menachem Mendel, her son Abraham lived with his grandparents Moshe and Esther and took the Westreich name. Abraham moved to Metz in the Alsace-Lorraine region of France in 1924 and, in 1934, he married Zlata and then moved to France. They had two children, Sali (Sal) and Michel. Upon the outbreak of World War II, they fled to St. Privat in southern France. Abraham, Zlata, and Michel perished in the Holocaust, but Sal survived because he was in school or on a class trip when the Jews of St. Privat were rounded up and subsequently deported. (The names of Abraham, Zlata, and Michel appear on the memorial wall in the courtyard of the French Holocaust Museum in the Marais section of Paris and a photo of Zlata and Michel is in the museum.) Sal spent the balance of World War II living with a Catholic French farm family. After the war, he was located with the assistance of the Red Cross and, in 1946, came to the US to live in New York City's Borough of Queens with his grandmother Leah and his aunt Naomi and her family. Sal received a PhD in history from Columbia University and was a professor of history at Pratt Institute in Brooklyn for about 50 years.

Leah and Menachem Mendel had three children that survived childhood – Yerma (Jeremiah)/Jerome (1906 - 2000), Boruch/Bernard (1908 - 1980) and Necha/Naomi (1910 - 1991) – and at least one that did not. Menachem Mendel was brought to the US prior to or during World War I by children from his first marriage. Leah and her three surviving children with Menachem Mendel (Jerry, Bernard, and Naomi) joined him in the US in December 1920 and lived in New York City. Menachem Mendel died in 1924.

Jerome married Ida Brier in 1930 and they had two children – Stanley and Marian. Jerry and Ida lived in the Bronx prior to moving to Toms River, NJ. After Jerry retired, they moved to Margate, FL. Bernard married Edith Moskowitz, and they too had two children – Sharon and Michael. They lived in the Bronx prior to moving to Clifton, NJ. Naomi married Charles Kassenoff in 1937 and they had one son – Melvyn. Naomi and Charles moved from the Bronx to Queens in 1939. Leah lived with Naomi and her family until her death at age 86 in 1960.

Nothing more is known about son **Abraham** (born 1879).

Son **Hyman** (1881 - 1932) married Sosche/Sophie Yahre in Manhattan in 1907 (see wedding photo below). Interestingly, Sophie's sister Rose married Abraham Westreich from the Brzesko branch of the Westreich family tree. Based on DNA results, Hy and Abe were cousins. Hy owned a Jewish bath house in Manhattan. Hy and Sophie had 5 children, all sons -- Milton (1910 - 1967), Albert (1912 - 2002), Gerald "Jerry" (1914 - 2000), Sherman (1916 - 2008), and Howard (1920 - 1999). See photo below with 4 of their 5 sons. The youngest 2 sons, Sherman and Howard, changed their last name to "Westrich." Hy died at the young age of 48.

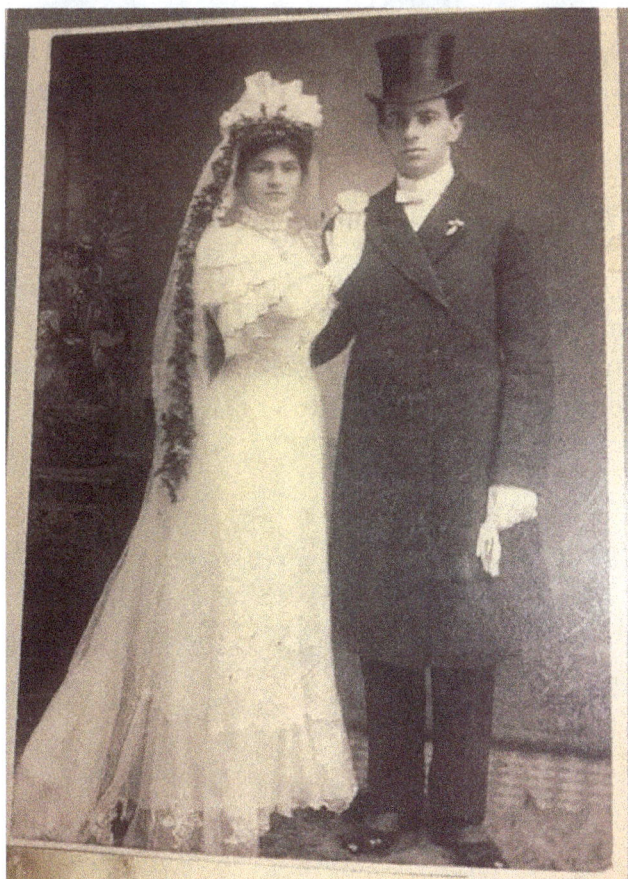

Wedding of Hyman Westreich and Sophie Yahre, 1907[80]

(L-R) Hy Westreich, Sherman, Jerry, Albert, Milton, Sophie,
Sophie's sister Selma/Sarah and her husband Victor Miller
posing in "boat" at Coney Island, Brooklyn circa 1917[81]

Son **Ovadia** (1883 - 1942, see photo below) was born in Chwalowice and died in the Holocaust. He married Meita Wilkenfeld. They lived in the town of Antoniow and had 9 known children -- Mordechai/Max, Avraham. Chanah/Anna, Yermiyahu, Menachem, Rivkah, Necha, Pinchas, and Hene. At least 5 of the children (Avraham. Rivkah, Necha, Pinchas, and Hene) died in the Holocaust.

Ovadia Westreich (center, with beard) with family (and friends?) in Poland,
wife Meita Wilkenfeld Westreich (left of Ovadia),
son Max Westreich (left of Meita)[82]

Son **Leibesh** was the only sibling who took his mother's maiden name, Silber, as his surname. Family lore says he did so in order to avoid serving in the Austrian army during World War I. He married Chaya Ita, moved to Germany in the 1920's (?), and after World War II immigrated to the US.

Leibish and Chaya Ita had 3 children -- Avraham/Adolf (1912 - 2004), Necha/Nettie (1913 - 2007), and Kalmen/Klemens (1914 - 2005) (see family photo below). Adolf was in Siberia during the war, followed by the Bergen-Belsen displaced persons camp (1945 - 1948). In 1948, Adolf emigrated to Brooklyn, New York and later owned a sweater factory. Nettie was also in Siberia during the war, followed by the Bergen-Belsen displaced persons camp (1945 - 1948). In 1948, Nettie emigrated to Israel. When Nettie passed away in 2007, she and her husband, Rabbi Chaim Berish Horowitz, had 4 children, 32 grandchildren, and 99 great-grandchildren. As of February 2019, there are over 300 descendants of Nettie and Chaim Berish, most of whom live in Israel. Klemens was in Denmark, Russia, Japan, and Brooklyn, NY (1941) during the war.

Leibesh Silber and family, 1920's[83]

Son **Yakov** (1891 - 1974) married Reizl Mohr (see photos below) and had 3 children -- Avraham, Rivkah, and Yermiyahu. Yakov survived the Holocaust and emigrated to Israel in 1948.

Yakov Westreich[84]

Reizl Mohr Westreich, wife of Yakov[85]

Yakov's son Avraham submitted the following information to Yad Vashem: "Avraham Westreich was born in Rozwadow in 1921. Avraham was deported to Lwow with his father and siblings. His mother remained in Rozwadow because she had relatives there whom she did not want to leave. In the end, she perished in Belzec. Avraham was deported from Lwow to a labor camp in Siberia and released in 1942. Afterwards, he served in the Anders' Army, located his father and siblings in Dzhambul, Kazakhstan, and remained there with them for a few years. In 1948, they made aliya to Eretz Israel."

(Yakov's son) Avraham had a son who was a pilot in the Israeli Air Force and, after he left the Air Force, worked for the Shin Bet (Israel's internal security service). In the mid-1980s, he was sent to Warsaw on business and, during some free time, he traveled to Rozwadow to see whether the house in which his father had been living in 1939 was still there. The Polish man who then lived in the house noticed him and came out and told him something along the lines of: "You're the son of Avraham Westreich; you look exactly like he looked when he left in 1939"!!

Daughter **Beila/Berta Chaya** (1893 - 1967, see photo below) married Sane/Nataniel Schreier and had 1 son -- Arno. The family fled to the Soviet Union in 1939 and successfully escaped the Holocaust. They emigrated to the US in 1949.

Siblings Beila Westreich Schreier (girl on left),
Leah Westreich Perlman (girl on right), and
Leibesh Silber (boy in front center)[86]

In spite of the many trials and tribulations of their ancestors, the descendants of this Westreich branch live on throughout the world today.

Rozwadow Branch 1a
of the Westreich Family Tree

Y-DNA match

Yermiyahu Westreich
(probable father of Solomon)
b. circa 1828
m. Necha
d. ??
|
Solomon Westreich
b. circa 1859
m. Ettel Perlmutter
d. ??
|
Abraham Abisz Westreich
b. 1889 in Wielowice
m. Feiga Silbert from Chwalowice
d. 1942 in Auschwitz
|
Netty Westreich
b. 1929 in Metz, France

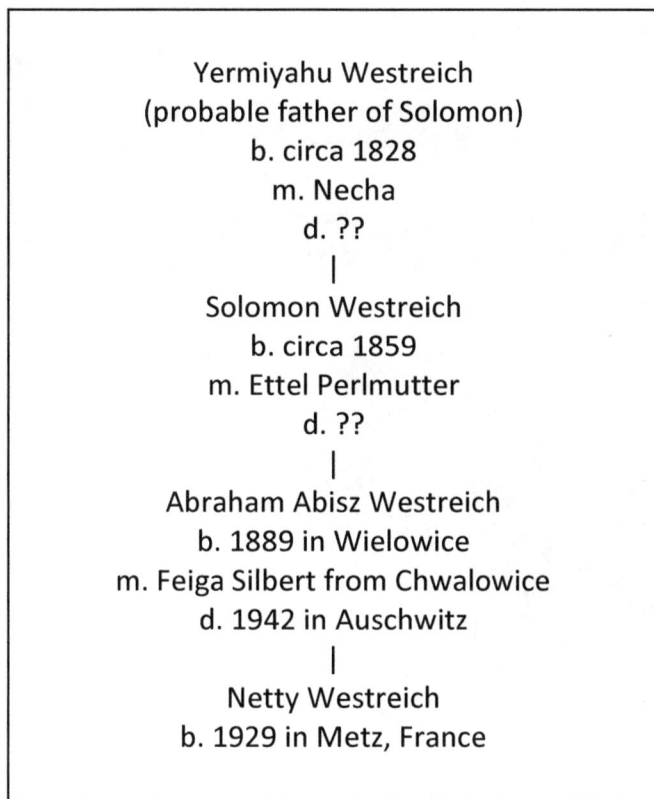

Rozwadow, previously a town of its own,
is now part of the town of Stalowa Wola in modern-day Poland,
formerly part of Galicia, Austria (1772 - 1918),
located 16 miles east of Tarnobrzeg.

Primary source:
Westreich Sisters
blog entry from
Resistance Polonaise en Saone-et-Loire
(*Polish Resistance in Saone-et-Loire*),
2013[87]

Edited by Allan Westreich

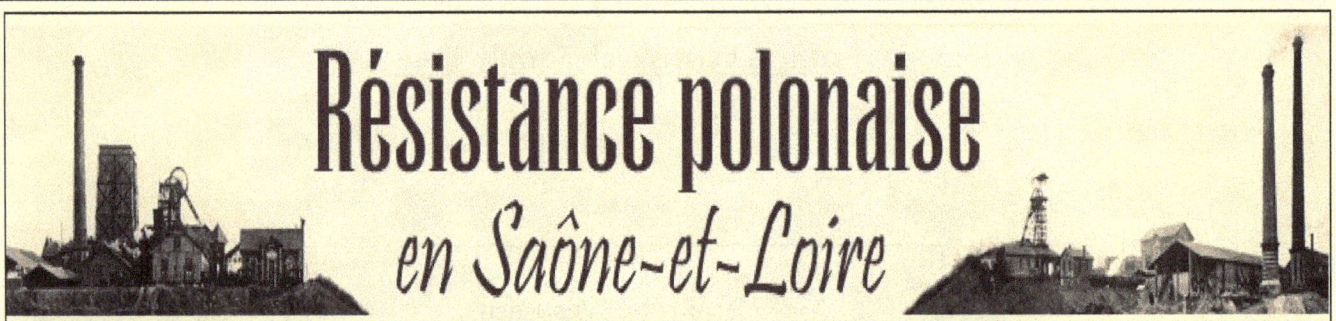

Résistance polonaise
en Saône-et-Loire

goods

Resistance FTP-MOI

POWN resistance

Outside the Montcellian basin

The liaison officers

+ SOCIAL FRAMEWORK

+ EVENTS ...

MAQUISARDS RUSSES -

Around the book

Those of the AS or the FTPF

PRESS - leaflets - posters

Biographies

TUES ET DEPORTES (cards and photos)

Jews

YOUR TESTIMONIALS ...

Disappearances ...

Memory

All items

Photo album

CALL TO RECOGNIZE ...

The sisters Westreich, survivors of raids and maquisardes ...

- In 1949, during the marriage of Mina -

The epic of the Westreich sisters, young Jews escaped from the October 1942 raid in Montceau-les-Mines, having spent the war years in several bushes, is frequently mentioned in the accounts of the Occupation. Most often the narratives are incomplete or simply erroneous.

This article is based on long interviews held in Paris in 2008 and 2009 with Mina and Netty Westreich ... It is published today with the agreement of Netty, while Mina is dead.

The parents

They came from eastern Poland: Abraham Westreich was born on 28 April 1889 in Wielowice. He married Feiga Silbert, born in Chwalowice on September 23, 1898. They then lived in Rozwadow, near Stalowa-Wola, where their first daughter Erna Ethel was born on 28 June 1922.

Feiga had a sister, Blima Silbert, also born at Chwalowice on 10 March 1900.

The couple and their first daughter emigrated to France in 1924, due to the conditions that prevailed in the young Polish republic after its independence (economic misery, waves of anti-Semitism).

The family settled in Metz where the father worked as a representative in the making. Two other girls were born, Mina in 1926 and Netty in 1929. By no means what administrative logic, Mina alone received French nationality, Netty being declared Polish, like her parents.

Usually speaking in Yiddish, they did not encounter any linguistic difficulty in adapting to Metz and the two sisters remembered a warm childhood in the Rue des Benedictins.

When the war came and the city of Metz was to be evacuated, the Westreich won Montceau-les-Mines, where Blima Silbert, who had married one Reicher, had two children, Theodore, born in Metz on 28 February 1929; Thérèse, also born in Metz on 3 May 1938. Both had French nationality.

The five Westreichs were initially housed at 2, rue Jean Jaurès, at Blima Reicher, whose husband had joined the free zone. They then found accommodation at 16, rue du Bois, not far from the place where Henri Pawlowski was going to establish his hideout three years later .

116

Polish Aviators

Communist Resistance

POWN resistance

All the pictures

slideshow

Connections

Search Links

Other Links ...

To discover

Chorale Traditions and

Mazovia

Polska Misja Katolicka -

Montceau

All partners

Submit a partner

Members

- The Westreich at Montceau (1941?) -

The father began his work as a hairdresser for the Polish clientele in the miners' quarters. Alas, this did not last, for the anti-Jewish laws promulgated by the Vichy government forbade him one day to work on his own account; He had to be hired as a laborer in a construction site, a profession that will be indicated at the time of his arrest.

Mina and Netty went to the girls' school, rue Carnot where Mina obtained her basic certificate.

Their cousin Theodore attended the boys' school in the rue Jean-Jaurès, close to his home.

- Netty - back 1941 at the complementary course of girls in Montceau -

The family was in contact with the other Jewish families of Montceau. Abraham was wanted to come and operate the ritual sacrifice of poultry at home.

Their elder sister Erna found work as an office worker and made a romantic relationship with a young man of the country, Andre Proudhon (born December 30, 1914 in Tunis), who worked for the mining company of Blanzy and Militated to the Socialist Youth. Pupil of the Nation, having also lost his mother, he then lived with his maternal grandmother, Jeanne Veillaud in the district of Georgets, commune of Sanvignes-les-Mines.

The girls do not seem to have lived the first two years in fear; At the beginning of June 1942, however, they had to bear the yellow star (German ordinance of 28 May 42), without seeming to suffer too much. A list found in the departmental archives of Mâcon reveals that of all the family, there was only the small cousin Therese to escape because it was less than 6 years.

Mina remembered her mathematics teacher, Mrs. Parriat, who one day, to her great embarrassment, had given her money to help the family, it had to happen after the father had lost his job ...

The arrests - See, taken from Physiophile, The tragedy of the Jews Montcelliens (2)

The Germans played no part in these arrests; The task was accomplished by the French police. It was then necessary to complete one of the first transports to Auschwitz, which was in preparation for the regrouping camp at Pithiviers; The Germans had planned 1000 people by train and there were no prisoners. Order was therefore given to the regional prefecture of Dijon to organize the raid of foreign Jews on the departments of its jurisdiction; The instructions were transmitted to the police by a telegram numbered by the regional prefect of Dijon, relayed by the departmental prefects. Those targeted were those in the 16 to 45 age group, crippled by being excluded, and Jews living in mixed marriages. The operation was scheduled to start on 12 July and to be completed on 13 to 20 hours, with orders to be delivered by 15 July at Pithiviers concentration camp (the word was then used to designate any regrouping camp).

EXTRAIT D'UN TELEGRAMME OFFICIEL CHIFFRE
————————

PREFET REGIONAL DE DIJON - 0006 - 393 - Texte II 2145. Instructions impéra-
tives autorités occupation - Tous les Juifs âgés de 16 à 45 ans, inclus, des
deux sexes de nationalité: Polonaise - Tchécoslovaque - Russe - Allemande
et précédemment Autrichienne - Grecque - Yougoslave - Norvégienne - Hollandai-
se - Belge - Luxembourgeoise et Apatride devront être immédiatement arrêtés
et transférés dans le camp de concentration de PITHIVIERS .

Juifs qui de visu sont reconnus estropiés ainsi que juifs vivant en mariage mixte ne devront pas être arrêtés. Arrestations devront être commencés
rigoureusement 12 Juillet courant. Elles devront être intégralement exécu-
tées le 13 Juillet à 20 heures. Juifs arrêtés devront être livrés pour le 15
Juilllet 20 heures dernier délai à camp concentration.

....

Copie conforme adressée à M. le Commissaire de Police de
MONTCEAU-LES-MINES pour exécution immédiate en ce qui le
concerne et en le priant de me tenir informé pour le 15
Juillet 1942 midi.
AUTUN le 12 Juillet 1942

Le Sous-Préfet délégué dans les fonctions
de Préfet pour la Saône-et-Loire occupée

signé: GOLDEFY

On July 13, 1942, the police officers of Montceau came to seize Ms. Westreich and her eldest daughter (20 years), both Polish.

The father, too old - 53 - was not taken away, neither were the two younger sisters, Mina because she was French, because she was too young. Aunt Blima was also taken; But not his children, both too young and French ... The monthly report - July 42 - of the Commissioner of Police of Montceau indicates that 34 people were then arrested and led the following day 14 July 1942 towards the camp of Pithiviers, under escort of 6 Police officers of Montceau.

The arrested spent the night in the fire hall, next to the police station, where they received a meal delivered by the Longueville restaurant. They left the following day by train to Pithiviers, joined in the station of Montchanin by the rafts of Le Creusot. At Pithiviers, they found people who had been interned for a long time, but also other people who had just arrived, like themselves, from the départements of Dijon. They were not to remain long, for the convoy No. 6 was now complete, and he set out at 6.15 am on 17 July 1942 for Auschwitz.

Feiga Westreich, her sister Blima and daughter Erna were gassed on 21 July.

The father remained alone at home with his two youngest daughters Mina (16 years), Netty (13 years) and nephews Théodore (13 years) and Thérèse (4 years). Unfortunately, only three months later, on October 9, 1942, the remaining Jews were apprehended by the French police and regrouped first at Le Creusot and then sent to Drancy. Most of them were leaving on 25 October in convoy No. 42 in the direction of Auschwitz. The daily reports of the police station of Montceau signal the action, this time affecting 17 people. Although the telegram of the sub-prefect of Autun still mentioned the only foreign and stateless Jews, this time also people of French nationality were caught, and among them the two young cousins Reicher, victims of the zeal of the only French police! A coach from the S & L transport authority had been chartered by the municipality to ensure the transfer to Le Creusot; The grocer Pons delivered a snack for the trip (sardines and pears). The corresponding invoices were methodically addressed by the Mayor of Montceau, for reimbursement, to the General Union of Israelites of France, UGIF, 19, rue de Teheran in Paris. They are in the archives of the Shoah Memorial; The Jewish community financed its own deportation!

WESTREICH Feiga
1898-1942

REICHER Blima
1900-1942

REICHER Théodore
1929-1942

REICHER Thérèse
1938-1942

Mina remembered the arrest of Theodore and Therese, who, on arrival of the police, had gone to hide in the garden. It was a friendly neighbor who pointed out the hiding place for the cops ... Mina and Netty escaped thanks to the intervention of André Proudhon, the friend of their big sister, who took them under his protection.

The escape

On October 9, 1942, André Proudhon led the two teenage girls to his grandmother Veillaud, to the Georgets. They had had time to take a suitcase with them, hastily packed some clothes, papers and photographs, including those listed above. The next day, all three of them set off, with a backpack in their hands, under the direction of Henri Parriat, professor of natural sciences and close friend of André. With a few others, including the music teacher Berthelon, they shared the same political position, whose content we know by the biography of Parriat (3): a pacifist socialism with a libertarian root marked by the struggle against Stalinism and threats of war.

They cross the demarcation line in the area of Croix Racot and St-Romain and then head towards the Perrons. Knowing them safe now since in the free zone, Parriat returns to Montceau, where he will participate in the rescue of other abandoned Jewish children. The first night, André Proudhon and his protégés sleep at the station of Mont-Saint-Vincent, from where leaves the bus to Macon.

- André Proudhon -

From that day, Andre will stay permanently with the two teenage girls, like a big brother protector; This departure marks for him the abandonment of his work at Montceau and the entry into the adventure of active resistance, which he will actually join some time later in the Ain.

In the free zone, the journeys are easier and are made by coach. The trio first headed for Louhans, where André had friends, the Desvaux, who lived at La Chapelle-Naude (4 km south of Louhans). They will stay there for about a month, Mina having fallen ill.

In November, they went to Ain, to an aunt of André, Margueritte Veillaud, who lived with her husband Michel Trombone in Billiat, near Bellegarde, a stone's throw from the dam of Génissiat. La Guitte is a midwife and Michel works at the construction site of the Génissiat dam, which began construction in 1937; He hires Andre. Michel is a Communist; We imagine the discussions between the two men ... Resistant action would bring them closer.

The three Montcellians would stay for 14 months at the Trombones (until February '44), in this region of Bellegarde, at the foot of the plateau of Retord, where the shepherds made such good cheeses.

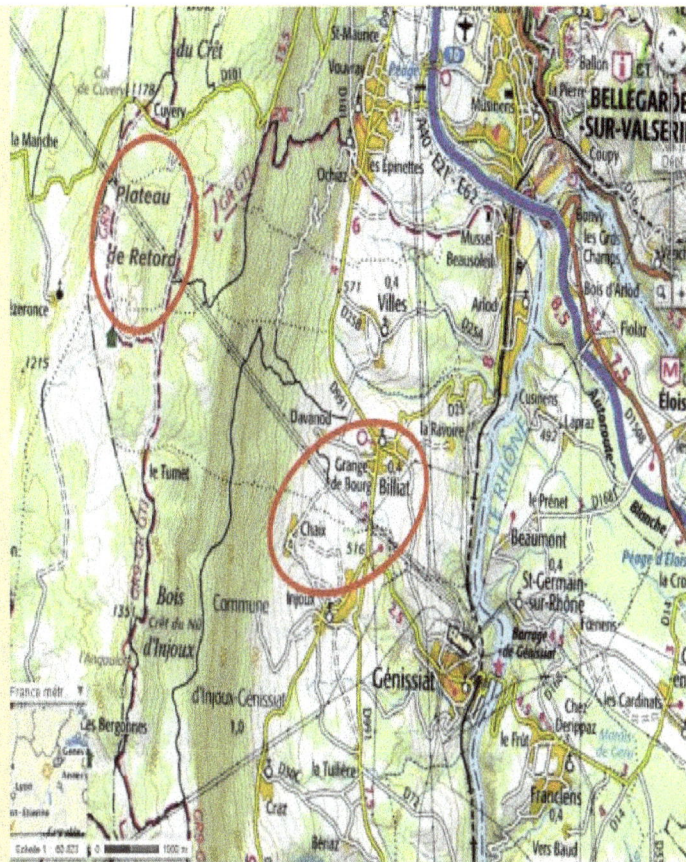

Resistant in the Ain

The girls do not go to school, so as not to attract attention, because their false papers are too rudimentary. They took the name of Proudhon, Madeleine (Mado) and Georgette, so-called cousins of André, coming from Morocco, which had a bit of probability because a branch of the family was really installed there. They have an identity card in their name, but no birth certificates ...

At the end of the year 1942 began the real resistance, where Michel Trombone and André Proudhon committed themselves. The house of the Trombones being at risk of being spotted, it is decided that André and the two daughters would go to lodge higher, in a mountain house, in the hamlet of Chaix ... André participates in actions of sabotage; The girls are entrusted with auxiliary tasks of liaison officer with the camps of the Retord where the maquis has fixed. Netty has the memory of having driven English airmen across the mountain; Frightened, they followed her too closely, while they were instructed to stay at a good distance ...

At one point, in the winter of 43-44, the Germans attacked the maquis of the plateau. The wounded maquisards have gone down to Chaix; Mina makes the nurse and heals the wounds in a bowl red with blood.

Their state of services, established after the war, mentions their contacts with the officers commanding the resistance in the sector: Lieutenant Trombone, Captain Fenestraz, Dr. Mallet.

The sisters retain a dazzled memory of this period, first of all by the intensity of the engagement of their resisting friends, united in the same struggle, in which political differences were of little importance; But also by the discovery of the country life, by the multiple new activities that they share with the young people of the country, throughout the seasons of this year 1943: breeding of pig, crops, participation in harvest ...

(After the war, Netty often went on vacation with the Trombones, while her sister worked at the PTT in Lyon).

In the maquis "Serge", in the Morvan

This period ends after the success of the sabotage of the Génissiat dam at the end of winter 43-44 , which triggered a tight repression on the part of the Germans. Spotted, the Resistance dispersed ... The shelter of Chaix burned, André decides to leave the area; The trio is reformed and they set out on foot in the snow, beginning with a harassing march of ten kilometers to immediately take the distance; Then by bike, the trio ended in February 1944, at Planchez in the Morvan (Nièvre), seat of the maquis "Serge" ...

In 1943, André had made contact with Gérard Drouin (captain "Serge"), who was running a maquis attached to the FTP (4). Drouin, a native of St-Vallier, a commune in the Montceau-les-Mines basin, had lived in Sanvignes for a long time and was one of Andre's friends. He had gone to fight in the Morvan, where his wife came from, after being active in a group of resistant sedentary miners and apparently spotted by the police ...

The two sisters, too, were well acquainted with Gerard Drouin and his family; They lodge at the Vial, in the family Brossier, which is one of the fixed points of the maquis ...

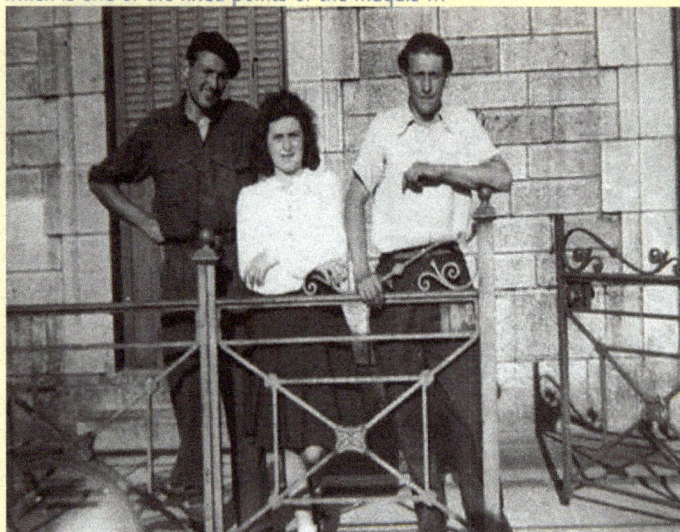

- In the Morvan, each of the sisters with André Proudhon (left) -

In the maquis "Serge", they find their function of liaison, Netty especially, who younger, has more ease to pass the controls. She goes several times by bike to Epinac and to a lawyer of Autun ... (password she remembers: "the sun ..." and in response: "... has appointment with the moon"); One day it returns a radio transceiver.

Mina, on the other hand, often goes on a mission to the pharmacist of Anost.

They both participate in parachute receptions. They learn how to erect / disassemble weapons and use them, in case the cantonment is attacked ...

Rigny-sur-Arroux

After the Germans attacked Planchez on 25 June 1944, at the end of which they fled to Autun, the situation was considered too dangerous for the two young girls; They are conducted to Rigny sur Arroux; They are lodged at "tante Francine", the wife of Pierre Thevenet, who is then in the maquis and will be killed there. They are there under the protection of Lucien Cabaretier, the head of the maquis AS "Lucien" installed then at the castle of Petite-Faye.

... But a drama soon arrives: Andre - "Lieutenant Guy" of the maquis "Serge" - who stayed in the Morvan, is shot down on July 9 while trying to flee after being arrested by the Germans following an action In Epinac (North of the S & L). Netty learns the news while she is on mission at Montceau.

For the two girls, it is a blow of a club; The pain is much more acute than that caused by the fate of the parents, which has long remained imprecise. Their memory will repress much of the whole period after André's death. It is only known that they continue as liaison officers; On the occasion of immense cycling trips, they made missions with Raymond Barault "Jean Roche", departmental director of the AS. In Montceau, they meet Paul Mercier "Benoît", the local chief of the AS, and Ms Forest, who holds the function of "mailbox".

Mina and Netty will stay in Rigny until the Liberation. They will then return to Sanvignes where they will find André's relatives, particularly his uncle Louis Veillaud (brother of Marguerite Trombone) and his wife (5), who will become their adoptive parents ... Netty will be formally adopted by Veillaud and will resume Studies in Montceau, then after his marriage, will settle in Brittany, while Mina will find a job at the PTT before marrying, in 1949, a pharmacist of Montceau, Jean Birgé.

Mina and Netty Westreich will be decorated with the medal of the Resistance.

(Click to read)

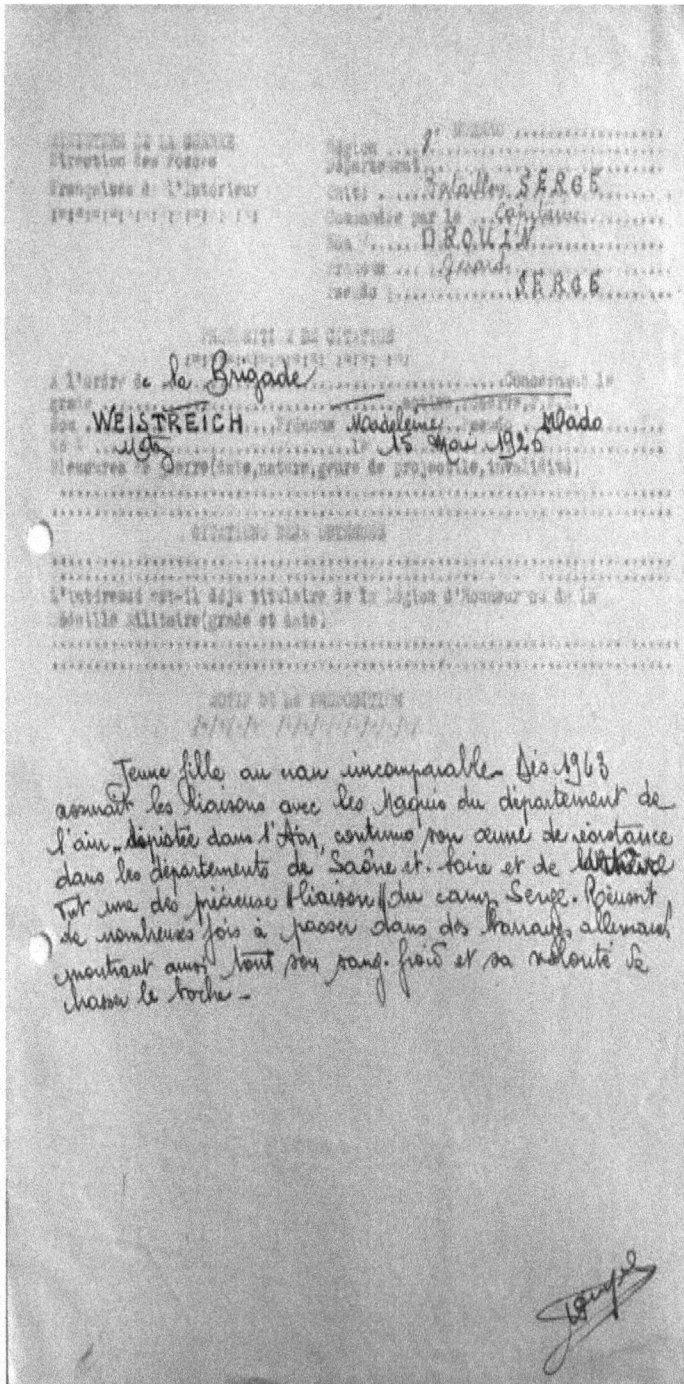

Proposal submission memorandum
Of the Resistance Medal

On January 15, 2004, Yad Vashem awarded André Proudhon the title of Just among the Nations (6).

_____

(1) First military leader of the Polish FTP-ME Resistance in Montceau (see his biography). Note the parallel between the stories of the two families.

(2) Georges Legras and Roger Marchandeau, *The tragedy of the Jewish Montcellians 1940-1945* , Physiophile, special issue, Montceau-les-Mines, 2010.

(3) *Biography of Henri Parriat 1910-1975* , Physiophile, Montceau-les-Mines, 1986. Order
(Click here).

(4) On this point, see Michel Villard , *Ombres et Lumières of the Occupation and the Liberation of Autun* , by the author, 1984 and André Jeannet, *Memorial of the Resistance in S & L* , JPM, Mâcon October 2005.

(5) Louis Veillaud was mayor of Sanvignes from 1945 to 1974.

(6) See the relevant page of the Yad Vashem website

Other sources :

OJ of 8 July 2001, which sets out the dates of death.

ADSL in Mâcon

Historical Defense Service, Resistance Office in Vincennes, BAVCC in Caen

Shoah Memorial.

Website of the commune of Sanvignes (pages mémoire) - click here

The pictures were entrusted to us by Netty.

03/17/2013   1 *Post a Comment* 🗨 *0 likes*👍

| G+ | 🐦 Tweet | 🔶 PARTAGER 🇫 ╘ ✉ … | 🖨 |

To print

To discover

Ottavio Tamponi 1 - a funny Polish

Michal Kokot, from the mine to the sea fishing ...

The KOCLEJDA, a committed family ...

comments

Zaidi-Marx Yeva · 4 November 2014

Very beautiful testimony of my grand mother netty and my aunt Mina (mado). This story is very detailed and allows to understand this story, thank you very much for this information and I am very proud of my grandmother, and congratulations for this site very complete.

👍 0 · Reply

Rozwadow Branch 1b
of the Westreich Family Tree

Y-DNA match

Yermiyahu Westreich
(probable father of Yakov)
b. circa 1828
m. Necha
d. ??
|
Yakov/Jacob Westreich
b. circa 1864
m. Cypora Federbush
d. 1926 in Tarnobrzeg
|
Itzhak Westreich
b. 1892 in Tarnobrzeg
m. Golda Weinman
d. in Holocaust
|
Moshe Westreich
b. 1923
m. Rivka Fershtman
d. 1998 in Herzlia, Israel

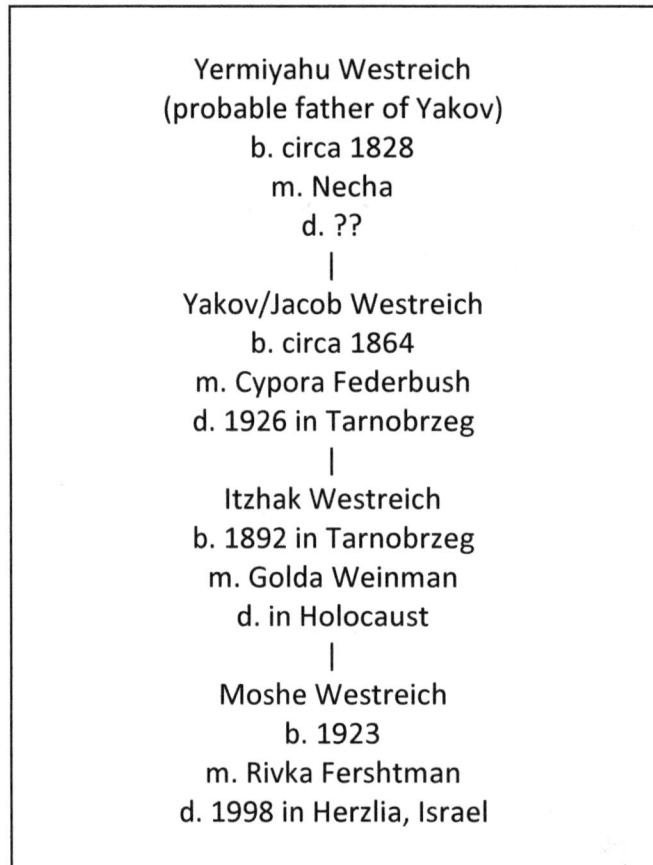

Rozwadow, previously a town of its own,
is now part of the town of Stalowa Wola in modern-day Poland,
formerly part of Galicia, Austria (1772 - 1918),
located 16 miles east of Tarnobrzeg.

Not much is known about the early generations of this branch.

Edited by Allan Westreich

Family Photos[88]

Itzhak and Golda Westreich, parents of Moshe

Twin brothers Moshe and Naftali Westreich, and younger brother Yakov

Twin brothers Moshe and Naftali Westreich

Moshe Westreich in Israel, 1996

Prisoner Registration ("Personal") Card[89]
Buchenwald Concentration Camp
Moshe Westreich, 1943

Name	Mozes Westreich
Birth	13 August 1923 in Tarnobrzeg
Marital status	single
Number of children	none
Residence	Lemberg, Galicia
Religion	Jewish
State	Poland
Registered (at Buchenwald)	4 September 1943
Reason	Political Polish Jew
Height	162 cm (5' 4")
Body type	strong
Facial type	long
Eyes	brown

Nose	curved
Ears	small, standing outward
Teeth	2 missing
Hair	black
Languages	Polish, German

Moshe Westreich survived multiple concentration camps:
- Buchenwald (near Weimar, Germany)
- Gross-Rosen (Gross-Rosen, Lower Silesia, Germany [modern-day Poland])
- Kraków-Plaszow (Plaszow, Poland)
- Janowska (Lwów, Poland [modern-day Ukraine])
- Sonnenburg (Sonnenburg, Germany [modern-day Poland])

Fortunately, he survived the Holocaust and went on to raise a family in Israel.

Galicia Branch 1
of the Westreich Family Tree

Y-DNA no match

David Westreich
b. circa 1846
m. Mollie Weinstein
d. ??
|
Abraham Westreich
b. 1876 in Galicia
m. Tobias/Tillie Gerscheidt from Brody
m. Hermina Hartstein from Czeke, Hungary
d. 1958 in NY

Alexander "Al" Westreich	Murray Westreich
b. 1909	b. 1923
m. Evelyn Ginsberg	m. Arlene Kutisker
(m. Helene Finaly)	---
d. 1987	d. 2013
Stanley Westreich	Neil Westreich

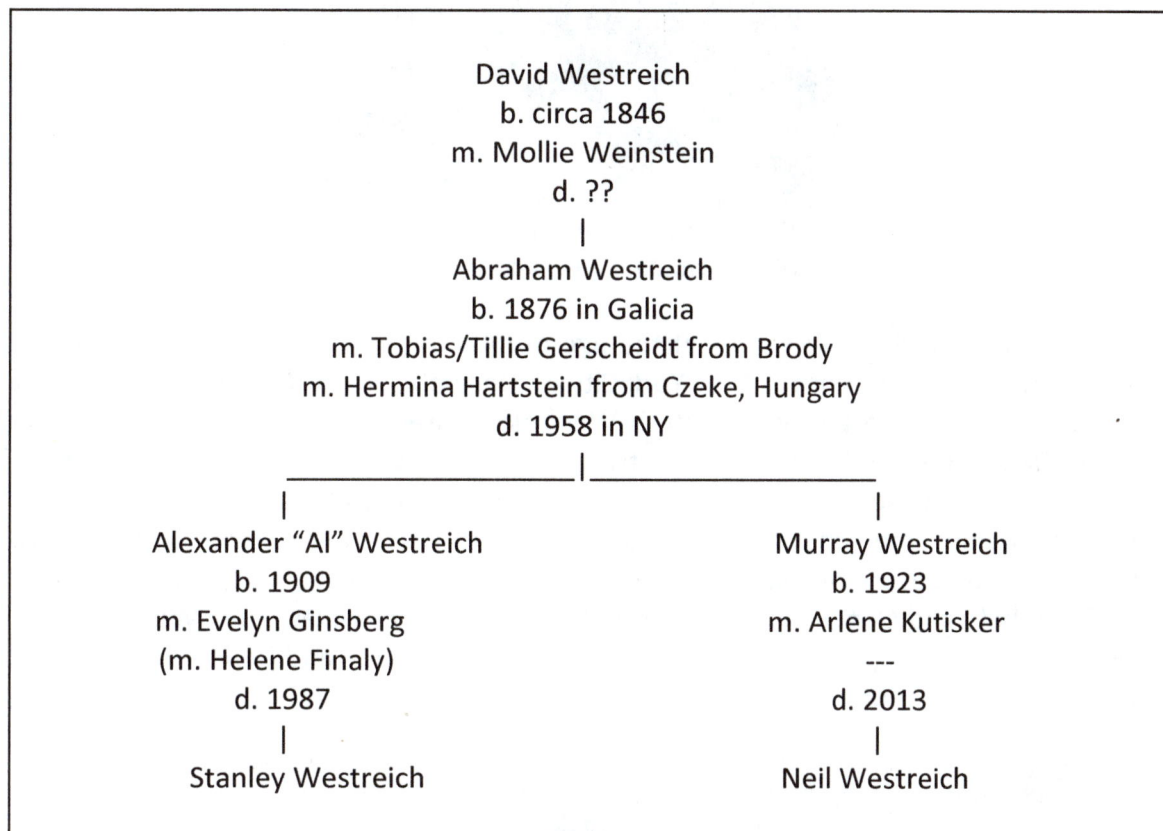

This branch originated in modern-day Poland or Ukraine,
formerly part of Galicia, Austria (1772 - 1918).

Edited by Allan Westreich

Not much is known about the early generations of this branch. Abraham Westreich's son Alexander started the very successful Lord West formal wear company.

Stanley Westreich's Legacy:
Real Estate Icon Was the Visionary Behind the Rosslyn Skyline[90]
APRIL 19, 2021

(L-R): Anthony Westreich (son), Dana Hirt (daughter),
Lauren Westreich (daughter) and Stanley Westreich

Stanley Irwin Westreich passed away at the age of 84 in his home in San Diego, California on April 11, 2021. Stanley was born in New York City on December 8, 1936 to Alexander and Evelyn Westreich. He is survived by his wife Ruth Westreich; three children Lauren Westreich (Bob Emerson), Dana Hirt, and Anthony Westreich (Tanya Zuckerbrot); four stepchildren Tim Landres, Claudia (Tim) Helmig, Jason(Angela) Merchey, and Kelly (Ariel) Haas; 19 grandchildren, Greta and Nathaniel Emerson, Oliver, Kalie and Quincy Hirt, Max and Gabriel Westreich, Tobey, Olivia and Juliette Beyer, Megan, Jacob and Matthew Landres, Camille, Charlotte and Billy Helmig, Campbell, and Genevieve and Corrine Haas; his former wives, Thea Westreich Wagner and Leslie Westreich; step-siblings, Gail White, Billy Cohen (Anne), and Dede Harris; and cousins Neil Westreich and Marjorie Westreich (Rob Berkson).

Anthony Westreich (son), Neil Westreich (cousin), Stanley Westreich,
Murray Westreich (uncle) and Alexander Westreich (father)

Stanley received his law degree from NYU and his undergraduate degree from the University of Miami. He served in the US Coast Guard in Cape May, NJ and on the USS Unimak. He moved to Washington, DC in1961 where he lived most of his life, before retiring in San Diego, California. Stanley, in partnership with Bill Brakefield, Sr. and Jared Drescher, formed Westfield Realty. Over the course of 50 years, Westfield built a commercial real estate empire and, with great vision, pioneered the development of Rosslyn, Virginia. Westfield developed 10 buildings in Rosslyn shaping the skyline, including the then-famed 'Gannett and USA Today Towers', and another four throughout Northern Virginia. In 1992 Westfield formed a partnership with Terry Eakin and Bob Youngentob to help launch their new rm, EYA. From 1992-2014, EYA in partnership with Westfield, developed 27 residential communities and over 3,000 homes throughout the greater Washington, DC-area.

Current Rosslyn skyline view because of Mr. Westreich's 10-building development

In addition to real estate, Stanley was a long-standing Board Member of Signet Banking Corporation and subsequently became a Founding Board Member of Capital One Financial Corporation in 1994. He served on the Board of Capital One from 1994- 2008. He also partnered with Gene Samburg and founded Kastle Systems in 1972. Stanley was an ambitious and entrepreneurial man yet pursued his business investments in a conservative way. He always believed that his "hand-shake" was more binding than any contract.

Stanley loved golf and bridge, playing both for most of his life. He had a keen mind for numbers and loved a good joke. He was an avid traveler, art lover, and philanthropist. He was always generous and kind. He loved his big family and was proud of the many accomplishments of his children and grandchildren, often bragging to whomever called about their successes.

In the year before his death, Stanley penned and published his autobiography entitled, "A Life Well Lived." He wrote the book for his children and their children to pass along the family's history. A memorial service will be planned in Washington, DC to celebrate his life when it is safe to gather.

© *citybiz*

From the Desk of Neil Westreich[91]

Dear Finely Tuned Friends,

As my daily musical diet has expanded to embrace live performances of discordant sounds emanating from my joints, I've concluded that I'm unlikely to find myself in Box 33 on March 7, 2075, when Carnegie Hall will presumably pull out all the stops to celebrate Maurice Ravel's 200th (and my 125th) birthday.

In an effort to face down this existential challenge, I've elected to include a bequest in my will for Carnegie Hall. I do it in the hopes it will enable a discriminating group of sentient music lovers to act as my proxies in savoring the pleasures of that and other future transcendent evenings at the Hall—assuming, of course, the corner of Seventh Avenue and 57th Street remains above sea level at that late date.

An unanticipated consequence of this act of generosity was my prompt elevation into the ranks of the Isaac Stern Society (informally known as the "Orpheus in the Underworld Association"), which is populated by other far-sighted, lugubrious music lovers who have also decided to express their appreciation for Carnegie Hall with their dying breaths.

Recently, my friends at Carnegie Hall asked me whether I could put into writing those circumstances that prompted me to make my bequest, presumably "to encourage others," as the French are fond of saying following a guillotining. This latest assignment seems the natural progression from my having been previously tapped to deliver welcoming remarks to fellow Patrons at selected dinners before Carnegie Hall concerts that have featured works such as Beethoven's *Missa solemnis*, Mahler's *Resurrection Symphony*, or Brahms's *Ein deutsches Requiem*.

At its simplest, of course, my decision to make a parting gift is a public declaration that my relationship with Carnegie Hall has been one of the longest, most passionate, and least contentious love affairs of my life. Although it often feels as if this romance, as in any good *National Geographic* episode, dates back to "time immemorial," my overflowing box of Playbills suggests that my introduction to the Hall took place on November 26, 1963—a notable evening in which The Philadelphia Orchestra, under Eugene Ormandy, did a quick change of programming and performed Brahms's *Ein deutsches Requiem* as a tribute to slain President Kennedy.

At the concert's conclusion, there was, by design, no applause, and the audience members filed out of the Hall in a silent, orderly manner. It was only later I came to learn that a typical evening at the Hall includes not only a stunning concert, but also vigorous applause, cheering and shouting, occasional foot-stomping, and, predictably, New Yorkers shoving one another as they frantically head to the exits.

In the four decades following that first encounter, whether pursuing academic studies or my career, I increasingly spent more memorable afternoons and evenings at Carnegie Hall. But, following the arrival of the new millennium and, shortly afterward, my early retirement, the relationship took on a whole new complexion. Each succeeding season found me subscribing to additional series, for despite having attended concerts for decades at the Hall, the arrival in January of each season's new brochure left me excited and amazed that, despite any carping by *The New York Times's* dyspeptic classical music critic, the artistic team had once again managed to assemble another season of fresh, imaginative, and compelling programming.

Apart from the concerts themselves, after several years as a card-carrying Patron, I was invited to join the Patrons Council and given the privilege of co-hosting, each year, a handful of convivial pre-concert dinners in the Shorin Club Room, where I often had the pleasure of meeting many like-minded devotees of Carnegie Hall and, occasionally, delivering the welcoming remarks (frequently peppered with some seemingly erudite comments on the evening's musical program, acquired earlier that afternoon through the magic of Wikipedia).

I also had the great privilege, during the decade that preceded the lockdown, of hosting a string of eight annual soirées at my home for Carnegie Hall Patrons, at which members of Ensemble Connect or the National Youth Orchestra of the United States of America rapturously performed leading works of chamber music repertoire in the sort of intimate setting for which much of that music had been composed, without a single complaint about seating or sight lines.

And so, having witnessed and experienced Carnegie Hall up close and personal over a lifetime, what do I think and how do I feel?

Even allowing for my natural hyperbole, it's clear to me that after 130 years, Carnegie Hall remains the greatest concert hall in the world, and we have the good fortune to be in the midst of one of its golden ages.

The awe in which the Hall is held by performers and public alike is not just the result of its great physical beauty, remarkable acoustics, and historical importance, but also because, year in and year out, its programming is unmatched in terms of creativity, variety, and quality. Its stages are home to an unending number of wide-ranging and sublime concerts, performed to the highest standards by the greatest orchestras and musical artists in the world.

Watching their faces as they scan the Hall, I have the impression that the superb artists who come to perform there are clearly awed by the experience and play their hearts out. More than one performer has said to me that there is only one Carnegie Hall, which I assume is meant to convey an insight beyond the merely numerical.

Finally, of great importance to me is the warmth and camaraderie that appear to infect almost everyone who works at the Hall, right through to the most charming and skillful ticket takers and ushers in New York City, who embrace everyone, apart from those audience members who seem determined not to leave Carnegie Hall without having electronically captured a flawless recording of the highlights of the evening's performance.

With so much to be grateful for, it seems obvious to me that when the time comes to swap my seats for a harp and a halo, I want to try to repay a small portion of the large debt I've incurred to Carnegie Hall over six decades of inspired entertainment and education.

Of course, it's never been a one-way street. Those of us who regularly fill Carnegie Hall's seats and coffers with generous annual gifts have been essential in enabling it to remain at the summit of the world's most treasured cultural institutions. And yet, despite the frequency with which I'm warmly thanked by Carnegie Hall for my support, I'm sure a proper accounting would confirm that I've always gotten the better part of the deal. Quite simply, it's impossible to place a price on rapture and transcendence. Other Patrons have frequently shared similar sentiments with me.

If "thank you" seems like more than a good enough reason to leave money to Carnegie Hall in my will, I also like to think that, if my pessimistic assessment of my long-term posthumous prospects proves to be ill-founded, perhaps my friends at the Hall will be good enough to treat a portion of my bequest as a downpayment on subscription tickets to eternity.

Wishing you all good things, including your preferred seating, for many years to come,

Neil Westreich

Abe and Tillie Westreich[92]

Abe and Hermina Westreich[93]

Lord West Tuxedos

TUXEDO MAKERS Weinstein and Westreich.

CROSSING THE RUBICON, FROM CHELSEA TO QUEENS

Beginning in 1917, West Mill Clothes Inc. had turned out Lord West tuxedos and other formal wear from a succession of loft buildings in Manhattan's Chelsea section, the most recent at 18th St. and Sixth Ave.

But in the spring of 1987, the firm's landlord told West Mill its lease would not be renewed when it expired in July 1988.

"We had three choices," recalls West Mill president Harvey Weinstein, "liquidate, move to nearby New Jersey, or move to Brooklyn, Queens or the Bronx — but out of Manhattan."

Lord West asked the city if there were tax breaks and other incentives to remain in New York.

The city came up with space in Woodside, Queens, and ways to save money. The savings added up to more than $4.5 million, including corporate tax credits of $1.9 million; real estate tax savings of $1.42 million; below-market financing and associated tax savings worth $335,900; a relocation grant of $110,000; an energy cost reduction of $703,200; and a commercial occupancy tax cut of $49,800.

"If we had relocated into New Jersey, our costs would have been substantially less," says Weinstein. "But we estimated we would lose maybe 35% of our work force."

The firm employed about 450. More than half lived in Brooklyn and Queens.

A personal pledge from Mayor Koch helped anchor West Mill to the city. It came while Weinstein and his partner, Murray Westreich, sat in the office of Deputy Mayor Alair Townsend in 1987.

"Mayor Koch walked into the meeting and stated unequivocally that Lord West would not leave," recalls Weinstein. "He and his staff were there to help us stay."

"Basically, you cross the Rubicon at some point, and we crossed the Rubicon, took a deep breath, and said we were going to make the investment."

"By relocating in Queens, we're in a position to warehouse a lot more merchandise. We have the ability of increasing our sales by 50% over the next five years."

— Franklin Fisher

New York Daily News, 1988[94]

Chorzow Branch
of the Westreich Family Tree

Y-DNA match

Edited by Allan Westreich

Leib/Leopold Westreich
b. circa 1900
m. Hinda/Helen
d. in Holocaust
|
Jacob "Jack" Westreich
b. 1923 in Chorzow, Poland
m. Anita
d. 2013 in Toronto, Canada

The following interview was transcribed by
Jack Westreich's grandchildren.

Testimony of Jack Westreich
USC Shoah Foundation[95]
(March 19, 1996)

I was born 1923 [in Chorzow, Poland, 45 miles WNW of Krakow]. My father had a store, maybe 8-10 people working. It was a very modern city where we lived. My mother was involved in this business too, before the war and she just came out Saturdays and Sundays because during the week he had a manufacturing business making permanent solution, shampoo, perfume, mostly to supply for barbers and beauty salons.

Tell me about the rest of your family.

I had another two brothers, my brother was born 1925 and the youngest was born 1928. The middle one was Max and the youngest was Ernst. My parents gave them German names. There were lots of - German Jews in our city. Before the first war, this part belonged to Germany. After this first war, this part belonged to Poland. Many Jews lived there for generations. Later, after the war people moved there-3 km from the border. I remember before the war, I went a few times to the German side- it was a very modern city, lots of professionals lived on the other side. It was a very nice city. It was so close that when it was Kristallnacht, people went closer to the border to see the flames.

Tell me about your family life, how did you get along with your brothers?

Very nice, everything was fine. My parents I will tell you were not religious because they worked Saturdays. But they kept Shabbas- they lit the candles. I remember come yontiv there was full supper. We had a meal at 12 when we came from school and at night we had fish and cake. Not a heavy meal. Only if it was Pesach or Rosh Hashana or Yom Kippur- we had lots of friends come over.

Did you go to synagogue at all?

Yes. My father didn't go so much- holidays, sometimes Saturdays.

Tell me about going to school.

Till 6 years, I went to a German kindergarten. Later, when I finished I went to a Jewish public school- mostly Jewish kids went. Only went from grades 1-6 and later for high school we had to join with other kids. You learned Polish but there were some subjects like German and French you could pick up. Hebrew we had afternoon like special classes. We had a private teacher whose house we went to. He made a deal with my parents that he would do private. He taught humash. Till 13 we slowed down but we had to know a seder. Every Saturday they changed the torah reading, we needed to know. Didn't go to a cheder.

What did you do when you didn't go to school?

First thing, I belonged to Maccabi from 6 years old. I went for exercises and all kinds of sports, till the war. I worked for Jewish organizations- I belonged to bet ar. People went to Akiba, other Jewish organizations. On Saturdays we all got together. It was a very nice Jewish community. Under circumstances, what was before the war you could not ask for better. There were rich, middle class and poor Jews.

Tell me about Beitar.

We got together. Talked about Israel. I enjoyed it because the last couple years I went to summer camp for the summer, the same places I later worked in the camp.

Did you have any non-Jewish friends?

We lived in apartment complex. In the middle was a playground, mostly there were gentiles because the parents were there for generations. They went to Polish school too, but we played with them.

What was the relationship between the Jewish and non-Jewish community?

It was very good. From the beginning it was not so bad. When Hitler came to power, everything changed. We had lots of Germans, they were Polish but when the Germans came in they were German. Not really anti-Semitism. When I belonged to Maccabi it was German instructor. Because people were living close. In our store, 50 percent of people that worked for my father were German. When the war broke out, we left and gave someone the keys to the store and when we came back they didn't want to give the store back.

Before the war you played soccer, tell me about that.

I played lots of soccer. First thing, my father was very active in the games, active in the group, was the best players in Poland, mostly they were German. The games were mostly on Sunday but some games were middle of the week. A lot of people went- 10-20 000. It was a big stadium.

Anything about yourself before the war?

I had a very nice life. My parents were not rich, they were comfortable. One thing they would spend- they would spend on kids, on clothes, on food, school. they tried their best.

Friday September 1, 1939 the war broke out, what did you hear about the Nazis?

Lots of Germans in 1938 and 1939 ran away on the other side. Older people knew what they were doing and the younger ones just wanted to be somebody.

Were the Jews afraid?

They were afraid, they didn't pay attention. The German Jews didn't think they would be touched.

Did Germans deport German Jews back to Poland before the war?

Yes they put them on neutral place- the Polish didn't want them and the Germans didn't want them. Later the Polish let them in. They went to Cracow or somewhere else.

Anything else before the war?

It was very nice, nice Jewish community. Maybe 10 000, nice Jewish synagogue- unbelievable architecture. Not too many orthodox. Not too many stores closed Saturday.

The war broke out, how did this affect you?

There was a feeling something would happen. My mother and brothers they took whatever they could, they sent it out to Auschwitz. My grandparents lived there in that city. So my mother and my brother went there before. I remember when the war broke out on Friday, my father was still in the store working but he had a feeling. We took a street car to Katowice, from there we almost caught the last train to Auschwitz and already German planes were flying. Everyone was running around- people were running away from evacuations so Saturday we decided to go too. But everyone stayed. My parents went. So we went, we had a ride, until we came to Krakow. My dad knew someone. They took us in for a few days. And in just a few days the Germans were there. There was nowhere to go anymore. Better to go home. We tried to go home. We had to pay for horse and buggy because there were no trains. We found out that our grandfather was shot from the Germans or hoodlum from Polish. So everyone was sitting shiva (in Auschwitz). My father stayed a few days. It was a very bad feeling to come back to the same place, we were only gone 2 weeks. It was the end of September. There was no more synagogue, a few Jews got together to pray. It was a bad feeling that people did not want to give us back the keys. These were people we left in charge of the store and apartment. Later they gave us back and we didn't stay too long. The same German kids that we played with on the playground didn't want to talk to you. Polish weren't as bad. Everything changed. Signs said Jews and dogs not allowed. People who owned the stores offered to bring food to them because they were afraid of being seen helping Jews.

What was the first bad thing that happened with German occupation?

They took over the store- they found someone to run business because they said you don't need it anymore. Bad experience was everyone needed to register in Jewish congress. In October, they took all the Jews from 20-50 to build a ghetto or work camp for the Jews from here so they rounded up all the Jews from Chorzow and Katowice and took them to the station and loaded them in cattle trains and sent them out. A week later they started with us. They rounded up people from 18 to 65 and they told them to take 25 pounds and a few days food because they will be in the train and they needed to meet in a gentile school in a gym on certain day and hour. My mom packed everything like we were going to camp. We came with a laundry basket. This wasn't the first time I saw the Nazis. They told us to give away all of our gold. I had a gold ring from my bar mitzvah. They said everyone need to show their hands. My ring was so stuck it took so long to take off. They took money, they took everything. My mother gave me money and we kept it. Younger people they didn't beat so much. They knew people know how to hide.

After this they took us to Katowice - we walked there. Maybe 4500. We were guarded with bull dogs. Later, we came to the station there and they loaded us up on the cattle trains. There was nowhere to go. They gave you a bucket to pee. The train went. It took us 4-5 days. My 16th birthday was in the cattle train. We got to a station, there was SS, all of the people were afraid. We didn't think too much. Later they got the group together. There was a bridge to go right from the station, went over mud. The SS- put this stuff on the buggies this way you don't need to carry the stuff. We were stupid so we just put them. We pushed the buggy across the river and then they ran away with our stuff. Me and my brother chased it to knock the stuff off and they started whipping us. We got some stuff down but the older people had nothing, nothing to wear. We looked around, where to go? We were afraid to go back across the river. This was a dividing line between a different Poland. We went on the other side. Some people thought- we aren't far from the Russian zone. We wanted to look for a train or horse and buggy to drive us closer to the border. We walked for a few days, we didn't have anywhere to sleep so we went to the farmers they were a little anti-semitic. They said we can't let you sleep here for free, you must have gold or something. We had nothing. We gave them a shirt or something, we had some clothes. We walked for a few days we got to a city where the train was running to Lemberg. The train was Lubachuv. They took us on the train and we jumped trains till we came to Voov. We didn't know anyone, there were lots of refugees. We met someone and asked if he knows my father. I was reunited with my father. I was with my brother. When we got to the Russian border, they were so friendly, they let us through. After a while, they threw us back to Germany. Later at night, we would smuggle over to Russia. Later I went to Lemberg. We met my father, he lost everything. Whatever the Germans asked for, he gave them. I stayed there. My father found himself a job. My brother ran away. He always wanted to go to Israel. Him and some friends ran away, we never saw him again. This was the middle brother. He wanted to go to Romania and from Romania to Israel. The younger brother stayed with my mother. My mother and brother were still in Chorzow. They made it Judenrein. They believed it belonged to the German Reich. My brother packed up, she got a mover and took everything to Auschwitz. Normal Jewish city and she lived with my grandparents. It was a normal city and she lived there. I was in Vuuv. I thought I should go home and see what my mother was doing. If everything was okay my father would come. A smuggler took me home, for money. Later, we went closer to the border to a small town. We needed to cross a river and it was frozen. This was January 1940. We went through, we got a farmer, he drove us to a train station in Yara, big Polish city. We didn't wear our Jewish band. There were German police everywhere. Later, I remember from there, from the morning till night, the Germans were checking papers. So we came to Auschwitz. Later I got together with my mother and brother. I lived there till March 15, 1941. There was Jewish community but no synagogue. They started to take people to forced labour. They would take certain ages. They took my uncles and cousin to Germany. They took me too, for 2-3 days to go out and work. The concentration camp was a Polish camp before, like an army. They started moving in 1940. The people in Auschwitz didn't know what they were building. I know they opened the camp in 1940 because lived in the city close the bridge near the camp and I saw trucks come in with people packed like herring. People didn't pay attention. German kapos came over and singing on the streets singing German songs and the blue stripes and later in 1941, march, again, they made it so we had to go for forced labour. My younger brother was there, but he was too young. He was only 12, this started at like 17. I registered and they took me to a camp. I remember again that my mother packed my things. Some days I feel like I should have stayed and hid, and stayed with my mother. But in some ways I was lucky, it was a good camp. In charge was a contractor. We have one picture with the work that we were doing.

Tell me about the camp, how did it look?

It was a farmer's house. It was a work place. There were still SS. We were lucky we had free movement. This place where I worked was maybe 30 people. The whole place maybe 300, different groups. The Germans/Romanians took over 10 farmers houses and kept the nicest for themselves and the rest they told us to demolish. We worked for the SS. I was in this camp for almost 2 years. Mainly I was demolishing houses. Other things were helping contractors build, renovate houses, like for the Germans, some for the Hitler yuden. The last camp I was in we worked on a river for flooding.

Let me ask you about your day.

This camp was not so bad, they got you up at 6. This camp was small farmers rooms for about 10 in a room and there were 3 women in the kitchen. We ate breakfast, whatever they had left over. Then we went to work. We ate at about 7. This place was not so bad. We ate bread. We went to farmers, if we had money, we could buy. Under circumstances, this was unbelievable. You could go to other towns on the train, meet relatives and come back. We always had lunch. I went to Polish farmers and told them a story, they would give me something to eat. The Romanian Germans spoke better Jewish than real Jews. In the summer we stopped work earlier, like 5. In the winter it depended on where you work. The women cooked dinner- soup, potatoes. No one was starving in this camp.

What did you do at night?

Stories, talking, not bad. I was young. People were married with kids, they would talk about how they got engaged.

What did people think would happen?

They didn't. They lived one day to the next. If you start thinking you are a lost person.

How long did you spend?

Till 1943, in March or April. In 1943, there were lots of small camps. But when everything turned over, the uprising in Warsaw, they started closing small camps. They made small ghettos, they started closing them up. There was a change. One day I remember, getting up in the morning. The SS came with big trucks and they rounded up the house and they told us pack up whatever you can and we will take you away. So many SS. So we got everything together and they loaded us up on a truck and they took lots of people from other small towns around us. All kinds of small cities had small camps with Jews and they sent us to Sosnowitz.

Did you hear anything about going on outside?

Yes. In 1943, I went to Benjing on a vacation. Like to leave for a few days. I didn't see cousins, other people, they disappeared. People knew very well. They took them to Majdanek, to Auschwitz, they knew. All of the people they took like garbage. We really knew. Because in 1941 where I worked on the other side was Romania, Hungary and Czech, there were trains going with people and people were waving. We were close we couldn't figure out where they were going. Later we found out they were going to Auschwitz.

Anything else?

The guy in charge tried his best to keep us okay. He supplied us with food, he gave us like 50 cents a day to go buy. He would give us a pay day every 2 weeks. We could buy cigarettes, food. Under the circumstances, we were treated better in comparison to others. He was a very nice man, after the war, he was in bad shape, hiding in Austria. He asked me to help contribute money (a friend) to help him and I gave him some. Thought he was worth it because what he did.

It was very bad. A few thousand Jews were put around the square. They started segregating- young, older, the kids. Who could work. The younger kids were separate, the women, the older men- all separate groups. They loaded the people up, like garbage and took them to Auschwitz. There was so much screaming but there was nothing to do. You couldn't open your mouth. All Nazis around. There was one guy who limped a little bit. We stayed a few days in Sosnowitz. They looked for gold and diamond. Later they sent me to work in the steel factory close to my city. There was a camp, maybe 300 people, we worked on the construction site. My younger brother and mother were deported from Auschwitz to Gerlitza near Krakow. I wrote to my mother and later lost track, maybe they sent her to Majdanek or Treblinka. I heard my brother was supposed to go to a camp to. People lied about their age. Some kids wanted to make themselves older. I don't understand when people say they were 10 when the war broke out because I was one of the youngest, but some people they used for experiments.

Tell me about Bismarckhutte.

We worked in a steel factory digging ditches- like rain, cold. You still came home, got a meal, they gave you bread and soup. No cakes, no oranges, no apples. You were lucky if you could fill up your stomach with bread.

What did it look like?

Like a town house, every room people. Like a complex. There were guards walking around , towers. It was not bad.

You had enough to eat?

Not really. The best thing was, when I worked on construction. It was muddy, cold. We were digging ditches. The guard tells me, because I spoke to German- I am from there too. What is your name? He knew my father. He said he worked for a Jew wholesale and he told me the guy

If something happened on the outside that was bad for the Germans they beat the Jews. You needed to know people, know what type of work to get. If you said you were a mechanic or tradesman. Just get out of heavy work.

How long did you spend at Reivesvel?

May or June 1944.

Are the Russians coming closer?

Still nothing. They closed this camp and they were trying to get everyone to concentration camps. So they sent us to Blechhammer. Blechhammer was –commando of Auschwitz. 184627. I acquired my number in Blechhammer.

May I ask you how you felt when you got the number?

I felt nothing. We came to this camp and we were maybe 3-400 people and they lined us up. They told us to take all of our clothes off because we were going for a shower, cut our hair and they gave us a number and gave us clothes. The trouble is I had German money I wanted to hide it. I put a ditch. Later we left everything, completely naked. Walked to the other room. They cut the hair, they gave us the number and then you were finished. You were lucky if you got to keep shoes. And that's all. They give us a room there was a place where I lived with all the people. This was in Blechhammer block 10.

Tell me about Blechhammer.

Big construction. They were a big farm industry- they were making gas from coal. It was a huge area. People were from all over the world- prisoners of war, Jews, gypsies. There were almost 10 000 people. They came and worked- Russian, Germans. Free Germans too. German prisoners who didn't want to go to the army. People who couldn't go to the front. But still it wasn't bad there. I had schlep. I knew people who worked in the kitchen from my city. They felt sorry for me- they would give me bread and soup. I had a friend who raised pigs. Whatever was left over I would eat. I couldn't ask for more in the camps.

What was your day like?

We were maybe 100 people in the room. The beds were 3 levels. There was a table in the middle. The worst was that you needed to have a watch man at night. There was a pail. You needed to take it out to the toilet. Or you had to wash the floor to keep it clean. Then you would fall asleep and if you were caught you were beaten up like crazy by the Germans.

Did you have a roll call in the morning?

Yeah every day you needed to be lined up. You needed to get up, they put all the commandos. The Jews would want to stand together to stay warm but they didn't like it. To keep warm I would take paper and put it around me like a sweater. The Germans didn't like it. They beat you up like crazy. The main SS was standing on a pedestal and sometimes music was playing.

When did your day end?

Blechhammer was under the circumstances a good camp. You can interview people and they will say the same thing. They were healthier when they were liberated. The trouble was that the work was coming to an end. The American and English came with the planes with the thousands and they bombed the construction site. Every time they bombed they would choose 5 or 6 people to hang. At night they would wake them up and they had to go watch them hang people. This was in 44.

Did you hear about the Russian advances?

Yes some people came free from other cities and came to work. I worked with a German soldier that couldn't go to the army. He was a mechanic. But the Polish guys that came went home every week and came back. They were free. A woman in charge of clothing from city brought me clothes. I would exchange it for bread.

When the bombs came we went into two separate rooms in the bunker. The other bunker got a direct hit and they all died. There were a lot of kids there. I remember when the bomb popped I was flying in the air and I ran out and the whole place was in smoke. But I survived.

Where did you go from Blechhammer?

Because the Russian were coming closer we went on evacuation. First thing I was lucky. This woman who gave me clothes- she had a sister. I begged her to give me shoes. It was like January 1945. She gave me good clothes but she was shot in Blechhammer because she didn't go. Maybe 200 women worked in the kitchen washing clothes. The first night was cold and stormy and these people didn't have clothes.

Tell me about the march?

The problem was that people froze. If they walked to the side, the Germans shot them right away. Before my eyes people were going crazy. Shoes was the most important thing. I had a sweater and a blanket. Later we went to a farmer. We were sleeping in barns. Some people had a hard attack, other people couldn't get up so they just shot them. We were walking maybe a week. A couple thousand died on the way- to gross Rosen. Some people ran away. I went to farmers, I told them I would work for nothing, I speak German, I come from a German family but they didn't want.

Tell me about Gross Rosen.

They put us in a big room but it was Polish kapos. They had a baseball bat and they would beat everyone to get bread. They were mainly political prisoners. Later I said I don't want the bread I should stay out. A few days later they went to open trains and started sending us to Buchenwald. I remember the weather was so cold. The Germans guard were in the train watching you.

How long was the train?

We went maybe 4-5 days. I remember one day the American trains were flying like crazy. I remember coming to a big city called Leipzig. They took us to Buchenwald. Before Buchenwald was a city called Weimar. American trains started bombing we jumped out. We looked for bread. We could have run away but there was nowhere to go.

Buchenwald was like a city. I liked to be the first to get out of the train. I remember I was one of the first ones at the gate. There was a special place to get the clothes. So they let us in, they took away our clothes. They told me whatever I want to keep I could put it on the side. Later they cut all the hair. Later you had to go into a special tank for disinfection. When you went into the tank you burned. We knew what they were doing in Auschwitz with the showers. We looked to see if water was going. We knew that they told people to go to the showers but it was gas. Later they gave us clothes and told me to go to a room. Block 49. It was a concrete place. I slept with 4 people in a bed. You got the lice back. Stayed there a few days. They took my name and sent me to another camp - Lundenshtein. It was February 1945. They sent me again on the cattle car. This was a camp just to die. In the mountains, muddy. We worked in the mountains. No food, no bed, no clothes, people were diarrhea. I thought that I would work night shifts. I figured out that in the day time I can sleep. But during the day the Nazis came in with whips and beat me up terribly- almost broken. I told him I work at night. These other people didn't work because they weren't fit to. A couple weeks later I changed for daytime. This camp was terrible. To save my life I learned that other people were dying of diarrhea. I burned wood and eat the charcoal to stop the diarrhea. I think someone had told me that people did that in the wartime.

So there was a lot of dysentery?

People were dying left and right. There were no doctors. In Blechhammer there were doctors. In this camp there was nothing. I was there till April 8. This was a camp to die. You can't believe it. The mud and the shit.

Was the routine the same?

Lots of people were there. Serbian, Ukrainian. The others were prisoners.

After April 8?

Again an evacuation. They took us away from the Americans. So we went 3-4 days again. You slept in a church, here or there. I always approached people to take me in. They would take a dog, a cat but not a Jew. The last stop I had- there was no food- I ate garbage I was so hungry. We came to a park in Bitterfeld. I remember a big Nazi- he must have been Hungarian or Romanian. He spoke better Jewish than me. He took the bread and dug the crust in the dirt. I ate it. That was it- I realized I needed to take a chance. We were walking- I talked to the German guards. They didn't care anymore. They knew that the war was going to end. I would say I have diarrhea I needed to go and I'd join back. So I ran away. This was Saturday. I lied down on the road. I went over the hill where there were all farmers houses. All the dogs barked. The third shed was open and there was a goat. I was so hungry I took the food from the goat and I ate it. I sat there in the corner until the morning when the man came to milk the goat. The woman opens the door and screams when she sees me. I said that I'm a German and that I'm hungry. I spoke in German. I asked for some bread. She said I'll give you bread, but my husband is a strong German. I knew he was a Nazi. She gave me two pieces and said run away. I ran in the bushes and I saw the guy with the dog, bike and whip looking for me but he couldn't find me.

Were you marked in any way to show you were Jewish?

I had the stripes and the yellow mark on the jacket that said I was a Jew. Later I went to the farmers again begging for bread. One gave me bread with jam. I hadn't eaten for months. This went on for a few hours. A German soldier caught me and said he would take me to the police. I told him I'm a German, I'm a kappo, I'm hungry I'll go back. He said you're lucky it's Sunday I don't want to get my hands dirty with a Jew. So he let me go. I walked and walked. Kids are pointing and laughing like I'm in the circus. I saw a brick factory. There was a watchman watching. I asked him if I can get some water. I looked, there was a small shack with the working clothes. I was so fast and I took the clothes and ran away and I changed the clothes from the stripes and I was no more concentration camp. And I walked I don't know where. I was thirsty. I wasn't feeling well. I walked to a house I was lucky. Nice German girl, she let me in. I told her I'm a German and she washed me up, and gave me food. Later the mother came home and I begged her. The mother said the American tanks are closing in here. But she told me that she couldn't keep me here. She told me to go to work in Bitterfeld. There was a coal mine. So she let me out, I walked, slept some place. Later, the next day I walked to Bitterfeld. I was walking and the German army was right beside me. My heart was beating. They asked where are you going, I said I'm going to work. If they could see a little bit of the clothes underneath they would have shot me. I followed a Polish prisoner into a store then gave a whole story I'm a Polish prisoner, I'm a political prisoner. He told me I will take you to where I live. Some people took me to a room, one guy gave me a shirt, pants. They threw my clothes in a lake. Gave me a bed to sleep in and I slept for maybe two days. I was sick- too much food. On the 21st we were liberated.

What was the first time you saw the Americans?

They were very nice. Once in the main street of Bitterfeld, I was walking alone it was Sunday and an American came and I showed him my number, I have no money or clothes, I was beaten. He said you want clothes, you want money I will give you. The guy went down got me two suits, shirts, socks, shoes. This is for you- take it to the camp.

The first time you saw an American and you knew you were safe and free how did you feel?

I couldn't believe that I'm a free man.

Family Photos[96]

Jack's father Leopold Westreich, 1939

Jack Westreich and mother Helen in Chorzow, 1938

Jack's brother Max, cousin Helen, brother Ernst, and cousin Chanka, 1938

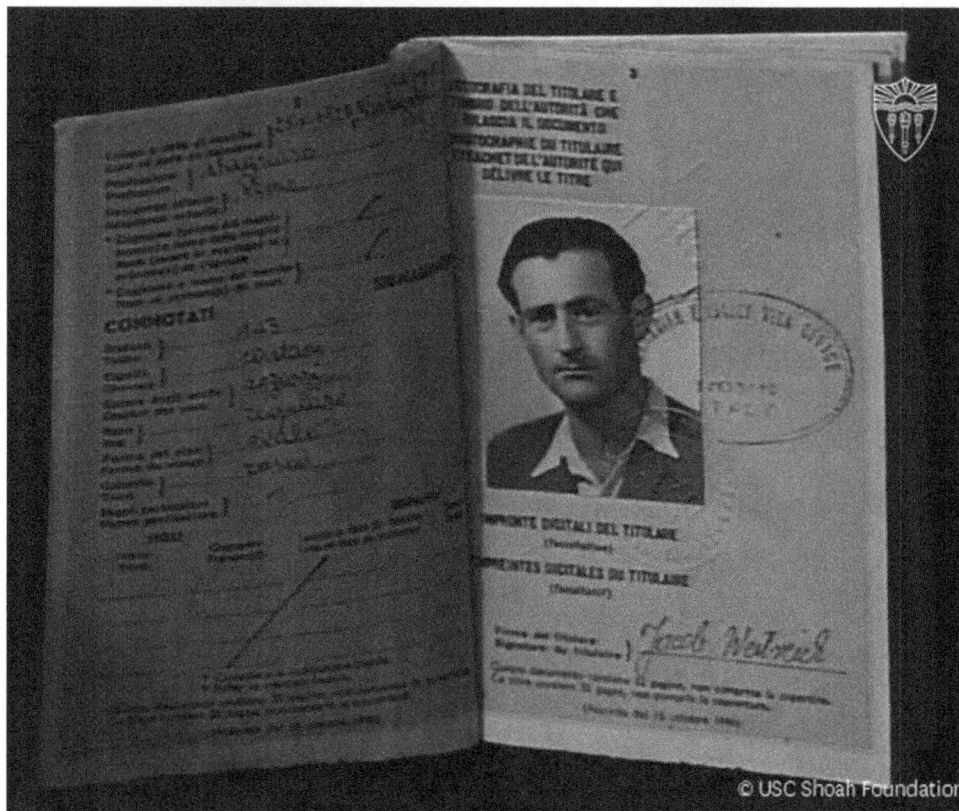

Jack's passport from Rome, Italy to Canada, 1951

Wedding of Anita and Jack, 1958[97]

Jack Westreich, USC Shoah Foundation interview, Toronto, Canada, 1996

Grebow Branch
of the Westreich Family Tree

Y-DNA match

Mordechai Westreich
b. circa 1850
m. Tova
(m. Blima Fortgang)
d. 1932
|
Abraham Isaac Westreich
b. circa 1872
m. Rose Krantz
d. 1906 in Manhattan, NY
|
Jacob/Jack Westreich/Vestrich
b. 1894 in NYC, NY
m. Martha Rodman
d. 1971 in Miami Beach, FL
|
Alan Irwin Vestrich
b. 1927 in NYC, NY
m. Dolores Gordon
d. 1996 in Falls Church, VA
|
Victoria Vestrich

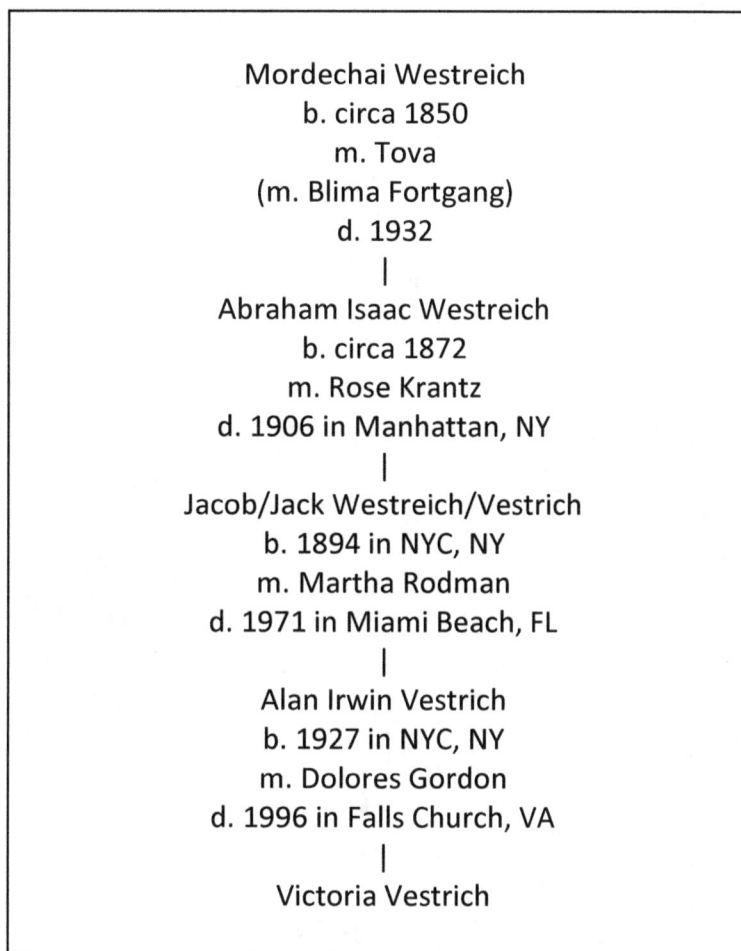

Grebow (aka Grembow) is a town in modern-day Poland,
formerly part of Galicia, Austria (1772 - 1918),
located 10 miles east of Tarnobrzeg.

Sources include:
email communications with Victoria Vestrich[98] and Steven Shatz[99]

Edited by Allan Westreich

Mordechai Westreich (b. circa 1850) is the earliest known patriarch of this branch. He had two wives -- Tova and Blima -- and had four known children with each of them.

Mordechai and Tova had the following four children -- Abraham Isaac (aka Isaac, b. circa 1872 - d. 1906), Laja/Lena (b. 1881 in Grebow), Chaia, and Leibish. Tova died at a young age.

Son (Abraham) Isaac Westreich immigrated to the US, arriving on June 8, 1892 at age 20 from Grebow (aka Grembow), Poland (actually Austria at the time). Sometime in the next year or so he married Rose "Rosie" Krantz and they had 6 known children from 1894 to 1904 -- Jacob/Jack, Tinnie, Hyman/Herman, Joseph, Louis, and Rebecca/Becky. Sadly, Isaac died in a streetcar accident at the young age of 33 in 1906 (see picture of gravestone below), resulting in Rosie putting the three youngest boys (Hyman, Joseph, and Louis) in an orphanage two weeks later. The oldest son, Jack, not quite 12 years old, dropped out of school to help support the family. Rosie took in boarders to help pay the bills. Rosie remarried 2 years later in 1908, and subsequently reclaimed the boys from the orphanage – Hyman in 1911, and Joseph and Louis in 1916.

Gravestone of Abraham Isaac Westreich, Washington Cemetery, Brooklyn, NY[100]

The descendants of Isaac Westreich changed their surname to either Vestrich or West.

As a young boy, Isaac's son Jacob/Jack Westreich/Vestrich (1894 - 1971) enjoyed submitting short articles and poems to the *Brooklyn Daily Eagle* newspaper. Below is one of the many he submitted.

Likes Checkers Best.

Checkers is one of my favorite games. It can be played by everybody, both young and old. When I have nothing else to do at night, I go to the gymnasium at Public School No. 147 of Brooklyn, and there, with my friends, play checkers part of the time. The game is limited to two players. There is not as much thinking as in chess.

The object of the game is to block and skip the other competitor with your own checkers. You are not to be caught napping. The result is the other player will skip your checkers, and has a good chance of winning the game.

JACOB VESTRICH (age 14).

Jacob Vestrich's submission to the *Brooklyn Daily Eagle*, 1911[101]

Jack went on to serve in the World War I U.S. Army as Divisional Sergeant Major of the 82nd Division. Jack married Martha Rodman and they had two children, Alan Irwin Vestrich (1927 - 1996) and Joan Vestrich (1930 - 2012 (?)). Jack worked for DeCoppett & Doremus, a bond trading firm on Wall Street, until he retired. He and his wife Martha moved to Miami, FL. Jack and Martha's children grew up in the Flatbush neighborhood of Brooklyn, NY attending public schools. Jack's son, Alan Vestrich, was selected to attend Brooklyn Technical High School for Science and Math, graduating at age 16. He entered the Navy towards the end of World War II. Alan attended Brooklyn College and graduated in 1950 with a B.S. in Geology. There he met Dolores Gordon (b. 1928 in NY, NY) in an Art History class. They married in September 1950 and took their honeymoon on a train to Austin Texas. Alan completed his MBA at the University of Texas in Austin in 1952.

Their son Mark was born in 1951 in Austin, TX. Their daughter Victoria was born in 1956 in Brooklyn, NY. In 1957, Alan was invited to a week of intense interviews in Washington, D.C. after passing the Foreign Service Exam for the U.S. State Department. He was selected to join the United States Agency for International Development (U.S.A.I.D.). In January 1958, the family of four left for their first overseas assignment in Kabul, Afghanistan. Through his thirty year career, Alan served in Pakistan, Vietnam, Nigeria, and Guyana with periodic assignments at the State Department in Washington, D.C. Alan and Dolores are proud grandparents of Adine Herron (Mark's step-daughter) and Colette Vestrich-Shade and Nathan Vestrich-Shade (Victoria's daughter and son). Dolores resides in Falls Church, VA. Mark resides in San

Francisco, CA and Victoria/Vicki resides in Baltimore, MD. Colette will be returning to Baltimore from Japan in summer 2019. Nathan currently resides in Manhattan.

Mordechai and his second wife, Blima Fortgang, had four children – Szaije/Joshua, Moshe, Chaim, and Shabtai. Shabtai married Helen Shifra Goldwasser (see picture below) in Grebow in 1924. Shabtai and at least two of his siblings perished in the Holocaust.

Helen Shifra Goldwasser, wife of Shabtai Westreich, circa 1923[102]

Brody Branch 1
of the Westreich Family Tree

Y-DNA match (with surname Solomowitz!)

by Benjamin Solomowitz

Salomon Joel Westreich
(1817 - ?)
m. Gische/Regina Feldmann
|
Ettel/Ethel Westreich
(1850 - 1929)
m. Shmuel/Samuel Mollet
|
Rebecca Mollet
(1884 - 1971)
m. Reuven David Natchitz/Nathanson
|
Shirley Nathanson
m. Murray Jacob Solomowitz
|
Benjamin Solomowitz

Brody is a town in modern-day Ukraine,
formerly part of Galicia, Austria (1772 - 1918).

Brody, a city located 54 miles east north east of L'viv, Ukraine, was the most Jewish of Galician cities when it was part of Galicia, Austro-Hungary. The town in the mid-1800's was 75% Jewish with many Rabbinical study houses. Close to the town center was the great synagogue. The Nazis blew it up during World War II, but due to its fortress-like construction, to this day, 3 walls of the synagogue are still intact.

My great-great grandparents Salomon Joel Westreich, born 1817, and Gische Feldmann, born 1815, lived at house number 358 according to the 1850 Brody Census. Gische's father might have been Heine Feldmann, landlord of house 358, according to the records of 1844. It is unknown if Salomon Joel and Gische were born in Brody.

They had three known children, all born in Brody in house number 358 – (1) Abraham Isaac Westreich, born August 2, 1840 and died at 11 years old on June 1, 1852 in Brody; (2) Hene Rive Westreich, born April 18, 1844; and (3) Ettel/Ethel Westreich (my great grandmother, see photo below), born April 6, 1850. All three children continued to live at house 358.

Hene Rive Westreich married Meyer Sitzer and had 3 daughters: Fannie, Gitel/Gussie, and Esther. Daughter Fannie (c. 1873 – 1963) married Benjamin Weiner and had 6 known children – Celia, Nathan, Beatrice, Henrietta, Rose and Helen. The first 2 children were born in Galicia, the last 4 in New York City. Daughter Gussie (born 1881) also immigrated to the US. Her husband David Moskowitz was a butcher. They had one son together, Nathan, who died in an elevator accident at Klein's department store in Manhattan shortly after his marriage. David Moskowitz had 3 children by a previous marriage -- Larry Marks and Ike Marks who sold clothing in Florida and Sonia Bloch who lived in Atlanta, Georgia. Little is known about daughter Esther.

Ettel Westreich married Shmuel/Samuel Mollet of unknown occupation, who must have died early because by 1904 Ettel was a widow living in Brody. They had five known children, all born in Brody – Schulem/Maurice (1871 – 1941), Gitcha/Gussie (1876 – 1940), Jacob Salomon (1882 – 1962, see photo below), Rebecca (my grandmother, 1884 – 1971, see photo below), and Bernard (? - ?).

Gussie married Phillip Nerlinger, had two children Helen and Samuel, and then immigrated to the United States in 1905.

Rebecca met and later married Reuven David Natchitz (David Nathanson), a runaway soldier from the Czar's Imperial Army who was going to be sent to Siberia to fight in the Russo-Japanese War. He crossed the border from Dubno, Russia into Brody, Austria where he met Rebecca. Rebecca and David, along with some of Rebecca's family (including her mother Ettel), immigrated to Paris, France. By 1906, their daughter Cecile was born in Paris, followed by sons Emile in 1910 and Albert in 1913.

During World War I, the family briefly went to San Sebastian, Spain to find employment and then moved back to Paris. David Nathanson, a tailor and Russian-trained soldier, was asked to enlist in the French Army during World War I, but instead left in July 1915 and crossed the

Atlantic Ocean to the United States. Rebecca, Cecile, and Emile followed in December 1915. The ship that brought them to the US was torpedoed by a German U-boat on its return voyage to France.

Young Albert was not able to go to the US with his family. As was customary in Paris, during the previous summer of 1914 he was sent with a nurse to a farm in the countryside. Unfortunately, the French town he was residing in, Amiens, was captured by the Germans and he remained there with the nurse for the duration of World War I. At War's end, the nurse brought him back to Paris to a relative's house, and in June 1919 he was brought to the US and written up in several US newspapers as the "war prisoner at 11 months." These articles proved valuable later in his life, when he needed proof of his arrival in the US to obtain his passport and he found microfilmed copies of his arrival in the NY Times and other newspapers.

Upon arriving in the US, Rebecca and David Nathanson initially moved in with Rebecca's sister Gussie in a tenement house on the lower East Side of Manhattan. Two additional daughters were born in the US, Shirley (Sylvia, my mother) born in 1918 and Rose born in 1920. Before Rose was born, the family bought and moved to a house in East New York, Brooklyn on Jersey Avenue and lived there for 10 or so years.

Ettel (Westreich) Mollet and her sons Jacob Salomon and Maurice remained in France. Ettel died in Paris in 1929. During World War II, some of their families were either arrested and detained in France and survived or deported to Poland and perished. Others were not arrested, but life was very difficult for them during the War years. The third brother, Bernard, a tailor, remained in Brody with his family, at times visiting his siblings in Paris. Unfortunately, he was presumed killed; the details are still unknown till this day.

A key document which helped identify the house where my great great grandparents lived was a picture postcard sent from Paris to Brody in the early twentieth century. It eventually made its way to relatives in the US. It was addressed to Ettel Mollet, 358 Synagogassen, Brody, Austria. My wife and I visited Brody, Ukraine in 1992 and were lucky enough to view the Metrical Books for Brody where we made the connection between house number, address, and how records were recorded in the Metrical Books by house number. With the transcribing of the Metrical Books by Gesher Galicia, I was able to find all people linked to house number 358 and construct family trees.

Others that lived at house number 358 in Brody and are assumed to be siblings of Gische Westreich (nee Feldmann) are Mayer Feldmann, a tailor who married Chaie Lea Reizes, and Ester Sima Feldmann, born 1809 and married Benjamin Zwengler born 1802. Benjamin Zwengler's siblings might also have been living at number 358, and they were Perl and Itzel Zwengler, who both married Isaac Schnitzer, and Sluwe Zwengler, who married Isaac Pitzel.

I submitted my mother's autosomal DNA to Family Tree DNA hoping to make a Westreich connection since my mother, Shirley, is a granddaughter of Ettel (Westreich) Mollet. I did make a connection with Allan Westreich who contacted me. What is surprising is that my Y-DNA, which comes from my father's family (surname Solomowitz), also showed a DNA connection to the Westreich family, which I cannot explain as of yet.

Family Photos[103]

Ettel Westreich Mollet in her 70's,
in Paris in the 1920's

(Ettel's daughter) Rebecca Mollet, Brody

L..J. BERTHOLET   101, Rue Ordener

(Ettel's son) Jacob Salomon Mollet and wife Gitel/Eugenie Wolicki,
in Paris in the early 1900's (?)

Possible Connection with Brody Branch 2 (from next chapter)

Two families named Westreich from the same Galician town of Brody. What are the odds that they are related? Although this seems quite likely, is there any evidence to support this? Quite simply, yes, as demonstrated by the many interconnections between the branches:

1. Same uncommon surname – Westreich.
2. Geographical parallels – Both families lived in Brody in the 1800's and then immigrated to Paris, France. Jacob Solomon Mollet (Branch 1) lived in the same apartment building in Paris (80 Rue Marcadet) as Clara Westreich Dubner (Branch 2). Members from both families temporarily moved to San Sebastian, Spain and then back to Paris circa 1916-1918 (Rebecca Mollet Nathanson and family from Branch 1 and Chane Rose Westreich Belfer and family from Branch 2).
3. Connection by marriage -- Both branches married into the same Dubner family. From Branch 1, Maurice Mollet (son of Ettel Westreich Mollet) married Rose Dubner. From Branch 2, Clara Westreich (daughter of Meyer Leib Westreich) married Jankel Dubner, brother of Rose Dubner. In the photo below of the wedding of Clara Westreich (Branch 2) and Jankel Dubner appears Jacob Solomon Mollet (Branch 1), brother of the brother-in-law (Maurice Mollet) of the groom (Jankel Dubner).

Wedding of Chaie/Clara Sara Westreich and Jankel/Jacob Dubner in Paris, 1905[104]
Clara Westreich (Branch 2) is bride in middle of bottom row.
Jacob Solomon Mollet (Branch 1) is leftmost in middle row.

4. Several birth, marriage, and death records from one branch were witnessed by members of the other branch.

Evidence of a direct blood relationship between the two branches is still awaiting.

Brody Branch 2
of the Westreich Family Tree

Y-DNA untested

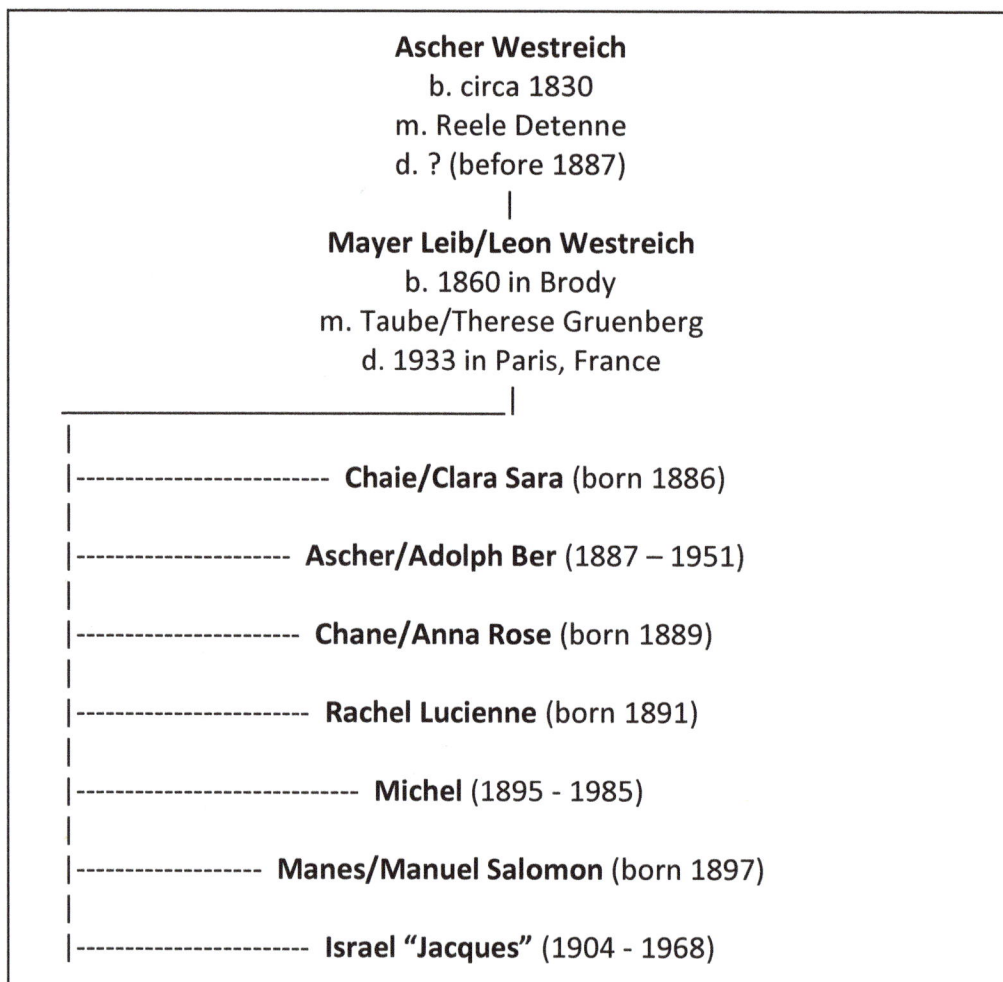

Ascher Westreich
b. circa 1830
m. Reele Detenne
d. ? (before 1887)
|
Mayer Leib/Leon Westreich
b. 1860 in Brody
m. Taube/Therese Gruenberg
d. 1933 in Paris, France
_____|
|
|----------------------- **Chaie/Clara Sara** (born 1886)
|
|--------------------- **Ascher/Adolph Ber** (1887 – 1951)
|
|---------------------- **Chane/Anna Rose** (born 1889)
|
|---------------------- **Rachel Lucienne** (born 1891)
|
|--------------------------- **Michel** (1895 - 1985)
|
|------------------- **Manes/Manuel Salomon** (born 1897)
|
|----------------------- **Israel "Jacques"** (1904 - 1968)

Brody is a town in modern-day Ukraine,
formerly part of Galicia, Austria (1772 - 1918).

Sources include:
email communications with Gary Pokrassa[105],
Rosalyn and James Boarer[106], Bertrand Biguadet[107], and Eliane Belfer[108]

by Allan Westreich

Ascher Westreich, born circa 1830, is the earliest-known patriarch of this branch. Ascher married Reele Detenne and they had 6 known children, all born in Brody, Galicia – Teme Reisel (born 1851), Rosche (1853 - 1854), Lea (1855 - 1855), Slamcze (1856 - 1858), stillborn (1859), and Meyer Leib/Leon (1860 - 1933). Only two of them survived childhood.

Ascher and Reele's son **Meyer Leib/Leon** married Taube/Therese Gruenberg and had 7 known children – Chaie/Clara Sara (1886 - 1972), Ascher/Adolph Ber (1887 – 1951), Chane/Anna Rose (born 1889), Rachel Lucienne (born circa 1892), Michel (1895 – 1985), Manes/Manuel Salomon (born 1897), and Israel "Jacques" (1904 – 1968). All of the children were born in Brody except the youngest, Israel. The family emigrated circa 1898 from Brody, Galicia to Paris, France where Israel was born. Below is a photograph of the Westreich family in Paris circa 1918.

The Westreich family in Paris, France circa 1918[109]
Front (L-R): Armand Dubner, Manuel Belfer, and Andre Dubner
Middle: Eugenie Dubner, Meyer Leib and Taube W., and Suzanne Belfer
Rear: Jankel and Chaie Sara Dubner, Manuel W., Israel W., Michel W., Chane Rose and Adolph Belfer
(all identities are not certain)

Meyer Leib and Taube's daughter **Chaie/Clara Sara** (1886 - 1972) married Jankel/Jacob Dubner (1880 – 1941) in 1905 in Paris – see photo below.

Wedding of Chaie/Clara Sara Westreich and Jankel/Jacob Dubner in Paris, 1905[110]

Chaie and Jankel Dubner had three children – Eugenie, Armand, and Andre. Daughter Eugenie (1906 – 2000) married Bernard Poznansky in 1931 in Paris, then later divorced and married Wolff Stein in 1959. Son Armand (1909 – 1985) married Emma Sieger in 1938 in Paris and had one known child, Jean-Jacques Dubner born 1946 in Paris (see photos below). Armand was a Prisoner of War in World War II in 1941 in Stalag I-B Hohenstein (near modern-day Olsztynek, Poland), but fortunately survived the brutal conditions. Son Andre (1913 – 1999) married Zysa Ryfka Dlugowska in 1939 in Paris.

Armand Dubner and Emma Sieger[111]

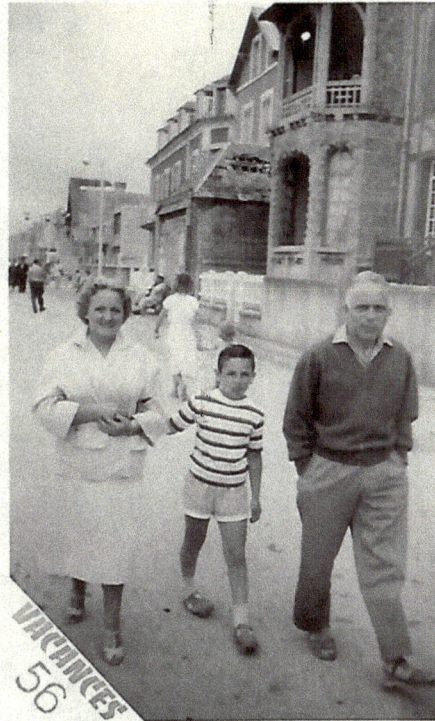

Emma, Jean-Jacques, and Armand Dubner, 1956[112]

Meyer Leib and Taube's son **Ascher/Adolph Ber** (1887 – 1951) married Leyka/Luisa/Lisa Pokrassa (1892 – 1982) in August 1913 in Paris, France, as announced in *Univers Israelite*, a French "journal of the conservative interests of Judaism" (see below). Adolph and Lisa immigrated to the US in 1915. Their first son David (1914-2002, see photograph below) was born in Paris, and their second son Julius "Jules" (1920-2002) was born in NYC. Adolph and his family changed their surname from Westreich to West.

Mariages de la Semaine

TEMPLE DE LA RUE NOTRE-DAME-DE-NAZARETH

Dimanche 17 août, à 1 h. 1/2. — M. Adolphe Westreich, 4, rue de l'Agent-Bailly, et Mlle Lisa Pokrasa, 3, rue des Trois-Frères.

Marriage announcement of Adolph Westreich and Lisa Pokrassa, August 1913, Paris[113]

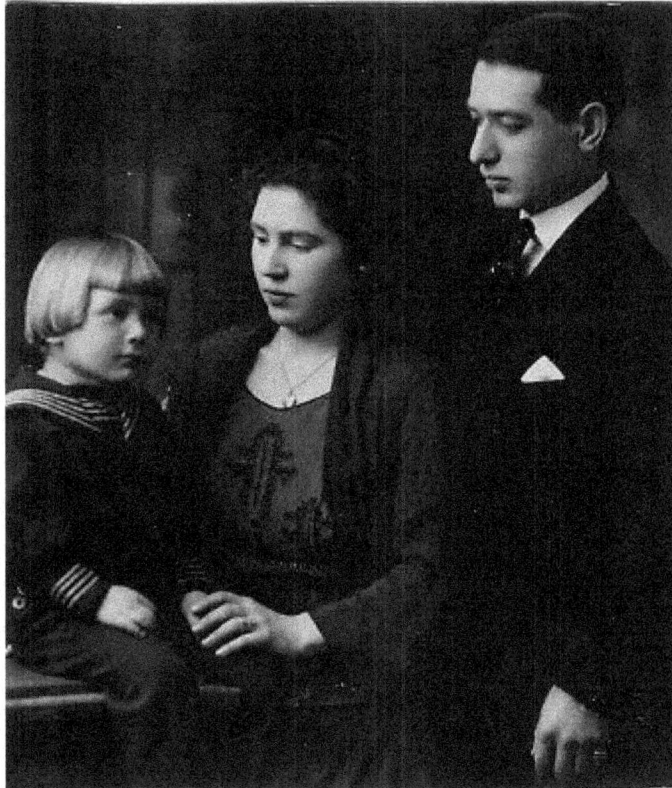

(L-R) David, Lisa, and Adolph West
circa 1917, NY[114]

Meyer Leib and Taube's daughter **Chane/Anna Rose** (born 1889) married Aron/Adolph Chaskel Belfer (1886 – 1942) in 1909 in Paris. They had two children – Suzanne and Manuel. Daughter Suzanne (born 1910 in Paris) married Albert Charles Heller (born 1910 in Chambery, France) in 1936 in Paris and had two daughters. Son Manuel was born 1916 in San Sebastian, Spain. The family later moved back to Paris – see 1936 Paris census record below.

NOMS DE FAMILLE	PRÉNOMS (un seul prénom)	ANNÉE de NAISSANCE	LIEU de NAISSANCE (Département ou nation)	NATIONA-LITÉ	ÉTAT MATRIMONIAL	SITUATION par RAPPORT au chef de ménage	PROFESSION	Pour les patrons, chefs d'entreprise, ouvriers à domicile, inscrire : patron. Pour les employés ou ouvriers, indiquer le nom du patron ou de l'entreprise qui les emploie. Pour tous, indiquer le lieu du travail (voir instructions spéciales).
Belfer	Adolphe	1886	Pologne		M.		tailleur	
	Anna	1889	Pologne		M	épse	meaut	
	Suzanne	1910	Seine		C	fille	stens gr	
	Manuel	1916	Espagne		C	fils	euy de bureau	

1936 Paris Census: Adolphe, Anna, Suzanne, and Manuel Belfer[115]

172

During World War II, Anna and Adolph were imprisoned in the Pithiviers internment camp approximately 50 miles south of Paris. They were later deported by convoy to the Auschwitz concentration camp on 9/21/1942. Adolph perished in Auschwitz; Anna apparently survived.

Meyer Leib and Taube's daughter **Rachel Lucienne** (born 1891) married Gaston Jules Fernand Cheville (born 1887) in 1917 in Saint Brieuc, Cotes-d'Armor, Brittany, France. They had two children – Fernande and Oscar. Daughter Fernande (1920 - 2013), born in Belgium, married Jean Machuraux. Son Oscar was born circa 1924, likely in Belgium also. The family moved to the former Belgian Congo (modern-day Democratic Republic of the Congo) in central Africa and later back to Belgium (Namur).

Meyer Leib and Taube's son **Michel** (1895 - 1985) married and divorced his first wife Marthe Juliette Marie Dupont in Paris. Like his older brother Adolph, he immigrated to New York, US (in 1921) and changed his surname to West. He met and married his second wife Pasha/Pauline Steinberg (1908 – 1990) from Kiev, Ukraine in Bronx, NY in 1925. They had four children – Frederick, Harvey, Leon, and Rosalyn. Below is a photo of Michel's and Adolph's families in NY.

West families (L-R): Michel, Pauline, Harvey, and Fred; Julius, David, Lisa, and Adolph circa 1930 in Bronx, NY[116]

Meyer Leib and Taube's son **Manes/Manuel Salomon** (born 1897) married Reine Cordier (1898 - 1974) in 1931 in Paris. See official marriage record below.

Le sept Mars mil neuf cent trente-un, Onze heures quinze •
devant Nous ont comparu publiquement en la maison commune : Manes Salomon WESTREICH, employé
de messagerie, né à Brody (Autriche Hongrie), le vingt-neuf décembre mil huit cent quatre • •
vingt-dix-sept, trente-trois ans, domicilié à Paris, 50, Rue Rodier, Fils de Mayer Leib WES-
TREICH, tailleur, et de Taube GRÜNBERG, sans profession, domiciliés à Paris, 50, Rue Rodier,
d'une part./ Et Reine CORDIER, sans profession, née à Courpalay (Seine et Marne), le treize •
Mai mil huit cent quatre vingt-dix-huit, trente-deux ans, domiciliée à Paris, 50, Rue Rodier
Fille de Alexandre Alphonse CORDIER, absent, et de Célestine TOURTE , son épouse, sans profession, domiciliée à Fontenay Trésigny (Seine et Marne), d'autre part. Aucune opposition •
n'existant. Les futurs époux déclarent qu'il n'a pas été fait de contrat de mariage. Manes • •
Salomon WESTREICH et Reine CORDIER ont déclaré l'un après l'autre vouloir se prendre pour • •
époux et Nous avons prononcé au nom de la Loi qu'ils sont unis par le mariage. En présence de
René PERRET, débitant de vins, 32, Rue Rodier, et de Elie POUGET, employé, Croix de Guerre,
11, Rue Rochechouart, à Paris, témoins majeurs, qui, lecture faite, ont signé avec les époux
et Nous, Auguste Pierre André TAILLAN, Adjoint au Maire du Neuvième Arrondissement de Paris.

1931 Manes Salomon Westreich and Reine Cordier marriage, Paris[117]

Meyer Leib and Taube's youngest child **Israel "Jacques"** (1904 - 1968) married Anna Besse (born 1908) in 1930 in Paris. They had one child – Renee. Daughter Renee (born 1933) married Bernard Bigaudet (1931 – 2010) in 1956 in Paris and had two children – Sylvie and Bertrand. Below are pictures of Israel's and Manuel's families.

Westreich brothers with their wives (L-R): Manuel and Reine, Israel and Anna[118]

(L-R) Renee with parents Israel and Anna Westreich[119]

From Brody, Ukraine to Paris, France to New York, US and beyond, and from Westreich to West, this family branch continues to thrive.

Tarnow Branch 1
of the Westreich Family Tree

Y-DNA no match

Schmuel Mendel Westreich
b. circa 1830
m. Breindel Grabkowicz
d. ?
|
Samuel Abraham Westreich/Weistreich
b. 1864 in Tarnow
m. Perel/Pearl/Pauline Klein
d. 1916 in Manhattan, NY
|
Dora
William
Minnie
Michael
Mollie
Louis
Freida
Milton

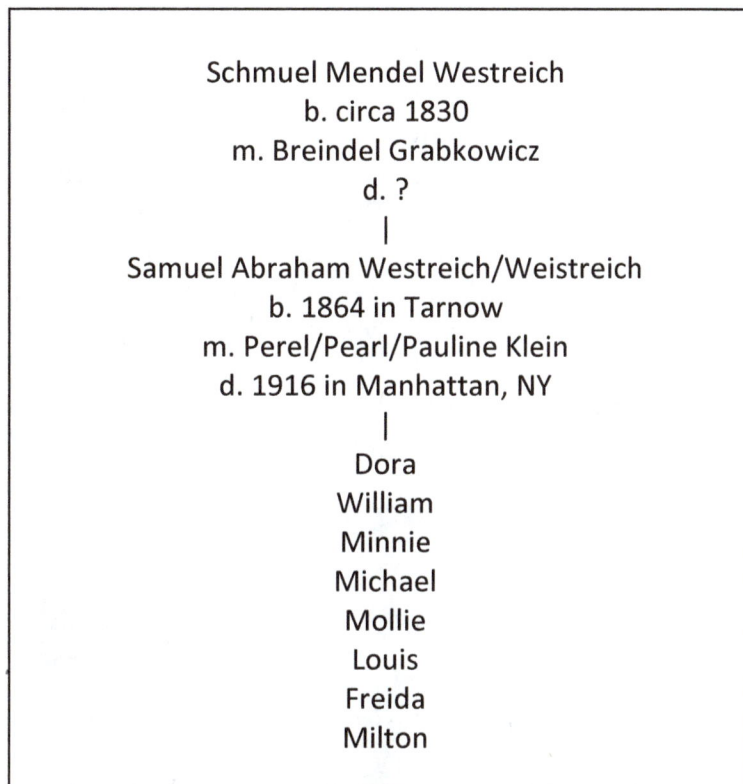

Tarnow is a town in modern-day Poland,
formerly part of Galicia, Austria (1772 - 1918),
located 50 miles east of Krakow.

By Allan Westreich

The earliest known ancestral couple of this branch is Schmuel Mendel Westreich and Breindel Grabkowicz. Schmuel was born circa 1830, presumably in Poland near Tarnow. His wife Breindel, daughter of Leib and Malka, was born on June 13, 1836 in Tarnow. Schmuel and Breindel had 9 known children – stillborn (1852), Chaje Sara (1854 - ?), Chane (1857 - ?), twins Chaim (1860 - ?) and Riwke (1860 - ?), Samuel Abraham (1864 – 1916), Pawe (1867 – 1868), Ruchel Lea (1873 - ?), and another stillborn (1877).

Son Samuel immigrated to the US in August 1894 and changed his surname to Weistreich (as if Westreich wasn't hard enough to pronounce in English to begin with!). He soon married Perel/Pearl/Pauline Klein (whom he was likely already married to in a Jewish ceremony back in the old country) in April 1895 in Manhattan. They had a total of 8 known children between 1889 and 1906, the first 3 born previously in Poland and the latter 5 born in Manhattan – Dora, William, Minnie, Michael, Mollie, Louis, Freida, and Milton. Pauline died in 1909, followed by Samuel in 1916 (see gravestone below), both in Manhattan.

Two members of this branch have tested their Y-DNA. Although they matched each other, they surprisingly did not match any of the other Westreich's that have tested. The puzzle continues.

Gravestone of Samuel Westreich (1864 – 1916)[120]
Mt. Zion Cemetery, Queens, NY

Tarnow Branch 2
of the Westreich Family Tree

Y-DNA untested

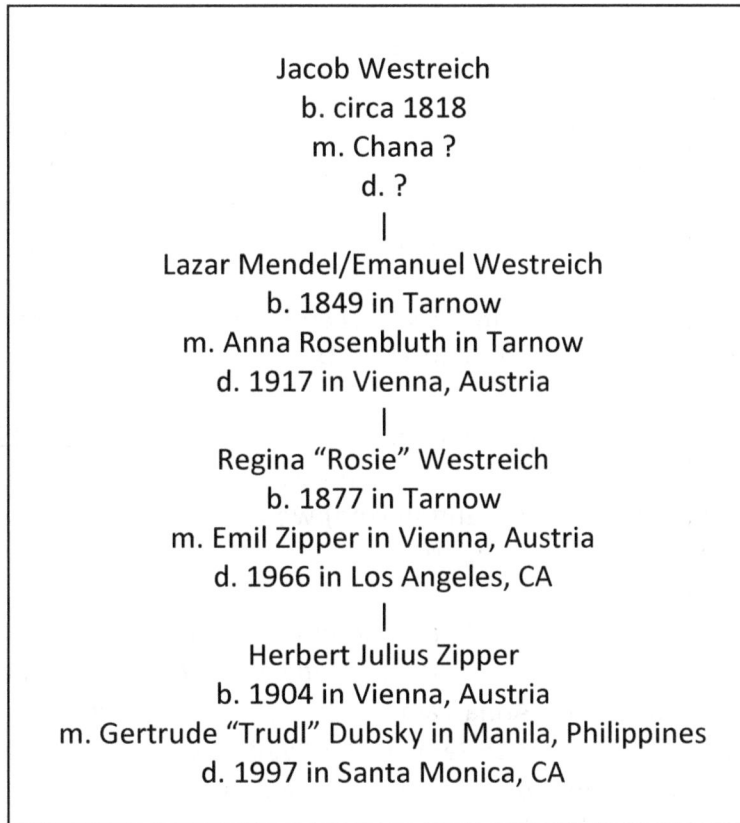

Jacob Westreich
b. circa 1818
m. Chana ?
d. ?
|
Lazar Mendel/Emanuel Westreich
b. 1849 in Tarnow
m. Anna Rosenbluth in Tarnow
d. 1917 in Vienna, Austria
|
Regina "Rosie" Westreich
b. 1877 in Tarnow
m. Emil Zipper in Vienna, Austria
d. 1966 in Los Angeles, CA
|
Herbert Julius Zipper
b. 1904 in Vienna, Austria
m. Gertrude "Trudl" Dubsky in Manila, Philippines
d. 1997 in Santa Monica, CA

Tarnow is a town in modern-day Poland,
formerly part of Galicia, Austria (1772 - 1918),
located 50 miles east of Krakow.

Written by Allan Westreich

Sources include:
Dachau Song: The Twentieth Century Odyssey of Herbert Zipper, Cummins, P., 1992

This branch of the Westreich family tree can be traced back to the ancestral couple Jacob and Chana Westreich, born circa 1818. They had 4 known children – Chawe, Mojzesz, Lazar Mendel/Emanuel, and Chaje – born between 1838 and 1858.

Daughter **Chawe** was born circa 1838 and died in 1921 in Tarnow. She married Mojzesz Schwinger in 1908 in Bobowa. They had 5 known children -- Leib, Mirl, Chaje, Josef, and Chaim.

Son **Mojzesz** was born circa 1843 and died in 1908 in Tarnow.

Jacob and Chana's youngest child, daughter **Chaje**, was born circa 1858. She married Mordechai/Markus Langer and had 3 children that survived infancy – Malka, Ernestyna, and Gitel/Gizela. Gizela died in 1922 in Tarnow at the young age of 22, before the Holocaust. Sadly, Chaje, Malka, and Ernestyna died in the liquidation of the Tarnow ghetto in September 1943.

More is known about son **Emanuel** and his descendants. He was born August 3, 1849 in Tarnow. He married Anna Rosenbluth (born circa 1856) in Tarnow in 1876. They had 4 known children –
Regina "Rosie" (1877 – 1966, married Emil Zipper), Berta/Bertha (1881 – 1943, married Julius Schreibner), Julius Heinrich (1885 – 1893), and Cornelia "Nelly" (1894 – 1971, married Arthur Paunzen). The first two children (Rosie and Bertha) were born in Tarnow, and the second two (Julius and Nelly) were born in Vienna, Austria.

Emanuel's daughter Rosie married Emil Zipper, an engineer, in Vienna on May 26, 1901. They had 4 children -- Walter (1902), Herbert (1904), Hedwig "Hedy" (1907), and Otto (1914). In 1914, Rosie's parents Emanuel and Anna came to live with the family in Vienna. The Zippers were an assimilated middle-class Jewish family who lived a secular Viennese life, even though Emil's father was a cantor and Rosie's father, Emanuel, was a rabbi. Emanuel was an intellectual man who was critical of World War I.

Rosie was described by her son Herbert as "the most lovable person [who] exuded life. She had the gift of drawing people out of their shells."[121] Rosie died in 1966, while living in the multi-generational California household of herself and husband Emil, daughter Hedy and her husband Fred Holt, and the Holt children Lucy and Henry.

While the Holocaust had a significant impact on the Zipper family, none of them perished in it. Herbert and Walter survived multiple concentration camps. In fact, Herbert composed a song while imprisoned in Dachau entitled *Dachau Song* which became an anthem of resistance across other concentration camps. Herbert later went on to become a world-renowned musical composer, conductor, teacher, public arts activist, and symbol of never giving up. He died in California on April 21, 1997.

With Music and Poetry, Herbert Zipper Reached for Humanity in Dachau[122]

by Julie Gruenbaum Fax, USC Shoah Foundation, 2022

Herbert Zipper, from his 1995 interview with USC Shoah Foundation

Herbert Zipper, a world-renowned conductor, composer and pioneer of the community arts movement in the United States, grew up in a Vienna of extremes: From his birth in 1904 until he fled in 1939, the Austrian capital transformed from the heights of science and culture to the depths of economic depression and the onslaught of violent antisemitism and Nazi rule.

Before World War I, Viennese culture inspired a belief that "every problem of humanity can be solved by science and technology, and that the good life could be forever if we just let science and technology work its way. That wars are obsolete, that security of all could be practically guaranteed … It meant that art became a way of life," Zipper said in a 1995 interview with USC Shoah Foundation, two years before he died at age of 92 in Los Angeles. His testimony is contained in the Visual History Archive. A selection of Zipper's work is being performed May 23, 2022 at a Library of Congress Concert, available for viewing online.

Culture and Poverty in Vienna

Zipper was the second of four children. His father was a successful engineer, and his mother a spirited intellectual who hosted Thursday afternoon teas and evening parties in their home. Herbert began his own study of the piano as a young child.

The brutality of WWI and the economic depression that followed shattered Zipper's illusion of security. He remembers wearing a winter coat made of paper to accommodate his teenage frame that was growing to over 6 feet tall.

"Before school, I went around to every market in the neighborhood with my bicycle, which had leather tires, because rubber was unavailable, just to find out where I could get some of these ugly beets and things just to fill your stomach with," he said.

He graduated gymnasium in 1921 and started at the State Academy of Music and the Performing Arts in Vienna, where among his instructors were Maurice Ravel and Richard Strauss.

When Zipper told Strauss he wanted to be a pianist, Strauss scoffed.

"He said, 'come on, a pianist? They're a dime a dozen.' He said, 'You're pretty tall...you should be a conductor.'" Zipper recalled.

In addition to working as a musician while a student, Zipper organized and played concerts in recreation halls in the working-class neighborhoods of Vienna—performances that filled up every Sunday.

An Unconventional Romance

Trudl (née Dubsky) Zipper

It was during this time that Herbert spotted Trudl Dubsky at a dance where he was chaperoning his sister.

"I saw this little girl just arranging her hair. And I saw those hands, and I was electrified by the movement and by the hair and by the way she moved," Zipper said in his testimony.

Trudl was a dancer, a student at the State Academy, and though only 14 and 4 foot 9, was already performing internationally. Sometimes, Herbert would accompany her dance class on piano, according to *Dachau Song*, his biography, by Paul Cummins.

"2 Dances for Trudl," a recently discovered composition that will be performed at the Library of Congress concert, was likely written during this time.

The Rise of Hitler

In 1932, Zipper was hired as a conductor in Dusseldorf, and Trudl moved to join a prestigious dance school in London. While in Dusseldorf, Zipper witnessed the rise of Hitler.

"I attended some of his meetings, some of his rallies in order to know, to learn what's happening because learning is a profession for me," Zipper said in his testimony.

After Hitler claimed the chancellorship in 1933, colleagues and mentors in Dusseldorf who had been Herbert's close friends would no longer speak to him because he was Jewish.

"One of the worst sights of my life – the day was May 10 [1933] – was when the book burnings started. That was a terrible experience. And when you see this, then you know this is really the greatest danger that we are facing," Zipper said.

Twice, he was warned by a sympathetic friend to flee Dusseldorf, but Zipper returned to finish out the school year. He returned to Vienna and traveled to Russia, Italy and England to conduct. In 1937 Trudl took a one-year appointment in Manila to establish a dance department at the University of the Philippines. After their respective assignments, the pair planned to move to the United States and get married.

Herbert also became involved in underground political cabaret – composing and performing satirical songs.

When the Nazis marched into Vienna after Germany annexed Austria in March 1938, Herbert decided he'd experienced enough while living in Germany to know it was time to get out.

"Those 180,000 Jews of Vienna became, overnight, complete outlaws. They could be robbed. They could be mishandled. They could be killed – as they would be," he said.

Herbert's father was in London when German soldiers marched in, and Herbert warned him not to return to Vienna. But he could not convince the rest of his family still in Austria to flee.

In Dachau, 'Shorn of Our Entire Past'

On May 27, 1938, Gestapo officers arrived at the Zipper home and arrested Herbert and his two brothers. They were shoved into a boxcar.

"Those 13 hours from Vienna to Dachau were the ... most beastly, most terrifying, most ugly, most inhuman, most ghastly experience of my life," Herbert said.

"We came [to Dachau], and immediately we were shorn. But we were not only shorn of our hair, from top to bottom, we were shorn of our entire past. What we have been. Through our education, through our social standing, through our friends, through the way we lived," he said.

Most of the prisoners, ostensibly arrested for being "political threats," were Jews. One of Herbert's brothers was released for medical reasons, and Herbert and his brother Walter, along with other prisoners, were put on labor details – digging ditches, pulling cement carts, hauling and crushing stones.

But a sense of humanity still prevailed.

A vegetable seller from Vienna inspired the prisoners to hold on to their identities. Zipper stood outside the barracks, reciting poetry from memory. Inmates gathered around him. Among the prisoners were 30 or 40 talented musicians. They gathered boxes and strings and scraps to fashion crude instruments. Herbert collected paper and wrote out scores from memory.

They began to hold secret concerts in the latrines on their few hours off on Sunday afternoons. Prisoners came in rotations, 25 to 30 at time.

On his way to the labor site every day, Zipper had to walk through a gate that read, "Arbeit Macht Frei" ("Work Makes You Free"). One day, while walking with his friend Jura Soyfer, a Vienna poet he knew from the underground cabaret, Herbert got angry.

"It was in hot August. I said, Jura, this is really too much, to write this thing on top of there. So he said, 'You know, we should write a song.' "

Within a few days Soyfer produced lyrics, a satirical spin on the work ethic of a slave labor prison, and Zipper set them to music. In the darkness of the barracks, Zipper taught "Dachau

Song" to other musicians. Just days later, on September 22, Zipper, his brother, Soyfer and 4,000 other prisoners were transferred to the Buchenwald concentration camp.

New Horror, Then Release

Buchenwald presented a new set of horrors. Herbert and his brother were forced to clean open-pit latrines. His brother got frostbite during a 19-hour roll call, during which Herbert never stopped moving.

"I was afraid about my hands, because … I lived by my hands," Zipper said.

His collaborator on "Dachau Song," Jura Soyfer, died of typhoid just days before Herbert and his brother Walter were freed in February 1939. Their parents, who had fled to Paris, had secured visas to Uruguay, which enabled them to petition for their sons' release.

On March 16, 1939, Herbert and Walter were reunited with the rest of the family in Paris, and two months later Herbert sailed for Manila, where he reunited with Trudl and conducted the Manila Symphony Orchestra – a position he had been offered after the director heard a composition Zipper had written for his bride-to-be.

Honeymoon in Manila

On October 1, 1939, Herbert and Trudl were married and, as they watched the war unfold in Europe, were able to live in peace until January 1942, when Japan invaded the Philippines. Within a few weeks, Zipper was arrested for his associations with high-ranking Americans and for a speech he had given that was critical of the Axis powers.

After several weeks of brutal interrogations and four months of incarceration, Zipper was released on the promise – which he did not intend to keep – that he would reconvene his orchestra for the benefit the Japanese occupiers. After his release, Zipper became part of an underground intelligence unit and, on May 9, 1945, conducted the Manila Symphony Orchestra in a concert to celebrate the liberation of the capital.

An Advocate for The Arts for All

Herbert and Trudl moved to the U.S. in 1946. First in Brooklyn and then in Chicago, Trudl danced and Herbert conducted, taught, and became a pioneering advocate for community arts programming and education. He returned to Manila to conduct every summer.

In the 1950s, Herbert received a letter from the East German Ministry of Culture to determine if he was the H. Zipper who had composed "Dachau Song." According to the Cummins biography, it was the first time Herbert learned that his composition had leaked out of Dachau and filtered through the concentration camps as an anthem of resistance and was now of interest to musicians and archivists.

In 1972, Herbert took a position as the project director for the School of Performing Arts at the University of Southern California, which, with pivotal steering from Zipper, eventually became the Colburn School, where several programs and spaces are named for the Zippers.

Trudl, who danced professionally her whole life, died of lung cancer in 1976. Herbert was active internationally in the arts until he died in 1997.

His story was featured in a 1995 Oscar-nominated documentary, *"Never Give Up: The 20th Century Odyssey of Herbert Zipper."*

"The tragic thing is that the best in the human race comes forward when it is in real trouble," Herbert said in his USC Shoah Foundation testimony. "The humdrum of every day buries it. … We become human when we find that we all actually face the same dangers, the same problems, and that we don't fool ourselves that we are immune to them."

Family Photos[123]

Engraving of Emanuel Westreich by son-in-law Arthur Paunzen

Front: Rosie and Emil Zipper; Back: Herbert, Trudl, and Otto Zipper; arrival in San Francisco, 1946

Tarnow Branch 3
of the Westreich Family Tree

Y-DNA untested

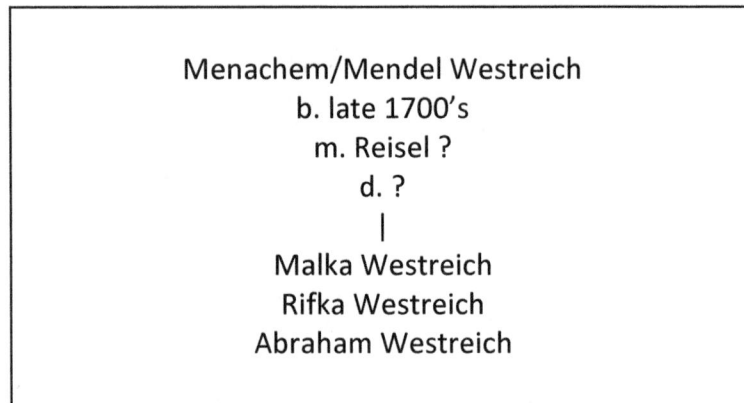

Menachem/Mendel Westreich
b. late 1700's
m. Reisel ?
d. ?
|
Malka Westreich
Rifka Westreich
Abraham Westreich

Tarnow is a town in modern-day Poland,
formerly part of Galicia, Austria (1772 - 1918),
located 50 miles east of Krakow.

Written by Allan Westreich

This branch of the Westreich family tree can be traced relatively far back to the ancestral couple of Menachem/Mendel and Reisel Westreich. Mendel was born in the late 1700's. Reisel was born circa 1786 and died on April 12, 1840 in Tarnow.

Mendel and Reisel had three known children – Malka, Rifka, and Abraham.

Daughter **Malka** was born circa 1800 according to her death record, although it is likely she was born somewhat later. She died in 1916 in Zabno, approximately 10 miles north of Tarnow. She married David Rosthal (1802 – 1899). They had one known child -- Josef (circa 1850 – 1918).

Josef Rosthal married his first wife, Chaja Sara Fryst, in 1874 in Tarnow. Josef and Chaja Sara had 6 known children between 1874 and 1884 – Rosa, Henoch/Heinrich, Emanuel, Fradel/Franciszka, Sabina Reisel, and Joachim. After Chaja Sara died in 1895, Josef married Henie Mehl in 1901 in Tarnow. Josef and Henie had a daughter Regina in 1899 and a stillborn baby in 1906. Regina, who married Wilhelm Fertig in 1921 in Tarnow, died in 1973 in Australia. Her father Josef died in 1918 in Vienna, Austria.

Daughter **Rifka** was born circa 1818 and died in 1892 in Brzesko (is there a connection to the other Brzesko Westreich branches?). Rifka married Samuel Goldstein and had three known children beginning 1855 – Freida, Anschel, and Israel. Freida married Markus Leib Vogelhut and had 9 known children. Anschel married Rachel Blaufeder and had 5 known children. And Israel married Gittel Eber and had 7 known children.

Son **Abraham**, was born circa 1823 and died November 15, 1903 in Tarnow (see death notice below). He married Marjem/Marie Bass (circa 1837 – 1916) in 1855 in Tarnow (see marriage record below) and they had 13 known children born in Tarnow from 1856 to 1878 – Reisel Sabina (married Leopold Susswein), Lea/Laura (married Izydor Menderer), Mendel Efraim, Pesach, Chaje, Rosa, Joseph (married Grete Dornbaum), Scheindel Guttel, Herman, Paulina (married Ignatz Agatstein), Fany, and two stillbirths. Several of Abraham and Marie's children moved to Vienna, Austria. Below is the gravestone of Marie and daughter Laura Westreich Menderer in Vienna.

Descendants of this branch are likely spread throughout the world today.

1855 Marriage Record[124]

1855		Vor- und Zuname des Bräutigams und dessen Aeltern sammt Wohnort	Vor- und Zuname der Braut nebst deren Aeltern sammt Wohnort
Tag	Monath		
27	april	*Übertrag* *Abraham Westreich* *aus dem Dorfe Biala*	*Marjam Bass* *Tochter d. Efraim &* *Süssel Bass in Tarnow*

Bridegroom: Abraham Westreich (from Biala)
Bride: Marjem Bass (parents Efraim and Sussel from Tarnow)
April 27, 1855, Tarnow

Tiefbetrübt geben die Unterzeichneten Nachricht von dem Ableben ihres innigstgeliebten Gatten, bezw. Vaters und Grossvaters, des Herrn

Abraham Westreich,

Kaufmannes, Gemeinderates und Assessors der Stadt Tarnow, Mitgliedes des Bezirksrates, Präses „Jad charurim", gewesener Vizepräses der Krankenkasse u. s. w.,

welcher am 15. November d. J. nach längerer schwerer Krankheit selig in dem Herrn entschlafen ist.

Tarnow, am 16. November 1903.

Marie Westreich,
als Gattin.

Sabine Süsswein, Laura Menderer, Anna Hainbach, Dr. Josef Westreich, Advokat, **Pauline Agatstein, Teofile Nussbrecher,**
als Kinder.

Leopold Süsswein, Isidor Menderer, Hermann Hainbach, Dr. Ignaz Agatstein, Advokat, **Dr. Leo Nussbrecher,** Advokat,
als Schwiegersöhne.

Sämtliche Enkelkinder.

(Loose translation)
Deeply saddened, the undersigned announce the death of their
dearest husband/father/grandfather, Mr. Abraham Westreich,
merchant, municipal councilor, and assessor of the city of Tarnow,
member of the District Council, former Vice President of health insurance company, etc.,
after a long and serious illness has passed away.
Tarnow, November 16, 1903.
Marie Westreich, as wife.
Sabine Susswein, Laura Menderer, Anna Hainbach,
Dr. Josef Westreich (advocate), Pauline Agatstein, Teofile Nussbrecher,
as children.
Leopold Susswein, Isidor Menderer, Hermann Hainbach,
Dr. Ignaz Agatstein (advocate), Dr. Leo Nussbrecher (advocate),
as sons-in-law.
All grandchildren.

Gravestone of Marie Westreich (d. 1916) and daughter Laura Westreich Menderer (d. 1921) in Wiener Zentralfriedhof (Vienna Central Cemetery), Vienna, Austria

Galicia Branch 2
of the Westreich Family Tree

Y-DNA untested

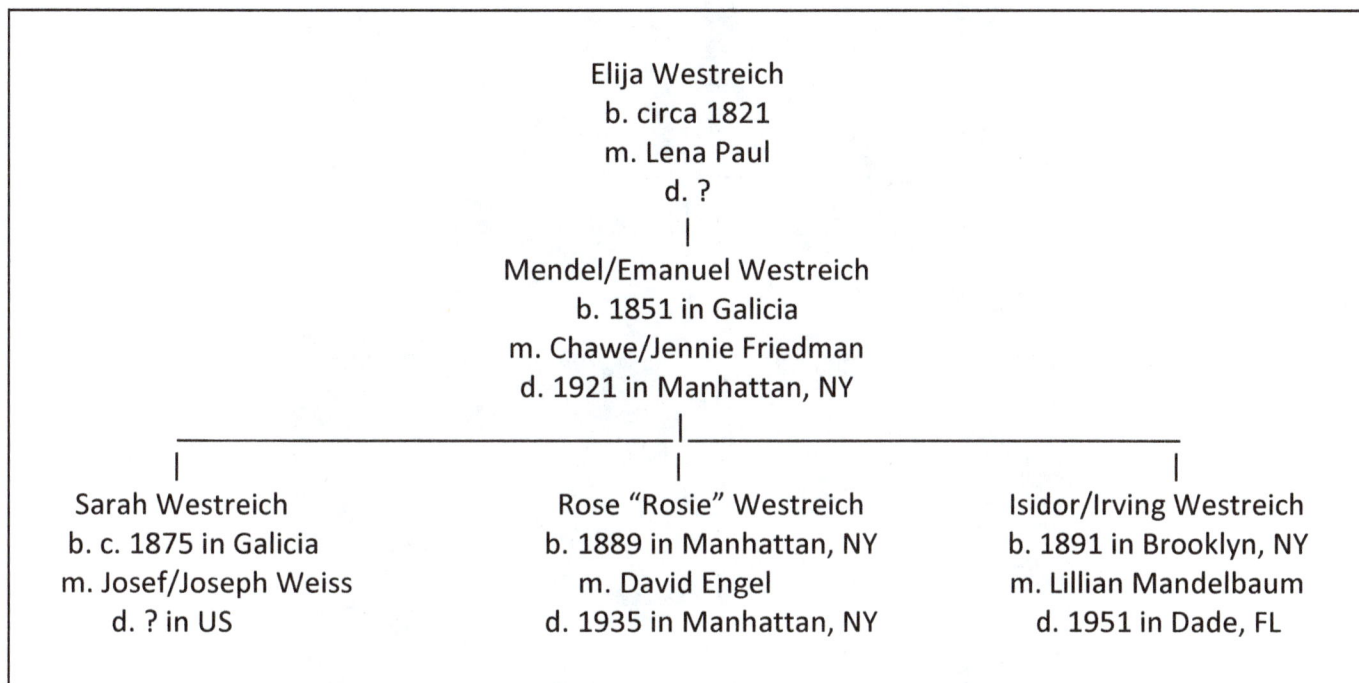

```
                        Elija Westreich
                         b. circa 1821
                         m. Lena Paul
                             d. ?
                              |
                  Mendel/Emanuel Westreich
                       b. 1851 in Galicia
                  m. Chawe/Jennie Friedman
                  d. 1921 in Manhattan, NY
                              |
        _____
        |                      |                          |
  Sarah Westreich       Rose "Rosie" Westreich    Isidor/Irving Westreich
  b. c. 1875 in Galicia  b. 1889 in Manhattan, NY  b. 1891 in Brooklyn, NY
  m. Josef/Joseph Weiss     m. David Engel         m. Lillian Mandelbaum
     d. ? in US          d. 1935 in Manhattan, NY   d. 1951 in Dade, FL
```

This branch originated in modern-day Poland or Ukraine,
formerly part of Galicia, Austria (1772 - 1918).

Edited by Allan Westreich

Little is known about this branch.

Gravestone of Emanuel and Jennie Westreich,
Washington Cemetery, Brooklyn, NY[127]

Rosie Westreich Engel, 1930[128]

Gorlice Branch
of the Westreich Family Tree

Y-DNA untested

By Allan Westreich

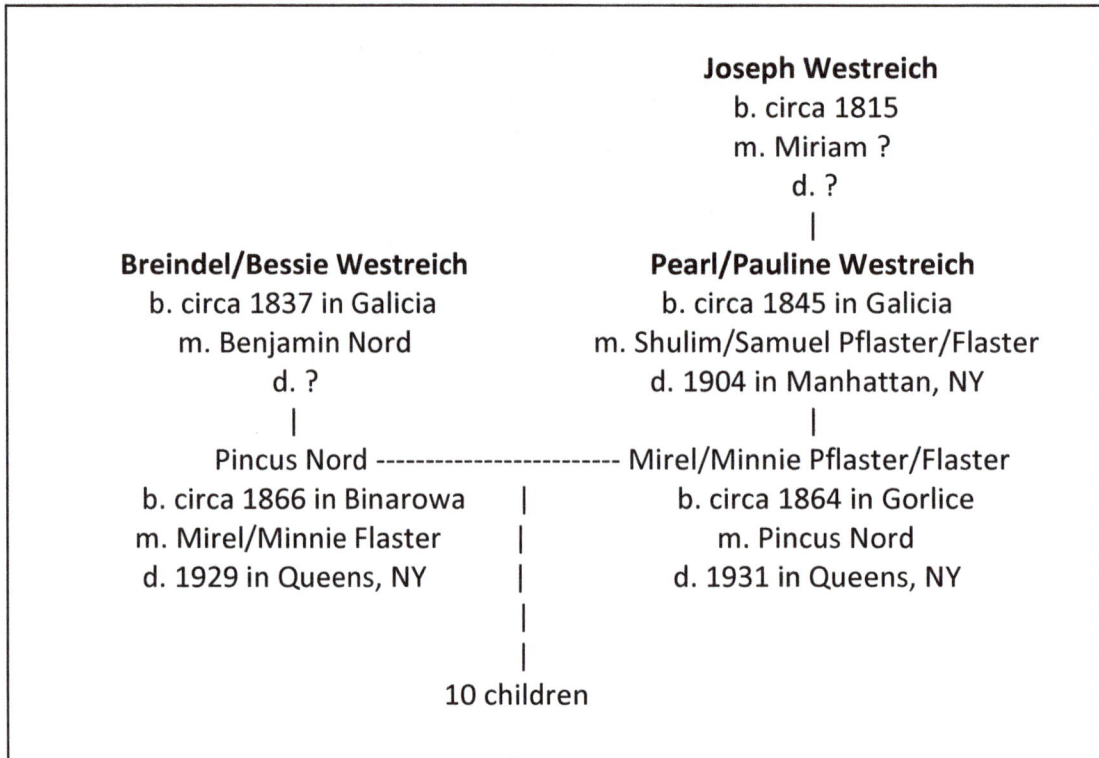

```
                                    Joseph Westreich
                                      b. circa 1815
                                      m. Miriam ?
                                          d. ?
                                           |
    Breindel/Bessie Westreich       Pearl/Pauline Westreich
      b. circa 1837 in Galicia        b. circa 1845 in Galicia
        m. Benjamin Nord         m. Shulim/Samuel Pflaster/Flaster
            d. ?                     d. 1904 in Manhattan, NY
             |                                |
        Pincus Nord ------------------------ Mirel/Minnie Pflaster/Flaster
    b. circa 1866 in Binarowa     |      b. circa 1864 in Gorlice
    m. Mirel/Minnie Flaster       |         m. Pincus Nord
      d. 1929 in Queens, NY       |       d. 1931 in Queens, NY
                                  |
                                  |
                             10 children
```

Gorlice is a town in modern-day Poland,
formerly part of Galicia, Austria (1772 - 1918),
located 62 miles ESE of Krakow.

Joseph and Miriam Westreich, born circa 1815, are the earliest known ancestral couple of this branch. They had one known child (and probably several others) – daughter Pearl/Pauline Westreich, born in Galicia circa 1845.

Pauline married Shulim/Samuel Pflaster/Flaster and they had 9 known children born between 1864 and 1888 – Mirel/Minnie, David, Hyman/Herman, Joseph, Miriam/Mary, Moses/Morris, Mayer/Max, Breindel/Bessie (see photo below), and Benjamin. At least several, if not all, of these children were reportedly born in the town of Gorlice (62 miles ESE of Krakow). The entire family (parents and children) immigrated to the US, not all at the same time, and died in New York. Parents Samuel (1899) and Pauline (1904) died in Manhattan.

The oldest child Minnie married Pincus Nord (see photos below). Of interest here is that Pincus' parents were Benjamin Nord and Bessie Westreich. Aha, another Westreich! While little is known about Bessie, born circa 1837 in Galicia, it would not be surprising if she was a sister of Pauline, and therefore the marriage of Pincus and Minnie was one of first cousins marrying each other, as was commonplace among Galician Jews at that time.

Pincus and Minnie Nord had 10 known children. Only one, the oldest Joseph Benjamin, was born in Galicia, on July 7, 1886. His birth record (see below) states that: Joseph was born in the village of Binarowa, approximately 8 miles NE of Gorlice; mother Minnie Flaster was from Glinik Mariampolski, a district of modern-day Gorlice; and father Pincus Nord was from Binarowa.

Pincus and Minnie's next 9 children were all born in New York, between 1888 and 1913 – Fannie, Esther, Solomon, Max, Philip Hyman, Rose (see photo below), Samuel, Abraham, and Paul. There are many living descendants throughout the US and likely the rest of the world.

1886 Birth Record of Binjamin Josef (Joseph Benjamin) Nord in Binarowa[129]

1	2 Der Geburt / Urodzenia					3 Der Beschneidung oder Namens-Beilegung / Obrzezania lub nadania imienia					4 Des Kindes / Dziecięcia				5 Eheliche, angeblich eheliche oder uneheliche Geburt / Ślubne, rzekomoślubne lub nieślubne	6 Vor und Zuname des Vaters, sowie Stand, Beschäftigung und Wohnort / Imię i nazwisko, stan, zatrudnienie i miejsca zamieszkania ojca
Fortlaufende Zahl / Liczba porządkowa	Tag / Dzień	Monat / Miesiąc	Jahr / Rok	Ort Miejsce	Haus-Nr. / Nr. domu	Tag / Dzień	Monat / Miesiąc	Jahr / Rok	Ort Miejsce	Haus-Nr. / Nr. domu	Name / Imię		Geschlecht / Płeć			
												männlich / męzka	weiblich / żeńska		
14	am 7 Ⅾ Aⅰⅼ		1886	Binarowa	125	am 14 Ⅾ Aⅰⅼ		1886	Binarowa	125	Binjamin Josef		1		männlich	

7 Vor und Zuname der Mutter, ihr Stand und Wohnort dann Vor- und Zuname, Beschäftigung und Wohnort ihrer Eltern / Imię i nazwisko, stan, miejsce zamieszkania matki i jej rodziców	8 Eigenhändige Unterschrift, Beschäftigung und Wohnort / Własnoręczny podpis, zatrudnienie i miejsce zamieszkania	9	10	11 todt geborene Kinder / Dzieci nieżywo urodzone	12 Anmerkung / Uwaga
	der Pathen oder Zeugen des Sandeks oder Schemes / kumów lub świadków Sandeka lub Schemes	des oder der Beschneidenden / obrzezującego lub obrzezujących	Der Hebamme oder des Geburtshelfers / akuszer lub akuszerki		
Mirl angeblich Ghattin des Pintas Nord in Binarowa Tochter des Salomon und Der Pearl Flaster Schauben in Glinik małopolski	Sandeta Israel Peller Beschneider in Biecz	Chaim Salamon Zinger Spryser Sandek obⁿ Markus Wag schaft Mohⁿ ... Sandek, beide in Biecz	Apolina Ryanerok in Binarowa		

Family Photos – 3 Generations[130]

Pincus Nord, 1910

Minnie Nord nee Flaster, 1910

Wedding of Paul Jacobs (son of Rose Nord Jacobs) and Leah Elkin, 1955
Couples (left-to-right): Paul and Leah,
Mimi Jacobs Sunkin (daughter of Rose Nord Jacobs) and husband Irving Sunkin, and
Rose Nord Jacobs (daughter of Pincus and Minnie) and husband Oscar Jacobs

Appendix A:
Using a Y-DNA Surname Project to Dig Deeper Into Your Genealogy
A Case Study

Journal: *www.jogg.info*
Originally Published: *Volume 8, Number 1 (Fall 2016)*
Reference Number: 81.009

USING A Y-DNA SURNAME PROJECT TO DIG DEEPER INTO YOUR GENEALOGY: A CASE STUDY

Author(s): Allan H. Westreich

Journal of Genetic Genealogy 9:1-14, 2017

Using a Y-DNA Surname Project to Dig Deeper Into Your Genealogy: A Case Study

Allan H. Westreich, Ph.D.

Address for correspondence:

Allan H. Westreich, Ph.D., 250 Route 28, Suite 206, Bridgewater, NJ 08807, allanwestreich@gmail.com

Abstract: The primary goal of this study was to test the value of genetic genealogy to help break through brick walls encountered with traditional genealogical methods. More specifically, a Y-DNA surname project was used to better understand the possible connections between separate family tree branches associated with the surname of Westreich. Each project member tested his Y-DNA with the 37-marker short tandem repeat (STR) test. By combining the DNA results with genealogical knowledge obtained through traditional methods, separate Westreich family tree branches were connected into a single merged tree, thus widening each individual tree with new-found cousins. Also, a deeper rabbinical branch enabled the other branches to extend several generations further back in time. Even a non-Westreich branch was connected to the tree. These conclusions were reached through an integrative genealogical approach which combined both genetic and traditional (non-genetic) genealogical methods, and not by either one alone. However, there are definite limitations to these conclusions, the primary one being they are not definitive but based on probabilities. For example, the primary conclusion that all of the project members belong to the same recent paternal lineage is "very likely." The secondary goal of this study was to clearly document the use of a Y-DNA surname group from start-to-finish to assist others in applying this relatively new technology to their family tree(s) of interest.

Introduction

Traditional paper-based genealogical research inevitably hits a brick wall, either temporary or permanent. In recent years, another tool has become available to help break through these roadblocks: genetic genealogy. Since each of us shares some DNA with our ancestors, and therefore with our siblings and cousins, the hunt for elusive distant (or sometimes close) relatives can be supplemented with looking for people with whom we share significant amounts of DNA.

The primary goal of this study was to test the value of genetic genealogy in better understanding the possible connections between separate family tree branches associated with the surname of Westreich, thereby demonstrating a generalizable framework useful for studying other surnames. Are the separate branches actually connected to each other? If so, members of one branch can incorporate information from the other branches to expand their genealogical knowledge both breadthwise (new cousins in recent generations) and depthwise (new ancestors in earlier generations).

The best type of DNA to use for a surname study is Y-DNA (Estes, 2016) since both surname and Y-DNA are transmitted relatively unchanged down the male line, father-to-son-to-son-to-son. Only males have Y-DNA. Therefore, candidates for DNA testing for this study are males with the surname of Westreich. The overall strategy is to compare the DNA of the tested individuals to determine the likelihood of blood relationships.

All of the currently known Westreich branches descend from Jewish ancestors from current-day southeastern Poland. This area was formerly known as Galicia, part of the Austro-Hungarian Empire from the late 1700s through the early 1900s. The paper trail stops for most of these family histories in the early 1800s.

The earliest known paper-based pedigree belongs to a branch of Galician Westreich rabbis dating back to the early 1700s (Wunder, 1981). It is not unusual for rabbis to have earlier-known family histories since they were considered the royalty of their time and their genealogies were often well-documented (Paull & Briskman, 2015). If descendants from the other Westreich branches are able to match their Y-DNA with descendants from the rabbinical line, then they will be able to extend their family branch back by another three or so generations. Similarly, several Jewish genealogical studies (Paull & Briskman, 2015; Paull, Rosenstein & Briskman, 2016; Paull, Briskman & Twersky, 2016; Akaha & Unkefer, 2015) have tried to identify the Y-DNA "signatures" of renowned rabbinical lines as references to which others can attempt to match and therefore extend back their family trees. Perhaps this strategy is most deftly called "is a rabbi hiding in your family tree?" (Akaha & Unkefer, 2015).

This study uses an integrative genealogical approach, which combines both genetic and traditional (non-genetic) genealogical data and methods. When weighing genealogical hypotheses, it is best to consider all available evidence, both genetic and non-genetic (Bettinger, 2016a; Bettinger, 2016b), whether supportive or dismissive. Even so, the solutions to complex problems are often probabilistic, not definitive.

The secondary goal of this study was to clearly document the use of a Y-DNA surname group from start-to-finish to assist others in applying this relatively new technology to their family tree(s) of interest.

Methods

A Y-DNA Surname Project was established with Family Tree DNA (FTDNA; Houston, Texas, USA). This provided the centralized "location" for DNA testing, DNA comparisons, and communication among the group members.

Candidates were identified for Y-DNA testing. The basic requirements were male gender with the surname of Westreich or one of its variants (e.g., Westrich, Vestraich, etc.). Ideal candidates would have a long-documented family tree, which would allow others in the group of testers to significantly extend their family trees back in time if their DNA matched. Already-known close relatives (e.g., brothers, first cousins) of another tester were not necessary as they would provide little, if any, new information. If female Westreich descendants were identified, they were a potential resource for finding male Westreich's in their local family branch, e.g., brother or paternal uncle.

Internet use was fundamental to finding and contacting these testing candidates. Useful sites included general search engines, genealogical records and sharing sites, online directories, and social networking sites. Sometimes the search process included "reverse genealogy" (Taylor, 2009), where the starting point was a known male Westreich from the past—such as Rabbi Israel Hill Westreich born circa 1720 (Wunder,1981)—and the search looked

forward in time for his living male Westreich descendents. This is the reverse of a typical genealogy search where the starting point is a living person and the goal is to find their earlier ancestors.

Male Westreich descendants from six separate Westreich family trees were identified and contacted. Four were successfully recruited to join the FTDNA Surname Project and test their Y-DNA. It took approximately 1 year to identify, recruit, and obtain the DNA results of these four participants.

Table 1 presents the basic genealogical information known about each group member's most distant known ancestor (MDKA), i.e., the highest link in each of the four separate family trees. The first names of the group members have been omitted for privacy reasons. The geographical location(s) associated with the MDKA is where the ancestor may have been born, lived, or died. Also, while these locations are all in modern-day Poland, they may have been part of Galicia, Austria during the lifetime of the MDKA.

The DNA test used was the Y-DNA 37-marker short tandem repeat (STR) test. This is the standard for initial testing of members in a DNA surname group (Gleeson, 2016a). As stated above, Y-DNA is used because both surname and Y-DNA are transmitted relatively unchanged down the male line, father-to-son-to-son-to-son. STR markers are locations on the Y-DNA that contain a variable number of repeated patterns of genetic information. Each marker tested yields a value, called an allele, which is the number of repeated patterns at that location. For example, marker DYS393 (DNA Y-Chromosome Segment 393) may have the value of 12, meaning that the genetic pattern of nucleotide bases AGAT (adenine-guanine-adenine-thymine; Wikipedia, 2016) was repeated 12 times. (Each marker has a different genetic pattern of nucleotide bases associated with it.)

STR values change (mutate) slowly over generations, so they are useful for testing for relatedness within a recent "genealogical timeframe" of existing surnames, paper records, etc. (roughly the previous several hundred years; Gleeson, 2015a). Descendants of a recent common ancestor should have the same or similar STR values for each of the markers tested.

Thirty-seven markers are generally considered to be optimal for initial testing (Gleeson, 2016a). More markers (e.g., 67, 111) can yield a slightly higher resolution at a greater expense, while fewer (e.g., 12, 25) may not adequately distinguish family lines from one another.

The primary results of each group member's Y-DNA test were their paternal haplotype and haplogroup. A haplotype is a list of the allele values for each of the markers tested. An example haplotype is shown in Table 2. In this example, for a tester named "Male1", marker DYS392 has its genetic pattern (TAT, or thymine-adenine-thymine;

Wikipedia, 2016) repeated 11 times. The values in this example are fictitious for the sake of confidentiality. Only 12 markers are shown for simplicity's sake; each member in this study tested at least 37 markers.

A Y-DNA haplogroup, similar to a Y-DNA haplotype, represents a group of men who share the same paternal ancestry. A new haplogroup is defined by a mutation of a single nucleotide polymorphism (SNP). SNP mutations occur on a random basis at a rate much, much slower than STR mutations. If SNP mutations did not occur, all men would belong to the same haplogroup. Compared to a haplotype, a haplogroup: (1) is much, much larger, consisting of groups and sub-groups (called sub-clades) of many more individuals; and (2) originates from much, much more ancient ancestry (dating back to tens of thousands of years ago), thus is not considered to be within a genealogical timeframe.

FTDNA reports a "predicted" haplogroup as part of the results from STR testing. This prediction is based on the STR haplotype. To confirm the haplogroup, SNP testing must be performed. Haplogroup names begin with letters, followed by numbers and letters to specify sub-groups. Some examples are B, J2a, and R1b1a. Since these names can get quite long, a shorthand notation has been developed, e.g., J2a1b is also called J-M67, where J is the topmost haplogroup and M67 is the bottommost SNP that defines the sub-branch.

At the heart of this study is using DNA to help determine whether two or more people descend from a recent common paternal ancestor and thus belong to the same recent paternal lineage group. Truth be told, DNA can never provide 100% proof of this. However, current DNA technology can help determine whether there is a high probability (or not) of this being true.

A high probability of recent relatedness is based on multiple potential sources of evidence, both genetic and non-genetic (Gleeson, 2015a). It is important to weigh the totality of the genetic and non-genetic evidence, both supportive and dismissive, when considering a genealogical hypothesis. The criteria to be considered for grouping members into the same recent paternal lineage are:

• Low genetic distance. The Y-DNA haplotype of a descendant should be the same as or very similar to the Y-DNA haplotype of their ancestor. Similarly, the Y-DNA of paternal relatives should be the same as or very similar to the Y-DNA of their most recent common ancestor (MRCA) and therefore to each other. The only differences are due to relatively infrequent random mutations of the STR values.

To determine how genetically close two haplotypes are to each other, the number of mutations to get from one to the other is approximated. This "genetic distance" is calculated (in most cases) as the sum of the absolute values of the arithmetic differences between the two haplotypes

(Estes, 2016). For example, the genetic distance of Male1 and Male2 in Table 3 is equal to (13-12) + (11-9) = 3.

A common method (Gleeson, 2015b) for determining the genetic proximity of a group of haplotypes is to compare each of them to an approximation of their MRCA's haplotype. This haplotype is often best estimated by the modal haplotype (Gleeson, 2015b) of the group, which is calculated as the haplotype consisting of the modal (most frequent) values on a marker-by-marker basis. See Table 4 for an example calculation of a modal haplotype. Continuing the example in Table 4, the genetic distances from the modal haplotype for each of the group members are: Male1 = 2, Male2 = 1, and Male3 = 2.

Now the question arises, what genetic distance is considered small enough to conclude that two people are related within a genealogical timeframe (roughly, the past several hundred years)? For 37-marker tests with people of the same surname, FTDNA reports possible "matches" if the genetic distance is less than or equal to 4 (FTDNA Learning Center, 2016c). More specifically, FTDNA uses the guidelines in Table 5 (FTDNA Learning Center, 2016a) for assessing the degree of relatedness based on genetic distance. Note that these are guidelines and are not absolute.

• Same haplogroup. The haplogroups must be identical for two people to be related. (Note that if one of the people has had additional SNP testing, two different haplogroups may be reported when one is actually a sub-group of the other. In this case, even though the reported haplogroups appear different, the individuals belong to the same haplogroup and possibly thus to the same paternal lineage.)

• Same MDKA. If separate family trees derived from paper-based genealogical research overlap, this is strongly suggestive of a relationship. However, keep in mind that paper-based trails are not always factual.

• Same surname. A common surname suggests relatedness. However, it is quite possible for two people with the same surname to not be related and for two people who do not have the same surname to be related.

• Similar geography. If ancestors can be located in the same or nearby locations, this is evidence supportive of a relationship.

• Shared rare marker values. Two haplotypes that share marker values uncommon within the larger haplogroup support a relationship.

• Same ethnicity and/or ethnic-based traditions. If two people, or ancestors of the two people, share the same culture, religion, language, etc., this is evidence for a relationship. Also, for example, if two separate Jewish families assign the same set of given names in the same respective time periods, they may be honoring the same set of ancestors; this is supportive evidence.

The simplest and most reasonable strategy for grouping members of a surname study into paternal lineages is to initially group them based on the same or similar haplotype, i.e., low genetic distance, and then use the additional genetic and non-genetic factors listed above for corroboration, particularly for borderline cases (Gleeson, 2015a).

After the Y-DNA results of the four recruited members were used to group them into recent paternal lineages, additional candidate group members were identified from their Y-DNA matches, who were already in the FTDNA database. These additional candidate group members will be discussed in the Results section below.

Once the paternal lineage groups were established, each of which consists of one or more members who have a high probability of sharing a recent common paternal ancestor, a more in-depth look at the closeness of the genetic connection between the members was undertaken. This was done by estimating the time to the most recent common ancestor (TMRCA) and then using this information along with relevant non-genetic evidence to merge the previously separate family trees. This process is detailed in the Results section below.

Results

The results of the Y-DNA STR 37-marker tests for the four recruited members of the Westreich surname project are presented in Table 6. An asterisk (*) denotes that the value is the same for all four testers for a given marker; the actual value is not specified for privacy reasons. Only the shaded values differ from the most frequent values of the other testers. At first glance, note that most of the STR values (144 of 148) are identical across all four members and that all four are considered a "match" to each other based on FTDNA guidelines (genetic distance is less than or equal to 4). We seem to be barking up the right (family) tree!

As stated above in the Methods section, the next step is to group the four testers into recent paternal lineage groups based on the following genetic and non-genetic criteria:

• Low genetic distance. The first criteria for grouping into the same paternal lineage is low genetic distance from the modal haplotype of that group, followed by the additional corroborating factors below. In this case, the modal haplotype is simply the haplotype of Male2 and Male4 Westreich. Male1 and Male3 Westreich each have a low genetic distance of 2 from the modal haplotype, with the three markers (DYS439, DYS389ii, and DYS456) that differ from the mode known to mutate at moderate rates (neither particularly fast nor slow) (Wikipedia, 2016). This suggests they are all recently related by FTDNA genetic distance guidelines (see Table 5). This is summarized in Table 7. All four testers meet the genetic distance criteria for belonging to the same recent paternal lineage group.

• Same haplogroup. As seen in Table 6, all four testers have the same predicted haplogroup of J-M172.

However, since the haplogroups were predicted from the haplotypes, there is no new information here. Independently-tested SNP values would be necessary to determine the true haplogroups to provide another meaningful piece of evidence.

• Same MDKA. None of the testers have the same MDKA.

• Same surname. All of the testers have the surname Westreich. While this evidence suggests that they share a recent paternal ancestor, it alone is not conclusive. Since the surname of Westreich was used in multiple districts across 19th-century western Galicia (Beider, 2004), the competing hypothesis that unrelated individuals adopted the same surname of Westreich is also a possibility.

• Similar geography. All of the testers descend from 19th-century ancestors from current-day southeastern Poland, formerly part of western Galicia, part of the Austro-Hungarian Empire from the late 1700s through the early 1900s. The earliest known ancestral towns of each of the branches lie within 90 miles of each other. And all of these ancestral towns are within 60 miles of Sedziszow Malopolski, the earliest ancestral town of the rabbinical branch and therefore possibly the source of all of the Westreich branches in this study. In addition, based on information obtained from traditional genealogical sources, both Male1 and Male4 have ancestors that lived in Brzesko (also known as Brigel in Yiddish), and Male3 and Male4 both have ancestors who lived in Grybow.

• Shared rare marker values. If testers share marker values that are uncommon in members of their larger haplogroup, this is evidence supportive of a relationship. Estes (2013) considers the frequency cutoff for "very rare" markers as less than or equal to 6% within the haplogroup. For the marker YCAIIa, all four testers have the value of 23 which occurs with a 1% frequency within the larger haplogroup of J2 (of which J-M172 is a sub-group) (Rootsweb, 2016).

• Same ethnicity and/or ethnic-based traditions. All of the testers' ancestors (as best as can be determined) share the same religion, Ashkenazi Judaism. It is a long-standing Ashkenazi Jewish tradition to name children after a deceased ancestor. If two Jewish family trees share given names, this is suggestive of common ancestors. The earliest known ancestor of Male4 is Rabbi Israel Hillel Westreich, whose grandson with the same not-so-common given name undoubtedly was named after him. Male1 also has an Israel Hillel Westreich in his family tree. Furthermore, the grandson Israel Hillel in Male4's tree lived in Brzesko and died in 1846 (Wunder, 1981). The Israel Hillel in Male1's tree also lived in Brzesko and was born in 1849, suggesting that he may have been named after his recently-deceased ancestor from Male4's tree.

After reviewing all of the above evidence in its totality—low genetic distances and significant corroborating evidence, both genetic and non-genetic—it is very likely that all four Westreich testers belong to the same recent paternal lineage, i.e., share a recent common paternal ancestor. It seems quite unlikely, given all of the above evidence, for the competing hypothesis of these Westreich's not being related, to be true.

Once the four recruited group members were assigned to a single paternal lineage group, additional candidate members were identified from their Y-DNA matches, comprising people who had previously tested with FTDNA. Particularly for those candidates who do not share the Westreich surname, they must have a very low genetic distance to the group modal haplotype as well as additional corroborating evidence in order to be considered part of the same recent paternal lineage group.

One such candidate surfaced. Male1 Taffel (given name again omitted for privacy) is a perfect 37 of 37 match with the modal haplotype, i.e., he has a genetic distance of 0 from the modal haplotype. In addition, there are several additional corroborating factors. His projected haplogroup of J-M172 is the same. His paternal ancestors are also from Galicia. More specifically, they lived in Sedziszow Malopolski (aka Shendishov or Shendishov Malopolski in Yiddish) which, very interestingly, is the same as the location of the earliest known Westreich rabbi ancestor of Male4 (Wunder, 2016). Male1 Taffel's haplotype shares the same rare marker value of 23 at YCAIIa. And his ancestors also share the same Ashkenazi Jewish religious background.

Based on the above evidence, Male1 Taffel is very likely to belong to the same paternal lineage group as the four Westreich members. The complete list of group members appears in Table 8.

The final challenge of this study was to combine the knowledge gained from the DNA testing with data obtained from traditional genealogical methods to produce a single, merged family tree of the group members. Before DNA testing, all of the family trees of the group members were separate from each other, as shown in Figure 1.

As a result of DNA analysis, the members have been grouped into a single recent paternal lineage, i.e., they all share a common paternal ancestor within a genealogical timeframe. Therefore, for each pair of separate family trees, the MRCA is the connecting point. If the number of generations from the testers to the MRCA can be determined for each pair of family trees, then the two trees can be merged. That number of generations is defined as the time to MRCA (TMRCA). (To approximate the number of years from the testers until the MRCA, simply multiply the number of generations by 30; Gleeson, 2016b.)

Merging two family trees based on TMRCA is illustrated in Figure 2 with an overly simplified example in which two men know their respective fathers and grandfathers and the TMRCA is five generations back from both tested men.

Keep in mind that the names of the MRCA and of all the generations from the MDKA up to and including the MRCA are not revealed by DNA and therefore still cannot be included in the tree.

To connect the separate trees of the four Westreich testers, the TMRCA needs to be identified between each pair of trees. Although the above simplified example uses a TMRCA of five generations, in practice the exact number is rarely known. The best we can do is to approximate a probable range of number of generations until the MRCA. Both genetic and non-genetic evidence can be very helpful in refining the endpoints of these ranges, as illustrated below.

Fortunately, in this example where all the individuals in the family trees have the surname Westreich and therefore their MRCA would very likely also have the Westreich surname, the early end of the TMRCA range is constrained by the time of adoption of Jewish surnames. Jewish surnames were mandated by the Austrian government in 1787, and specifically in western Galicia in 1805 (Paull & Briskman, 2014). Before this time period, Ashkenazi Jews typically did not have surnames with the possible exception of rabbinical lines.

Therefore, the first man in the Westreich rabbinical line to adopt the surname Westreich was highly likely to be either Israel Hillel (born circa 1720) or Yosef Yoska (born circa 1750) (Wunder, 2016). And therefore, the earliest possible MRCA between the rabbinical line and each of the other Westreich trees is highly likely to be either Israel Hillel (born circa 1720), Yosef Yoska (born circa 1750), or an unknown brother of Yosef Yoska.

The recent end of the range of possible MRCA's is also fairly tightly constrained in this example. For Male1 and Male2, based on birth year of their MDKA, the latest possible MRCA with the rabbinical line is Israel Hillel Westreich (born circa 1780). For Male3, based on the birth year of his MDKA, the latest possible MRCA with the rabbinical line is Yosef Yoska (born 1810). In fact, this is quite possible since Male3's MDKA Abraham Westreich (born 1845) as well as Yosef Yoska Westreich (born 1810) were born in Grybow, Poland.

In summary, the MRCA for the rabbinical tree with each of the other Westreich trees lies in the range of Israel Hillel Westreich (born circa 1720) and Israel Hillel Westreich (born circa 1780), with the possible exception for Male3 extending down to Yosef Yoska (born 1810). The resulting merged Westreich family tree is illustrated in Figure 3.

The last step is to merge the Westreich tree with the Taffel tree, thus creating a single merged tree of all the testers in the single paternal lineage. The most likely reason that these branches have individuals with different surnames is that the MRCA lived before the adoption of Jewish surnames (although this could also be explained by a "non-paternity event"; Estes, 2016). Using the same reasoning as above, the first Westreich ancestor without the Westreich surname is likely Israel Hillel (born circa 1720) or his father. So that is the recent end of the TMRCA range.

Since we have no paper-based information to determine the early end of the TMRCA range, genetic tools are used. FTDNA estimates the TMRCA given the genetic distance between two haplotypes (see Table 9; FTDNA Learning Center, 2016b). TMRCA is calculated as a set of probabilities that the MRCA lived no longer than "x" number of generations ago. In our example, we want to calculate the TMRCA between the merged Westreich tree and the separate Taffel tree. Therefore, we compare the modal haplotype of the Westreich testers with the haplotype of the Taffel tester. In this case, they are the same, i.e., the genetic distance is 0. Therefore, there is a 50% chance that the MRCA lived no longer than two generations before the testers, a 90% chance within five generations, and a 95% chance within seven generations.

FTDNA also has a TiP (time predictor) tool (International Society of Genetic Genealogy Wiki, 2016) that further refines the TMRCA estimate. In addition to genetic distance, it also takes into account the average mutation rates for each marker to give a more precise estimate. Continuing with our example, the TiP estimates are 59% chance that the MRCA lived no longer than two generations before the testers, 93% chance within six generations, and 97% chance within eight generations.

Given that these estimates are far from exact (Estes, 2012) and often overestimate the TMRCA (Akaha & Unkefer, 2015; Paull, Briskman & Twersky, 2016), a conservative estimate (Unkefer, 2014) for the early end of the TMRCA is eight generations. This corresponds with Israel Hillel's father (born circa 1690), who is also in the recent end of the TMRCA range. The resulting merged group family tree is illustrated in Figure 4 and is consistent with the MDKA's of the Westreich rabbinical tree and the Taffel tree both having lived in the same location, Sedziszow Malopolski.

Conclusions

The goals of this study were to:

  • take a test drive with genetic genealogy, specifically with a Y-DNA surname project, to determine if it adds value to traditional paper-based genealogical methods;

  • illustrate the value of integrating both genetic and non-genetic data and methods; and

  • clearly document the process to assist others to do the same for their family tree(s) of interest.

This Y-DNA project contributed significantly to breaking through some of the brick walls that had been reached in studying the Westreich family. By combining the genetic results with information obtained from traditional genealogical methods, separate Westreich family tree branches were connected into a single merged tree, thus widening each individual tree with new-found cousins. The deeper

rabbinical branch enabled the genetic branches to extend several generations further back in time. And even a non-Westreich branch was connected to the group.

However, there are definite limitations to this study, as with genealogical research in general. First and foremost, conclusions drawn from genetic genealogy alone are not definitive, particularly for positive results. Even when combined with known evidence from traditional genealogical methods, all of the conclusions in the above paragraph are "very likely" and not absolute, including the fundamental one that all of the group participants belong to the same recent paternal lineage. The number of generations in DNA-connected branches is approximate at best, and the names of the missing generations will never be supplied by DNA alone.

The net result is that the addition of a Y-DNA surname project to information already gathered by traditional genealogical methods has generated some very interesting and significant hypotheses regarding the Westreich family genealogy that are very likely to be true. This, in turn, points to future work to further examine and test these new hypotheses:

  • add more testers to see whether their results support or refute the newly-generated hypotheses;

  • perform additional genetic testing of the current testers, such as:

    o STR testing with more markers (more than 37) to generate haplotypes and resulting conclusions with a higher resolution; and

    o SNP testing to confirm haplogroups and identify sub-haplogroups, possibly including large-scale "BigY" testing;

  • use future genetic technology/methods for further refinement as they become available, as this field is currently in its infancy; and

  • continue with traditional paper-based research to generate new evidence to support or refute the new hypotheses.

Hopefully this article has also met its secondary goal of clearly explaining the methods of a Y-DNA surname project from start-to-finish to assist others in applying this technology to their family tree(s) of interest. One does not have to be a DNA expert, professional genealogist, or rabbinical scholar to conduct this type of research. The primary requirements are logic and persistence. Or as Thomas A. Edison (1901) said, "1 percent inspiration and 99 percent perspiration."

Acknowledgments

The author would like to thank all of the Y-DNA Surname Project participants, without whom this research would not have been possible.

Conflicts of Interest

The author declares no conflicts of interest.

References

Akaha J, Unkefer R (2015) Is a Rabbi Hiding in Your Family Tree?: Lessons from Genetic Genealogy for Traditional Genealogists. Avotaynu, XXXI (3): 15-20.

Beider A (2004) A Dictionary of Jewish Surnames from Galicia, page 573. Avotaynu, Bergenfield, NJ.

Bettinger B (2016a) The Genetic Genealogist: The DNA Era of Genealogy. http://thegeneticgenealogist.com/2016/12/17/the-dna-era-of-genealogy/. Accessed February 2017.

Bettinger B (2016b) The Genetic Genealogist: What is a Genetic Genealogist? http://thegeneticgenealogist.com/2016/12/27/what-is-a-genetic-genealogist/. Accessed February 2017.

Edison TA (1901) Doing One's Best. Idaho Daily Statesman (Idaho Statesman), Boise, Idaho, May 6, 1901, Page 4, Column 3.

Estes R (2012) DNAeXplained -- Genetic Genealogy: Averages, TIP Calculator and One Size Fits All. https://dna-explained.com/2012/11/29/averages-tip-calculator-and-one-size-fits-all/. Accessed Oct 2016.

Estes R (2013) DNAeXplained -- Genetic Genealogy: Triangulation for Y-DNA. https://dna-explained.com/2013/06/18/triangulation-for-y-dna/. Accessed Oct 2016.

Estes R (2016) DNAeXplained -- Genetic Genealogy: Concepts -- Y-DNA Matching and Connecting with your Paternal Ancestor. https://dna-explained.com/2016/04/14/concepts-y-dna-matching-and-connecting-with-your-paternal-ancestor/. Accessed Oct 2016.

FTDNA Learning Center (2016a) If two men share a surname, how should the genetic distance at 37 Y-chromosome STR markers be interpreted? https://www.familytreedna.com/learn/y-dna-testing/y-str/two-men-share-surname-genetic-distance-37-y-chromosome-str-markers-interpreted/. Accessed Oct 2016.

FTDNA Learning Center (2016b) Paternal Lineages Tests. https://www.familytreedna.com/learn/dna-basics/ydna/. Accessed Oct 2016.

FTDNA Learning Center (2016c) Y-DNA -- Matches Page. https://www.familytreedna.com/learn/user-guide/y-dna-myftdna/y-matches-page/. Accessed Oct 2016.

Gleeson M (2015a) Farrell DNA Project: Criteria for Allocating Members to Specific Genetic Families. http://farrelldna.blogspot.com/2015_01_01_archive.html/. Accessed Oct 2016.

Gleeson M (2015b) The Gleason/Gleeson DNA Project: Genetic Distance, Genetic Families, & Mutation History Trees. http://gleesondna.blogspot.com/2015/08/genetic-distance-genetic-families.html/. Accessed Oct 2016.

Gleeson M (2016a) DNA and Family Tree Research: Should I Upgrade My Y-DNA Test to 67 or 111 Markers? http://dnaandfamilytreeresearch.blogspot.com/2016/06/should-i-upgrade-my-y-dna-test-to-67-or.html/. Accessed Oct 2016.

Gleeson M (2016b) Spearin Surname Project: Big Y Results - Comparing TMRCA Estimates. http://spearinsurnameproject.blogspot.com/2016/04/big-y-results-comparing-tmrca-estimates.html/. Accessed Oct 2016.

International Society of Genetic Genealogy Wiki (2016) TiP. http://isogg.org/wiki/TiP/. Accessed Oct 2016.

Paull JM, Briskman J (2014) History, Adoption, and Regulation of Jewish Surnames in the Russian Empire. Surname DNA Journal. http://www.surnamedna.com/?articles=history-adoption-and-regulation-of-jewish-surnames-in-the-russian-empire/. Accessed Oct 2016.

Paull JM, Briskman J (2015) Y-DNA Genetic Signature of the Savran-Bendery Chassidic Dynasty: Connecting to the Great Rabbinic Families through Y-DNA. Surname DNA Journal. http://www.surnamedna.com/?articles=y-dna-of-the-savran-bendery-chassidic-dynasty/. Accessed Oct 2016.

Paull JM, Briskman J, Twersky Y (2016) The Y-DNA Genetic Signature of the Twersky Chassidic Dynasty. https://www.academia.edu/26048275/The_Y-DNA_Genetic_Signature_of_the_Twersky_Chassidic_Dynasty?auto=download/. Accessed Oct 2016.

Paull JM, Rosenstein N, Briskman J (2016) The Y-DNA Genetic Signature and Ethnic Origin of the Katzenellenbogen Rabbinical Lineage. Avotaynu Online. http://www.avotaynuonline.com/2016/03/y-dna-genetic-signature-ethnic-origin-katzenellenbogen-rabbinical-lineage/. Accessed Oct 2016.

Rootsweb (2016) Y-STR Allele Frequencies for Haplogroups Listed in Ysearch and Public Projects. http://freepages.genealogy.rootsweb.ancestry.com/~geneticgenealogy/yfreq.htm/. Accessed Oct 2016.

Taylor M (2009) Trace Your Family Forward. Family Tree Magazine. http://www.familytreemagazine.com/article/reverse-genealogy-resources/. Accessed Oct 2016.

Unkefer R (2014) Interpreting Y-DNA Markers: A Primer. Avotaynu, XXX (1): 5-6.

Wikipedia (2016) List of Y-STR Markers. https://en.wikipedia.org/wiki/List_of_Y-STR_markers/. Accessed Oct 2016.

Wunder M (1981) Meorei Galicia: Encyclopedia Lekhakhmei Galicia (Encyclopedia of Galician Rabbis and Scholars), Vol. 2: pages 928-931. The Institute for the Commemoration for Galician Jewry, Jersulam.

Wunder M (2016) Personal email correspondence. July 4, 2016.

Table 1. Recruited members of the Y-DNA Surname Project

Name	Most Distant Known Ancestor (MDKA)
Male1 Westreich	Gershon Westreich; born circa 1810; Brzesko, Poland
Male2 Westreich	Mojzesz Westreich; b c 1825; Skopanie and Jaslo, Poland
Male3 Westreich	Abraham Westreich; b 1845; Grybow and Gorlice, Poland
Male4 Westreich	Rabbi Israel Hillel Westreich; b c 1720; Sedziszow Malopolski, Poland[1]

Abbreviations: b, born; c, circa.
The geographical location(s) of the MDKA is where the ancestor may have been born, lived, or died.
[1] (Wunder, 2016)

Table 2. Example haplotype

Name	DYS 393	DYS 390	DYS 19	DYS 391	DYS 385a	DYS 385b	DYS 426	DYS 388	DYS 439	DYS 389-I	DYS 392	DYS 389-II
Male1	12	23	15	10	14	14	11	12	11	12	11	30

Table 3. Genetic distance calculation

Name	DYS 393	DYS 390	DYS 19	DYS 391	DYS 385a	DYS 385b	DYS 426	DYS 388	DYS 439	DYS 389-I	DYS 392	DYS 389-II
Male1	12	23	15	10	14	14	11	12	11	12	11	30
Male2	13	23	15	10	14	14	11	12	9	12	11	30

Genetic distance = (13-12) + (11-9) = 3

Table 4. Modal haplotype calculation

Name	DYS 393	DYS 390	DYS 19	DYS 391	DYS 385a	DYS 385b	DYS 426	DYS 388	DYS 439	DYS 389-I	DYS 392	DYS 389-II
Male1	12	23	15	10	14	14	11	12	11	12	11	30
Male2	13	23	15	10	14	14	11	12	9	12	11	30
Male3	12	23	15	9	14	14	11	12	9	12	11	29
Modal Haplo-type	12	23	15	10	14	14	11	12	9	12	11	30

Table 5. FTDNA guidelines for genetic relatedness (within a genealogical timeframe) for the 37-marker Y-DNA test for males with the same surname[1]

Genetic Distance	Relationship	Interpretation
0	Very tightly related.	
1	Tightly related.	Share a common male ancestor.
2	Related.	
3	Related.	
4	Probably related.	May share a common male ancestor.
5	Possibly related.	
6	Not related.	Not likely to share a common male ancestor.
>6	Not related.	Do not share a common male ancestor.

[1] (FTDNA Learning Center, 2016a)

Table 6. Y-DNA test results for group members with the surname Westreich

STR Marker	Male1 Westreich	Male2 Westreich	Male3 Westreich	Male4 Westreich
DYS393	*	*	*	*
DYS390	*	*	*	*
DYS19	*	*	*	*
DYS391	*	*	*	*
DYS385	*	*	*	*
DYS426	*	*	*	*
DYS388	*	*	*	*
DYS439	12	13	14	13
DYS389-I	*	*	*	*
DYS392	*	*	*	*
DYS389-II	30	29	29	29
DYS458	*	*	*	*
DYS459	*	*	*	*
DYS455	*	*	*	*
DYS454	*	*	*	*
DYS447	*	*	*	*
DYS437	*	*	*	*
DYS448	*	*	*	*
DYS449	*	*	*	*
DYS464	*	*	*	*
DYS460	*	*	*	*
Y-GATA-H4	*	*	*	*
YCAII	*	*	*	*
DYS456	15	15	16	15
DYS607	*	*	*	*
DYS576	*	*	*	*
DYS570	*	*	*	*
CDY	*	*	*	*
DYS442	*	*	*	*
DYS438	*	*	*	*
Haplogroup	J-M172	J-M172	J-M172	J-M172

* denotes STR marker value is the same for all members. Shaded values are different from the modal haplotype. Haplogroups are predicted.

Table 7. Genetic distance from modal haplotype

Group Member	Genetic Distance
Male1 Westreich	2
Male2 Westreich	0
Male3 Westreich	2
Male4 Westreich	0

Table 8. All Y-DNA Surname Project members

Name	Most Distant Known Ancestor (MDKA)
Male1 Westreich	Gershon Westreich; born circa 1810; Brzesko, Poland
Male2 Westreich	Mojzesz Westreich; b c 1825; Skopanie and Jaslo, Poland
Male3 Westreich	Abraham Westreich; b 1845; Grybow and Gorlice, Poland
Male4 Westreich	Rabbi Israel Hillel Westreich; b c 1720; Sedziszow Malopolski, Poland[1]
Male1 Taffel	Eliakum Taffel; b c 1816; Sedziszow Malopolski, Poland

Abbreviations: b, born; c, circa.
The geographical location(s) of the MDKA is where the ancestor may have been born, lived, or died.
[1] (Wunder, 2016)

Table 9. Probability that the common ancestor lived no longer than the specified number of generations ago[1]

Genetic Distance	50%	90%	95%
0	2	5	7
1	4	8	10
2	6	12	14

For 37-marker Y-DNA test.
[1] (FTDNA Learning Center, 2016b)

Figure 1. Separate family trees before DNA testing

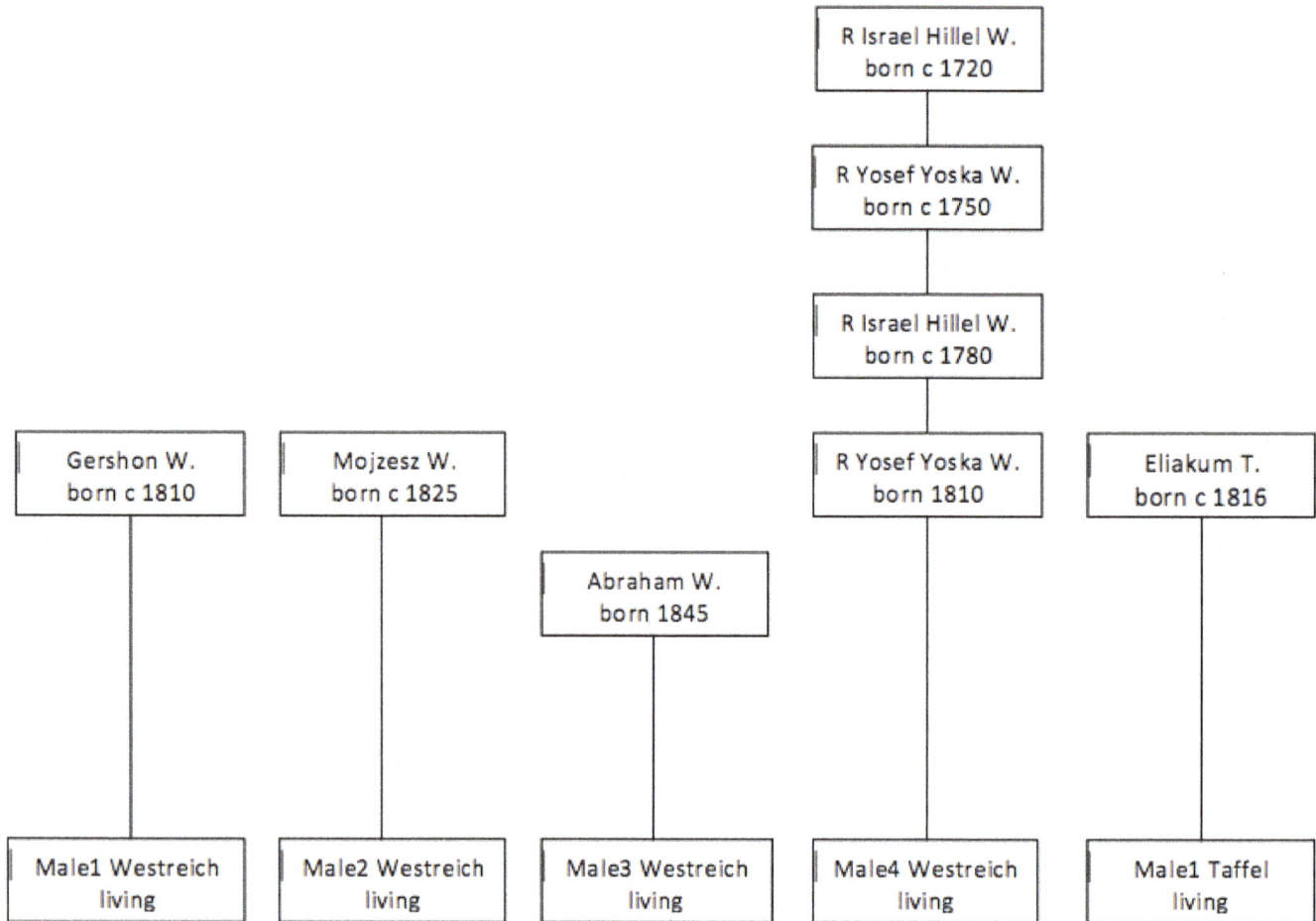

Abbreviations: c, circa; W, Westreich; T, Taffel; R, Rabbi.
Some birth years have been approximated using an estimate of 30 years as the length of a paternal generation (Gleeson, 2016b).

Figure 2. Simplified example of merging two family trees based on TMRCA

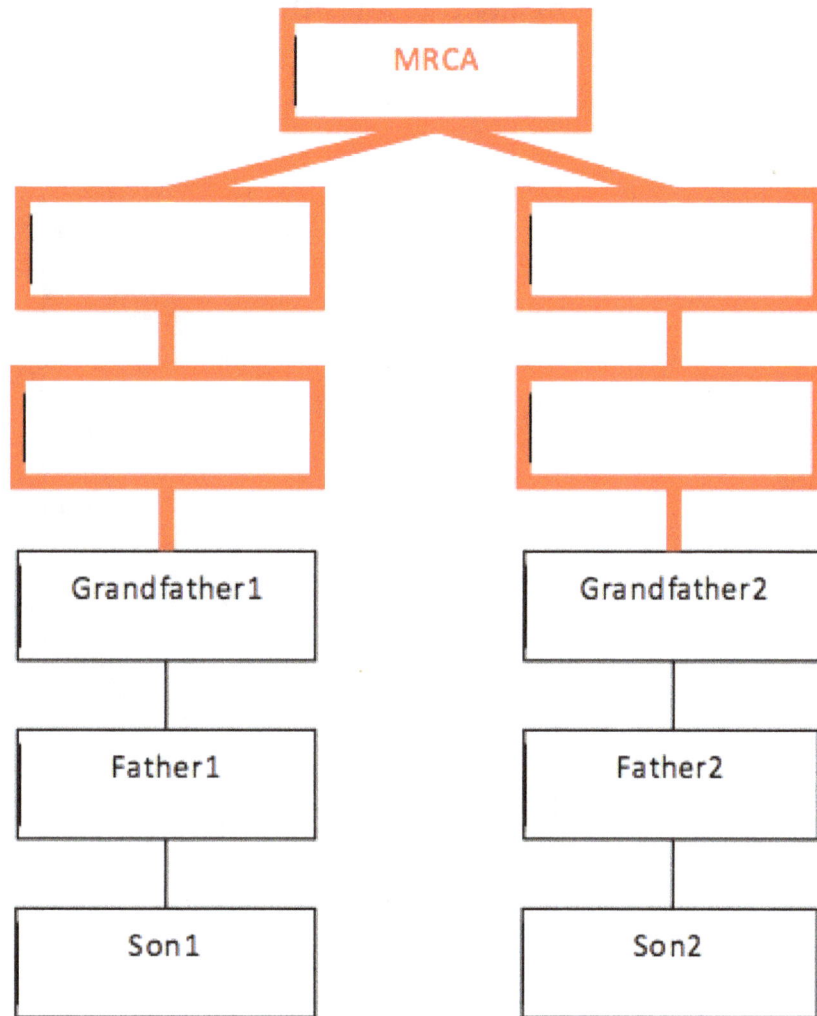

Red updates are based on TMRCA=5.

.Figure 3. Merged Westreich family tree after DNA testing

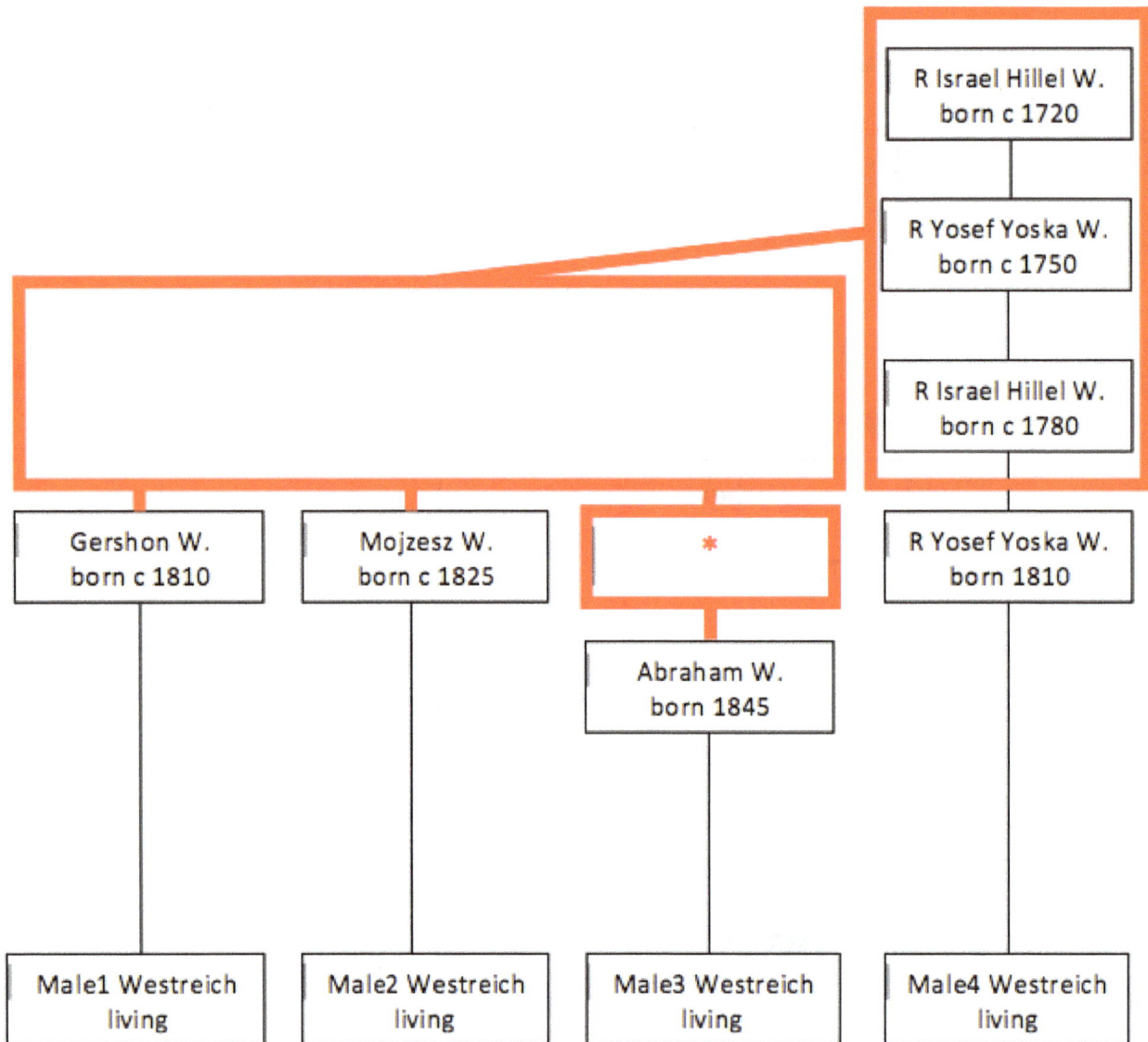

Abbreviations: c, circa; W, Westreich; T, Taffel; R, Rabbi.
Red updates are based on DNA results.
* This could be Rabbi Yosef Yoska Westreich (born 1810).

Figure 4. Merged group family tree after DNA testing

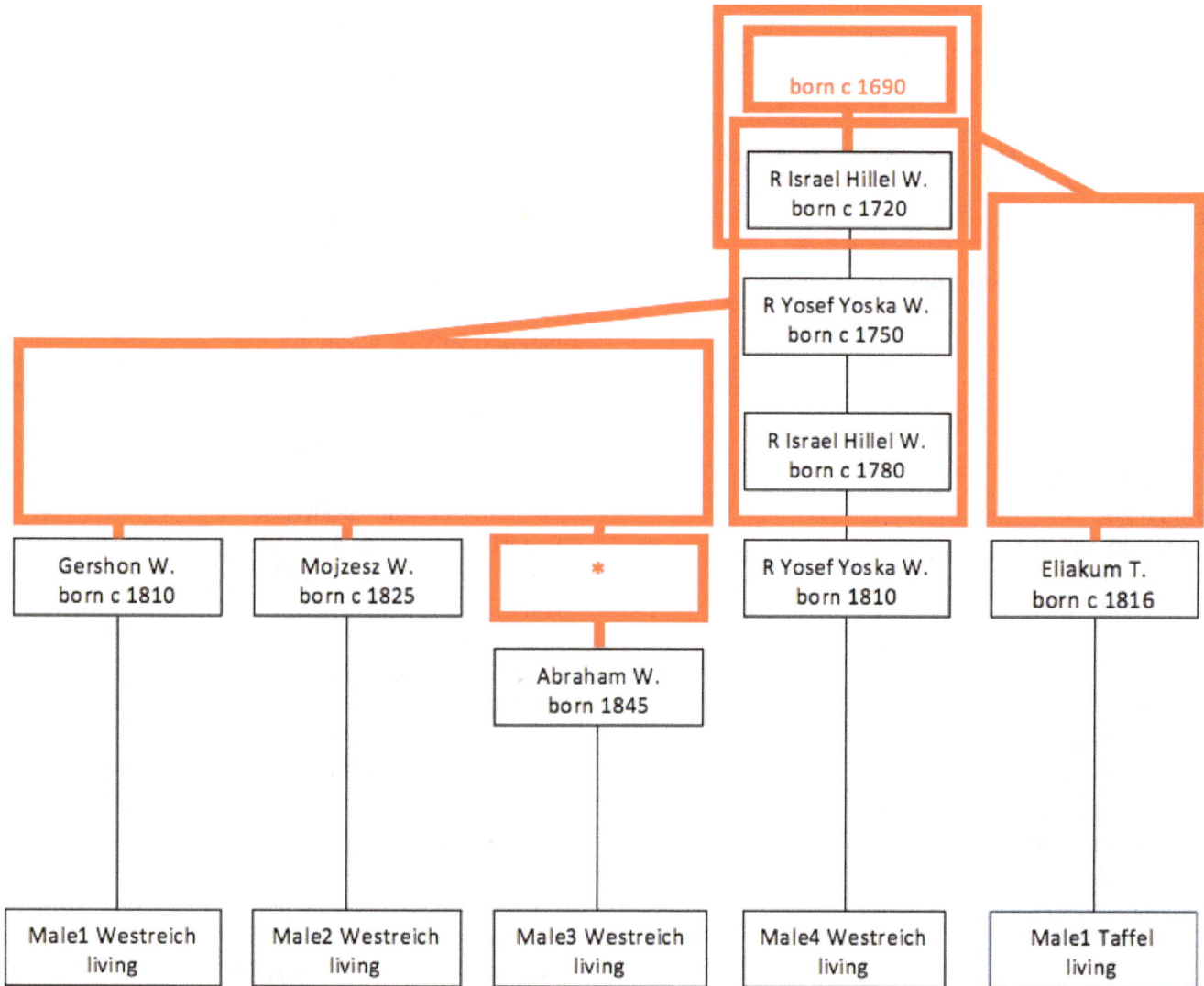

Abbreviations: c, circa; W, Westreich; T, Taffel; R, Rabbi.
Red updates are based on DNA results.
* This could be Rabbi Yosef Yoska Westreich (born 1810).

14

Name Index

Source Citations

[1] Image reprinted with permission of the State Bar of Wisconsin.

[2] Translated adaptation reprinted with permission of M. Wunder.

[3] Photograph reprinted with permission of M. Naor.

[4] Source: Blog entry from *Blood & Frogs: Jewish Genealogy and More, Communities tied to Rzeszow (Reisha), Poland via marriage*, August 4, 2018, https://bloodandfrogs.com/2018/08/communities-tied-to-rzeszow-reisha-poland-via-marriage.html. Image reprinted with permission of P. Traurig.

[5] Photographs reprinted with permission of the Israel State Archive.

[6] Photograph reprinted with permission of M. Bar-Hillel.

[7] Photograph reprinted with permission of M. Bar-Hillel.

[8] Photograph reprinted with permission of L. Westreich.

[9] Photograph reprinted with permission of L. Westreich.

[10] Invitation reprinted with permission of B. Westreich.

[11] Photographs reprinted with permission of the Auschwitz-Birkenau Memorial Place and Museum.

[12] Reprinted with permission of E. Westreich.

[13] Blog post (https://mirabarhillel.wordpress.com/2015/09/07/had-he-lived-longer-my-father-would-be-100-years-old-today-i-raise-a-glass-to-his-memory/) reprinted with permission of M. Bar-Hillel.

[14] Photographs reprinted with permission of M. Bar-Hillel.

[15] Photograph reprinted with permission of M. Naor.

[16] Photograph reprinted with permission of M. Naor.

[17] Photograph reprinted with permission of M. Naor.

[18] Photograph reprinted with permission of M. Naor.

[19] Photograph reprinted with permission of M. Naor.

[20] Photograph reprinted with permission of M. Naor.

[21] Photograph reprinted with permission of M. Naor.

[22] Photograph courtesy of F. Baileson.

[23] Photograph reprinted with permission of A. Brzyska.

[24] Photograph courtesy of F. Baileson.

[25] Photograph reprinted with permission of A. Westreich.

[26] Photograph reprinted with permission of V. Levy.

[27] Photograph reprinted with permission of V. Levy.

[28] Courtesy of *Brooklyn Chat*, defunct newspaper. In public domain.

[29] Courtesy of *Brooklyn Chat*, defunct newspaper.

[30] Courtesy of *Keyport Weekly*, defunct newspaper. In public domain.

[31] Courtesy of *Brooklyn Chat*, defunct newspaper.

[32] Photograph reprinted with permission of A. Westreich.

[33] Source: NYC Municipal Archives, 1940s Tax Department Photograph Collection, Photograph 3960-30 BK. Photograph reprinted with permission of Municipal Archives, City of New York.

[34] Photographs reprinted with permission of A. Westreich.

[35] Photograph courtesy of I. Westreich.

[36] Photograph courtesy of I. Westreich.

[37] Photograph reprinted with permission of A. Westreich.

[38] Photograph reprinted with permission of S. Linder.

[39] Photograph courtesy of I. Westreich.

[40] Photograph reprinted with permission of S. Linder.

[41] Photograph reprinted with permission of United Synagogue Burial.

[42] Courtesy of National Archives & Records Administration. In public domain.

[43] Photograph courtesy of G. Bogod.

[44] Photograph reprinted with permission of A. Westreich.

[45] Photographs reprinted with the permission of E. Witjas.

[46] Photograph reprinted with the permission of A. Brzyska.

[47] Reprinted with permission of Karlsruhe City Archive.

[48] Photograph reprinted with permission of R. Mohl.

[49] Photograph reprinted with permission of Foundation for Documentation of Cemeteries in Poland.

[50] Photograph reprinted with permission of Foundation for Documentation of Cemeteries in Poland.

[51] Photograph reprinted with permission of A. Brzyska.

[52] Reprinted with permission of E. Westreich and H. Westreich.

[53] Reprinted with permission of E. Westreich.

[54] Photograph reprinted with permission of H. Westreich.

[55] Reprinted with permission of H. Westreich.

[56] Photograph reprinted with permission of H. Westreich.

[57] Photograph reprinted with permission of G. Collins.

[58] Photograph reprinted with permission of G. Collins.

[59] Photograph reprinted with permission of Yavneh Memorial and Educational Centre, Cologne, Germany.

[60] Photograph reprinted with permission of Foundation for Documentation of Cemeteries in Poland.

[61] Photograph reprinted with permission of D. Minc.

[62] Photograph reprinted with permission of L. Markson.

[63] Photograph reprinted with permission of L. Markson.

[64] Source: Some family information was obtained from the USC Shoah Foundation Institute testimony of Jack Minc, http://sfi.usc.edu, Interview Code: 14699, 1996.

[65] Story and photograph reprinted with permission of S. Furst.

[66] Source: *Celebrating Shabbos*, 2017. Story reprinted with permission of S. Furst.

[67] Source: *Nanny's Gift of Memories: Rayna Gillman*, blog entry from *Subversive Stitchers: Women Armed With Needles*, July 14, 2009, https://subversivestitch.blogspot.com/search?q=nanny. Blog entry reprinted with permission of R. Gillman.

[68] Photographs reprinted with permission of R. Gillman.

[69] Courtesy of M. Haas.

[70] Article reprinted with permission of the *Record Gazzette*.

[71] Photograph reprinted with permission of the *Record Gazzette*.

[72] Photograph from 1941 *US Declaration of Intention* (for naturalization), National Archives and Records Administration. In public domain.

[73] Article reprinted with permission of the *Record Gazzette*.

[74] Source: *Master Chef*, https://www.epicurus.com/food/recipes/no-16-sandwich/35130/, 2018, defunct.

[75] Book excerpts from *I'm Still Alive* by Robert Westreich, 2017. Reprinted with permission of R. Westreich.

[76] Photographs reprinted with permission of R. Westreich.

[77] Courtesy of M. Kassenoff.

[78] Photograph reprinted courtesy of M. Kassenoff.

[79] Photograph reprinted courtesy of M. Kassenoff.

[80] Photograph reprinted courtesy of B. Diznoff.

[81] Photograph reprinted courtesy of B. Diznoff.

[82] Photograph reprinted courtesy of W. Westreich and Yad Vashem, Hall of Names photograph collection.

[83] Photograph reprinted courtesy of M. Kassenoff.

[84] Photograph reprinted courtesy of M. Kassenoff.

[85] Photograph reprinted courtesy of Yad Vashem, Hall of Names photograph collection.

[86] Photograph reprinted courtesy of M. Kassenoff.

[87] Source: Blog entry, https://www.respol71.com/les-soeurs-westreich-rescapees-des-rafles-et-maquisardes. Translated from French to English by *Google Translate*. Reprinted with permission of G. Soufflet.

[88] Source: Photographs reprinted with permission of the USC Shoah Foundation – The Institute for Visual History and Education, http://sfi.usc.edu, Interview Code: 23214, 1996.

[89] Source: Incarceration Documents > Camps and Ghettos > Buchenwald Concentration Camp, Reference Code 01010503 002 049 101, Document ID 7408654, ITS Digital Archive, Arolsen Archives. Permission not required for original document.

[90] Article reprinted with permission of *citybiz*, https://www.citybiz.co/article/44037/stanley-westreichs-legacy-real-estate-icon-was-the-visionary-behind-the-rosslyn-skyline/.

[91] Letter (2022) reprinted with permission of N. Westreich, The Carnegie Hall Corporation and the Isaac Stern Society, https://legacygiving.carnegiehall.org/meet-our-donors/neil-westreich.

[92] Photograph reprinted with permission of N. Westreich.

[93] Photograph reprinted with permission of N. Westreich.

[94] Article reprinted with permission of *New York Daily News*.

[95] Transcript of interview of Jack Westreich reprinted with permission of the USC Shoah Foundation – The Institute for Visual History and Education, http://sfi.usc.edu, Interview Code: 10348, 1996.

[96] Photographs from interview of Jack Westreich reprinted with permission of the USC Shoah Foundation – The Institute for Visual History and Education, http://sfi.usc.edu, Interview Code: 10348, 1996.

[97] Photograph reprinted with permission of J. Westreich.

98 Reprinted with permission of V. Vestrich.

99 Reprinted with permission of S. Shatz.

100 Photograph reprinted with permission of E. Broch.

101 Source: *Brooklyn Daily Eagle*, defunct newspaper. In public domain.

102 Photograph reprinted with permission of S. Shatz.

103 Photographs reprinted with permission of B. Solomowitz.

104 Photograph reprinted with permission of B. Solomowitz.

105 Reprinted with permission of G. Pokrassa.

106 Reprinted with permission of R. and J. Boarer.

107 Reprinted with permission of B. Bigaudet.

108 Reprinted with permission of E. Belfer.

109 Photograph reprinted with permission of R. Boarer.

110 Photograph reprinted with permission of B. Solomowitz.

111 Photograph reprinted with permission of E. Belfer.

112 Photograph reprinted with permission of E. Belfer.

113 Source: *L'Univers Israelite*, defunct newspaper. In public domain.

114 Photograph reprinted with permission of R. Boarer.

115 Source: Population Census Records, 1936, Paris Archives (https://archives.paris.fr/s/11/denombrements-de-population/?), DZM8 580. No permission required.

116 Photograph reprinted with permission of R. Boarer.

117 Source: Civil Status Records of Paris, Marriage (1860-1947), Paris Archives, (https://archives.paris.fr/s/4/etat-civil-actes/?), 9M 335. No permission required.

118 Photograph reprinted with permission of B. Bigaudet and S. Dechambenoit.

119 Photograph reprinted with permission of B. Bigaudet and S. Dechambenoit.

120 Photograph reprinted courtesy of Mt. Zion Cemetery, Queens, NY.

121 Interview of Herbert Zipper, 1995, USC Shoah Foundation – The Institute for Visual History and Education, http://sfi.usc.edu, Interview Code: 833.

122 Source: USC Shoah Foundation – The Institute for Visual History and Education, https://sfi.usc.edu/news/2022/05/33491-music-and-poetry-herbert-zipper-reached-humanity-dachau, *Voices From The Archive: With Music and Poetry, Herbert Zipper Reached for Humanity in Dachau*, J. Gruenbaum Fax, 2022. Article reprinted with permission of USC Shoah Foundation – The Institute for Visual History and Education.

123 Source: *Dachau Song: The Twentieth Century Odyssey of Herbert Zipper*, Cummins, P., 1992. Photographs reprinted with permission of P. Cummins.

124 Source: Polish State Archives, https://www.szukajwarchiwach.gov.pl/, Tarnow vital records, Reference Code 33/276/0/-/28. Reprinted courtesy of Polish State Archives.

125 Source: *Neue Freie Presse*, No. 14091, November 18, 1903. In public domain in Austria and United States.

126 Source: *Find a Grave*, database and images (https://www.findagrave.com/memorial/101012879/marie-westreich: accessed 04 August 2023), memorial page for Marie Westreich (unknown–Feb 1920), Find a Grave Memorial ID 101012879, citing Wiener Zentralfriedhof, Vienna, Wien Stadt, Vienna, Austria; Maintained by Daryl & Barbara (Biggs) Mallett (contributor 46984947). Photograph reprinted with permission of M. Davidson.

127 Source: *Find a Grave*, database and images (https://www.findagrave.com/memorial/244740488/emanuel-westreich: accessed 04 August 2023), memorial page for Emanuel Westreich (unknown–19 Nov 1921), Find a Grave Memorial ID 244740488, citing Washington Cemetery, Brooklyn, Kings County, New York, USA; Maintained by JIRCPA (contributor 47766572). Photograph reprinted with permission of J. Rosenthal.

128 Photograph reprinted with permission of R. Keats.

129 Source: Polish State Archives, https://www.szukajwarchiwach.gov.pl/, Biecz vital records, Reference Code 60/1116/0/-/2. Reprinted courtesy of Polish State Archives.

130 Photographs reprinted with permission of M. Schulman.